The Consolations of History: Themes of Progress and Potential in Richard Wagner'ʘ *Götterdämmerung*

In this book on Richard Wagner's compelling but enigmatic masterpiece *Götterdämmerung*, the final opera of his monumental *Ring* tetralogy, Alexander H. Shapiro advances an ambitious new interpretation which uncovers intriguing new facets to the work's profound insights into the human condition. By taking a fresh look at the philosophical and historical influences on Wagner, and critically reevaluating the composer's intellectual worldview as revealed in his own prose works, letters, and diary entries, the book challenges a number of conventional views that continue to impede a clear understanding of this work's meaning. The book argues that *Götterdämmerung*, and hence the *Ring* as a whole, achieves coherence when interpreted in terms of contemporary nineteenth-century theories of progress and, in particular, G.W.F. Hegel's philosophies of mind and history.

A central target of the book is the article of faith that has come to dominate Wagner scholarship over the years – that Wagner's encounter in 1854 with Arthur Schopenhauer's philosophy conclusively altered the final message of the *Ring* from one of historical optimism to existential pessimism. The author contends that Schopenhauer's uncompromising denigration of the will and denial of the possibility for human progress find no place in the written text of the *Ring* or in a plausible reading of the final musical setting. In its place, the author discovers in the famous Immolation Scene a celebration of mankind's inexhaustible capacity for self-improvement and progress. The author makes the further compelling case that this message of progress is communicated not through Siegfried, the traditional male hero of the drama, but through Brünnhilde, the warrior goddess who becomes a mortal woman. In her role as a battle-tested world-historical prophet she is the true revolutionary change agent of Wagner's opera who has the strength and vision to comprehend and thereby shape human history.

This highly lucid and accessible study is aimed not only at scholars and researchers in the fields of opera studies, music and philosophy, and music history, but also Wagner enthusiasts, and readers and students interested in the history and philosophy of the nineteenth century.

Alexander H. Shapiro is a practicing lawyer and independent scholar based in New York, U.S. His published works include "McEwan and Forster: The Perfect Wagnerites" in *The Wagner Journal* (2011), and "'Drama of an Infinitely Superior Nature': Handel's Early English Oratorios and the Religious Sublime" in *Music & Letters* (1993).

Routledge Research in Music Series

Masculinity in Opera
Edited by Philip Purvis

Music, Performance, and the Realities of Film
Shared Concert Experiences in Screen Fiction
Ben Winters

Burma, Kipling and Western Music
The Riff from Mandalay
Andrew Selth

Global Percussion Innovations
The Australian Perspective
Louise Devenish

Double Lives
Film Composers in the Concert Hall
James Wierzbicki

John Williams
Changing the Culture of the Classical Guitar
Michael O'Toole

Paul Dukas
Legacies of a French Musician
Edited by Helen Julia Minors and Laura Watson

The Consolations of History: Themes of Progress and Potential in Richard Wagner's *Götterdämmerung*
Alexander H. Shapiro

For more information about this series, please visit: www.routledge.com/music/series/RRM

The Consolations of History: Themes of Progress and Potential in Richard Wagner's *Götterdämmerung*

Alexander H. Shapiro

LONDON AND NEW YORK

First published 2020
by Routledge
2 Park Square, Milton Park, Abingdon, Oxon OX14 4RN

and by Routledge
52 Vanderbilt Avenue, New York, NY 10017

Routledge is an imprint of the Taylor & Francis Group, an informa business

First issued in paperback 2021

British Library Cataloguing-in-Publication Data
A catalogue record for this book is available from the British Library

Library of Congress Cataloging-in-Publication Data
A catalog record for this book has been requested

ISBN: 978-0-367-24321-0 (hbk)
ISBN: 978-1-03-208799-3 (pbk)
ISBN: 978-0-429-28172-3 (ebk)

Typeset in Times New Roman
by Apex CoVantage, LLC

**For my wife Susanna and my daughters Sarah and Penelope –
the sweet lights of a new consolation**

"Nothing in the world wants to go backwards," an old lizard said to me, "Everything strives forward, and, in the end, a great advancement of nature will occur. Stones will become plants, plants will become animals, animals will become people, and people will become Gods."

"But," I cried, "What will become of those good people, of the poor old Gods?"

"That will take care of itself, dear friend," the lizard answered, "Probably they will abdicate, or be placed into retirement in some honorable way."

I learned many other secrets from my hieroglyph-skinned *Naturphilosoph*; but I gave my word to reveal nothing. I now know more than Schelling and Hegel.

Heinrich Heine, "Lucca, the City" in
Travel Pictures, Part IV (1831)

Contents

Acknowledgements

I extend my thanks and gratitude first to Barry Millington. He has been a true mentor, and his faith in me and this project has proved vital. This book would also not have been possible without the support of my extraordinary wife Susanna and incredible daughters Sarah and Penelope who have tolerated with enduring patience the invasion of the living room with endless piles of books, long hours logged in the library and at the dining room table, car rides dominated by the music of the *Ring*, and my monomaniacal focus on the minutiae of nineteenth-century history and philosophy. I am also very grateful to the family and friends who have provided critical moral and intellectual encouragement, and support of all kinds throughout this process: Joan and Theodore Shapiro, Carol and Josef Sirefman, Aaron Rappaport, Jeffrey and Lauren Rosen, Jesse Cohen, Alexi Worth, Erika Belsey, David Levene, Stan Harrison, Maaja Roos and Ruth Smith. I thank Matthew Rye for his excellent work in creating the music excerpts, and Zoe Blecher-Cohen for her great bibliographic efforts on my behalf. Last but not least, Laura Sandford deserves special recognition for believing in the book and recognizing that Routledge was just the right platform for sharing these ideas.

Preface

In late January 1854, Richard Wagner sent to August Röckel, his former colleague and co-revolutionary, a lengthy *apologia* for his dramatic poem *Der Ring des Nibelungen*, the ambitious and visionary text for the opera tetralogy which he had just begun to compose. Röckel was at the time serving out the fifth year of what would become a 13-year sentence at Waldheim prison in Saxony for his role in the Dresden uprising of May 1849. Wagner, himself implicated in the rebellion, was safe in exile in Switzerland. In the course of that letter, Wagner took time to refute Röckel's assessment of the French Republic's Reign of Terror of 1793–94: "I deny 'Robespierre' the tragic significance which he has hitherto had for you. . . . [H]e was not conscious of any higher purpose in the attainment of which he had recourse to unworthy means; no, it was in order to conceal his lack of any such purpose and his very real want of resource that he had recourse to the whole terrible machinery of the guillotine."[1] The purpose of this book is to demonstrate why it was no accident that the subject of the Reign of Terror and Maximilien Robespierre's role in history, tragic or otherwise, arose in the context of a discussion about the *Ring*.

The French Revolution had a scarring impact on the political, social, and psychological landscape of Europe, and during Wagner's formative years, politicians, philosophers, and historians were still trying to make sense of the cataclysm. As late as 1837, Thomas Carlyle, in his monumental account of the period, *The French Revolution*, would refer to the historic episode as "that world prodigy . . . whereat the world still gazes and shudders."[2] From Adolphe Thiers, Alphonse de Lamartine, and Francois Mignet in France to Archibald Alison and Thomas Carlyle in England, historians of the early decades of the nineteenth century wrote exhaustive narratives of the fall of the *ancien régime*, meticulously piecing together the myriad factual details in the hopes of better understanding the historical forces at work.[3] The sheer scale and sweep of events from the storming of the Bastille to the glorious rise and ignominious fall of Napoleon seemed to reduce individuals to mere playthings of historical forces beyond any one person's control. And how to account for the sorrowful turn from inspiring Enlightenment ideals of *liberté*, *égalité*, and *fraternité*, as eloquently articulated and logically derived from first principles by Voltaire, Rousseau, and other *philosophes*, to the brazen indifference to human life shown by Robespierre and his Committee on Public Safety?[4] As Carlyle was forced to acknowledge in his book – hailed by John Stuart Mill in the *London and Westminster Review* as "not so much a history, as an epic poem"[5] – there was no precedent for that "new amazing Thing" called the Terror, and "History" would simply have to "admit, for once, that all the Names and Theorems yet known to her fall short."[6] A new vision of time and man was needed to comprehend and encompass the magnitude of these events, to place the political dislocations and anarchic violence into some form of intelligible framework.[7]

It fell to Georg Wilhelm Friedrich Hegel, an unsalaried lecturer at the University of Jena, to articulate a philosophical answer to the historical challenge. The French Revolution was a major catalyst for Hegel's intellectual development and had a critical impact on his philosophy.[8] As he explored in his *Phänomenologie des Geistes* (*Phenomenology of Spirit*) of 1807, hastily completed as Napoleon's troops were entering the city and the Revolution itself descended on Prussia, and would teach years later in his lectures at the University of Berlin, history marked a gradual but inevitable process of human spiritual enlightenment, ensuring an ever growing manifestation of freedom and reason in the world. From Hegel's Olympian perspective on time and human affairs, the French Revolution was not an aberration, an ineradicable scar in the European psyche, but merely a stage in a grander program of human evolution. The great principles of the Enlightenment thinkers which had first inspired the Revolution would still prevail in the long term. In this way Hegel succeeded in "domesticating" the Terror, bringing this fatal moment into perspective, and discovering the enduring benefits to mankind of such a bloody struggle.[9] Hegel's impact on European thought cannot be overstated,[10] and his groundbreaking historicist and historically confident mindset defined the thinking of the century from the Young Hegelian theories of Ludwig Feuerbach and David Friedrich Strauss to the historical and social commentary of Thomas Carlyle to the early socialism of Pierre-Joseph Proudhon and Karl Marx. As a result of Hegel's influence, "confidence in the march of civilization reached an unprecedented peak" in the nineteenth century.[11]

The poem of the *Ring* is singular for having been written in reverse order from 1848 to 1852 and then set to music in logical sequence over a period of over 20 years from 1853 to 1874. As a result, the last opera of the tetralogy, *Götterdämmerung*, curiously encapsulates both Wagner's first germinal intentions for the work, as well as his last mature conclusions. In his compelling but famously tendentious guide to the *Ring*, *The Perfect Wagnerite* (1898), George Bernard Shaw rejected *Götterdämmerung* as a mere operatic regression, unworthy of the completed music drama of the future and fully inconsistent with its philosophical aims. This jaundiced view of the work has continued to shape contemporary analysis. Wagner scholar Simon Williams, for one, has observed that "with *Götterdämmerung*, the *Ring*, it has sometimes been claimed, appears to lose coherence."[12] This judgment, with varying degrees of fervor, is widely expressed among recent commentators.[13] But this tendency to give *Götterdämmerung* the back of the hand is highly problematic; whatever structural failings the opera may have, it is the beginning and end of Wagner's artistic vision for the *Ring* and therefore worthy of every consideration. The purpose of this book is to attempt to rehabilitate the fourth opera of the tetralogy by giving greater credence to its original dramatic and philosophical aims, and thus rescue it from the critical disdain it has received over the years.

Commentators on the *Ring* over the last 100 years have almost uniformly identified love and compassion as the essential message of the work. But from the very start, Shaw rejected this view. Instead of love Shaw argued that the thesis of the *Ring* was a celebration of the life force of evolutionary growth: "The only faith which any reasonable disciple can gain from *The Ring* is *not in love, but in life* itself as a tireless power which is continuously driving onward and upward – not, please observe, being beckoned or drawn by *Das Ewige Weibliche* [sic] or any other external sentimentality, but growing from within, by its own inexplicable energy, into even higher and higher forms of organization."[14] My intention here is to salvage a version of this largely forgotten nineteenth-century interpretation and to show moreover – *pace* Shaw's spirit – that it is *Götterdämmerung* which most forcefully makes this point. Although expressed with a late nineteenth-century Darwinian inflection, Shaw's thesis statement is essentially an eighteenth-century postulate – originally articulated by Gottfried Wilhelm Leibniz and then Immanuel Kant – of progress as immanent in nature. This theory of nature's inevitable trajectory of self-improvement is augmented in Wagner's case by a Hegelian faith in human agency to order the course of history. A number of scholars have already recognized Hegel's impact on Wagner, but none has attempted to make sense of *Götterdämmerung*, and hence the *Ring* as a whole, in terms of Hegel's philosophy of history.[15] The thesis of this book is that *Götterdämmerung*, first conceived during the intellectual and political tumult of the revolutionary mid-century, is as much a story about the process and promise of history, and the consequent demands it makes on individuals caught up in its currents, as about the triumph of the human spirit. I argue that *Götterdämmerung*, and hence the *Ring* as a whole, achieves coherence when read in terms of contemporary nineteenth-century theories of progress.

Shaw glorified Siegfried as the robust symbol of iconoclastic activism, dismissing Brünnhilde as the purveyor of a trite dream of *amor vincit omnia*. Following on Shaw, the standard view of Siegfried is that he represents the revolution, its aspirations as well as its failures. But as I will argue, Wagner's message of progress is not communicated through Siegfried, but through Brünnhilde – and moreover, not Brünnhilde in her familiar and stereotypical guise as the paragon of love and compassion, a quality disparaged by Shaw but welcomed by many commentators since then,[16] but as a battle-tested Hegelian world-historical hero who has the strength and vision to comprehend and thereby shape human history. In this way, I not only take issue with the recurring view of Siegfried as an epoch-making revolutionary, but also qualify the standard reading of Brünnhilde as the untarnished standard-bearer of transcendent love. Neither of these traditional modes of interpretation adequately accounts for their roles in the drama.

But just as important, I also challenge the article of faith that has come to dominate Wagner scholarship, namely that Wagner's encounter with the philosophy of Arthur Schopenhauer in 1854 conclusively altered the final message of the *Ring*. In this reading both the revolutionary exuberance of Siegfried and the paeans to love associated with Brünnhilde cede pride of place to the *Weltschmerz* of Wotan and a pessimistic message of renunciation.[17] Carl Dahlhaus, in his seminal study *Richard Wagner's Music Dramas* (1971), was among the first of the twentieth-century scholars to methodically challenge the Schopenhauerian interpretation, but his tersely argued points need to be qualified, elaborated, and updated as I attempt to do here.[18] It is my contention that whatever appeal Schopenhauer's philosophy had for Wagner – and I do not deny that it was great – Schopenhauer's uncompromising denigration of the will and denial of the possibility for human progress find no place in the written text of the *Ring*, nor in a plausible reading of the final musical setting. Instead, it is my intention to show, as a corollary to the principal theme of historical progress, that the *Ring* as completed in 1874 is fully consistent with Wagner's philosophical program of 1848–54 which embraced a sanguine faith in the march of history and the promise of human spiritual and cultural evolution.

Although a conductor and composer thoroughly devoted to his craft, Wagner was not at all insulated from the philosophical and political trends of his day. As a young man he was a committed follower of the reform agenda of the Young Germany movement.[19] While in Paris living the *vie de bohème* from 1839 to 1842, he was also likely introduced to the socialist theories of Proudhon, whose treatise published there in 1840 asked *Qu'est que la Propriété? (What Is Property?)* and provocatively responded, "property is theft!"[20] Wagner's interest in radical political ideology did not diminish upon his joining the ranks of the establishment in 1842 as Royal Kapellmeister to the Dresden court of King Friedrich August II of Saxony. His assistant conductor Röckel was a disciple of Proudhon and deeply immersed in the political and social philosophies of the day. In the course of their professional collaboration and friendship, Röckel would have a profound intellectual influence on the composer.[21] Thus, while in Dresden, Wagner not only engaged further with the thought of Proudhon but also explored the writings of Hegel – his *Phenomenology of Spirit* and his Berlin lectures on *Die Philosophie der Geschichte* (*Philosophy of History*) first published in 1837 (2nd edition, Karl Hegel, 1840), a copy of which he had in his Dresden library[22] – as well as those of the Young Hegelians, among them David Friedrich Strauss, Bruno Bauer, and Ludwig Feuerbach.[23] During this period of intellectual and political ferment, Wagner also fell under the spell of the revolutionary Mikhail Bakunin, a personal associate of Karl Marx, whose apocalyptic brand of utopian socialism was heavily influenced by Feuerbach's writings.

In the late 1840s Wagner began to give shape to his own political voice and sought to match his artistic endeavors to the same aspirations. In September 1848, he gave a speech at the Harmonie-Gesellschaft in Dresden on the occasion of the Tercentenary Festival of the Dresden Königliche Kapelle in which he toasted "the future of the Kapelle" with a distinctly Hegelian formula, noting that the present day was "the period of the human spirit's evolution to ever more distinct self-consciousness: in it that spirit has sought with surer tools to grasp its destiny."[24] Some two months later, Wagner completed his verse draft of *Siegfried's Tod* (the libretto that would become *Götterdämmerung*) and turned his attention to a number of other dramas on heroic figures: *Friedrich I*, on the reign of Holy Roman Emperor Friedrich Barbarossa; *Achilleus*, inspired by Greek mythology;

and *Jesus von Nazareth*.[25] In February and March 1849, Wagner is believed to have tried his hand at a number of political tracts – *Die Revolution* (*The Revolution*) and *Der Mensch und die bestehende Gesellschaft* (*Man and Established Society*), although there is some circumstantial evidence that these may have been drafted by Röckel – and a poem, "*Die Noth*," in the Feuerbachian vein, all of which were published in Röckel's radical-left journal *Volksblätter*.[26] The Dresden uprising took place in May. On the eve of revolt, Wagner actually took editorial control over Röckel's publication while Röckel was in hiding in Prague. Once Prussian troops entered the city and crushed the reformist opposition, Wagner himself became a wanted man and political refugee. He fled first to Zurich and then immediately on to Paris. With the spirit of revolution re-ignited, the precedent of the French Revolution came into focus once again. Wagner had kept a copy of Mignet's two-volume history of the period, *Histoire de la Révolution Francaise, depuis 1789 jusqu'en 1814* (*History of the French Revolution from 1789 to 1814*; 1824) on his shelves in Dresden, and while briefly sheltered in Paris in 1849 immersed himself in Lamartine's more recent account *Histoire des Girondins* (*History of the Girondists*; 1847).[27] Back in Zurich a month later Wagner returned to Proudhon and undertook a more rigorous study of Feuerbach.[28] In November 1849 he confessed to Karl Ritter, a friend from Dresden, his great indebtedness to Feuerbach, and some years later, in September 1852, he recommended that philosopher's writings to Röckel as "uncommonly stimulating reading."[29] It was in Zurich that Wagner integrated his thinking on music, culture, and social reform in three remarkable theoretical prose works, *Die Kunst und die Revolution* (*Art and Revolution*; 1849); *Das Kunstwerk der Zukunft* (*The Artwork of the Future*; 1849), dedicated to Feuerbach; and somewhat later *Oper und Drama* (*Opera and Drama*; 1851). Out of this intense intellectual engagement with the progressive thought of his day blossomed Wagner's full elaboration of the *Ring* cycle in the form of three operas to precede *Siegfried's Tod*.

In Switzerland Wagner had ample time on his hands to ponder the revolutionary moment in Europe and its failure to spark meaningful political change in Germany. But even after the disappointments both political and personal of 1848–49 there is little question that Wagner continued to embrace the optimism of his time and to maintain a faith in history.[30] In *The Artwork of the Future*, for example, Wagner confessed that "after a long battle between hope within and despair without, I gained the keenest, most steadfast belief in the future" (AF 19).[31] Years later, in 1872, as he was completing the score for *Götterdämmerung* and at the same time organizing the publication of his collected works, Wagner prefaced his reprint of that essay with a quote from Thomas Carlyle that ecstatically anticipated the "Heroic Wise" of the future. Wagner made clear that at the time he wrote his revolutionary treatise "I was in complete accord with the last words of this summons of the grey-headed historian" (AF 24).

Taking this cue from Wagner himself, I place great reliance in the course of this book on Carlyle's writings as a guide to understanding the philosophical issues that Wagner confronted in the *Ring*. Indeed, there are few authors of the nineteenth century who so completely capture the spirit, fervor, and logic of Wagner's own thought as Carlyle does. Immersed as Carlyle was in German philosophy and literature of the late eighteenth and early nineteenth centuries, it is not hard to understand how his thinking and that of Wagner might converge. Although there is no conclusive evidence in the historical record that Wagner read the philosopher and historian earlier than the 1870s, it is certainly true that by the time he came to complete the *Ring* he had come to know and respect the historical and philosophical insights of this English scholar.[32]

In addition to Carlyle, I use a Shakespeare play as a framework for approaching Wagner's dramatic agenda for *Götterdämmerung*. There is no question that Wagner identified strongly with Shakespeare and viewed himself as the heir to that playwright's legacy. As he announced in *Opera and Drama*, "the Drama of the Future, in strict keeping with its nature, will be born from the satisfaction of a need which Shakespearian Drama has aroused but not yet stilled."[33] His Dresden library held the complete works in translation by Schlegel and Tieck,[34] and from the start of his career Wagner was indebted to Shakespeare's plays for inspiration. Wagner's earliest creative efforts were based directly on the bard's work, most notably his play *Leubald: A Tragedy*, which followed *Hamlet*, *Macbeth*, and other Shakespearean precedents; the opera *Das Liebesverbot* (*The Ban on Love*; 1836), based on *Measure for Measure*; and *Die Feen* (*The Fairies*; 1834), which shares thematic and dramatic elements with *A Midsummer Night's Dream* in its opposing worlds of fairies and humans. Cosima recorded in her diary Wagner's appraisal of Shakespeare's importance: "Shakespeare does not really belong to literature at all. . . . Through Shakespeare one can to some extent form a picture of a figure like Homer."[35] Wagner was not alone in his homage. Throughout the nineteenth century, Shakespeare was lionized among the Germans as one of the world's great poets, esteemed highly enough to stand alongside native sons Goethe and Schiller.[36]

Notes

1 Letter to Röckel, 25/26 Jan. 1854, *Selected Letters of Richard Wagner*, trans. Stewart Spencer and ed. Barry Millington (London 1987) (hereafter "SL"), 305–6.
2 Thomas Carlyle, *The French Revolution: A History* (Modern Library 2002), 606.
3 Mike Rapport, *1848: Year of Revolution* (Basic Books 2008), 105: By 1848, "the great French revolution of 1789 had been studied carefully by reactionaries, reformers and revolutionaries alike for lessons and warnings."
4 Aileen Kelly, *The Discovery of Chance: The Life and Thought of Alexander Herzen* (Harvard University Press 2016), 190.
5 Fred Kaplan, *Thomas Carlyle: A Biography* (University of California Press 1993); Robert T. Kerlin, "Contemporary Criticism of Carlyle's 'French Revolution,'" *The Sewanee Review*, Vol. 20, No. 3 (July 1912), 288.
6 Carlyle, *French Revolution*, 676–7.
7 Nathan Rotenstreich, "The Idea of Historical Progress and Its Assumptions," *History and Theory*, Vol. 10, No. 2 (1971), 197. Kelly, *Discovery of Chance*, 95: "The destruction wrought by the Revolution of 1789 and the Napoleonic wars, the political and social upheavals in France culminating in the revolution of 1830 . . . intensified the need for some overarching explanation of existence that would make positive sense of the chaos of the present as a transitional stage in the passage to a state of earthly bliss. This was supplied by the concept of progress and its inevitability."

8 Larry Krasnoff, *Hegel's 'Phenomenology of Spirit': An Introduction* (Cambridge University Press 2008), 3; Rebecca Comay, *Mourning Sickness: Hegel and the French Revolution* (Stanford University Press 2011), 5: "French Revolution will remain the burning center of Hegel's philosophy"; Steven B. Smith, "Hegel and the French Revolution: An Epitaph for Republicanism," *Social Research*, Vol. 56, No. 1 (Spring 1989), 240–1: noting the "enduring grip of the French Revolution upon [Hegel's] thought" and his belief that the Revolution represented "one of the great watershed moments in modern history"; Kelly, *Discovery of Chance*, 190.

9 Smith, "Hegel and the French Revolution," 235: "It was Hegel's attempt ultimately to domesticate the revolution by regarding it as a 'moment' but only a moment in the collective *Bildung* of humanity."

10 Sandra Corse, *Wagner and the New Consciousness: Language and Love in the* Ring (Farleigh Dickinson University Press 1990), 16–17; Daniel H. Foster, *Wagner's 'Ring' Cycle and the Greeks* (Cambridge University Press 2010), 6–9; Hollinrake, "Philosophical Outlook," in *The Wagner Compendium: A Guide to Wagner's Life and Music*, ed. Barry Millington (Thames and Hudson 1992), 143; Roger Scruton, *The Ring of Truth: The Wisdom of Wagner's* Ring of the Nibelung (Allen Lane 2014), 19: in 1831 when Wagner enrolled at the University of Leipzig "it was Hegelian philosophy that dominated the faculties and captured the imagination of the young."

11 Rotenstreich, "The Idea of Historical Progress and Its Assumptions," 197; Kelly, *Discovery of Chance*, 95.

12 Simon Williams, *Wagner and the Romantic Hero* (Cambridge University Press 2004), 94.

13 Barry Emslie is the most vehement proponent of this view, stating in a recent article in the *The Wagner Journal* that *Götterdämmerung* is the "climax on every level of something of which it is no longer worthy." Barry Emslie, "The Kiss of the Dragon-Slayer," *The Wagner Journal*, Vol. 7, No. 1 (2013), 23; see also Barry Emslie, *Richard Wagner and the Centrality of Love* (The Boydell Press 2010), 87–92: referencing "knockabout story." John Deathridge notes the "alarming changes of personality and stagy effects (Shaw rightly abhorred them) that are still hard to take." John Deathridge, *Wagner Beyond Good and Evil* (University of California Press 2008), 72. Barry Millington concedes in *The Sorcerer of Bayreuth* that the opera is the "most stylistically regressive writing in the entire tetralogy." Barry Millington, *The Sorcerer of Bayreuth: Richard Wagner, His Work and His World* (Oxford University Press 2012), 106. Philip Kitcher and Richard Schacht likewise observe in *Finding an Ending* that the "mechanics of *Götterdämmerung* are creaky and cumbersome." Philip Kitcher and Richard Schacht, *Finding an Ending: Reflections on Wagner's* Ring (Oxford University Press 2004), 192. Foster comments, "Something is wrong with *Götterdämmerung*. Its music jars stylistically with the rest of the *Ring* and its plot does not seem to follow from *Siegfried*'s optimistic ending." Foster, *Wagner's 'Ring,'* 197.

14 George Bernard Shaw, *The Perfect Wagnerite: A Commentary on the Niblung's Ring* (Dover Publications Inc. 1967), 67.

15 A number of scholars have identified and explored compelling connections between Wagner's *Ring* and Hegel's thought. See Geoge G. Windell, "Hegel, Feuerbach and Wagner's *Ring*," *Central European History*, Vol. 9, No. 1 (1976); Corse, *Wagner and the New Consciousness*; Foster, *Wagner's 'Ring'*; Richard H. Bell, "Teleology, Providence and the 'Death of God': A New Perspective on the *Ring* Cycle's Debt to G.W.F. Hegel," *The Wagner Journal*, Vol. 11, No. 1 (2017); Richard Wagner, *The Artwork of the Future*, trans. Emma Warner, special edition of *The Wagner Journal* (recognizing Wagner's extensive use of Hegel's terminology). Windell, most notably, concludes, as I do, that Brünnhilde, not Siegfried, is Wagner's world-historical figure, but does not explore this insight in much depth. Windell, "Hegel, Feuerbach and Wagner's *Ring*," 46. Instead he examines how emotion and self-interest drive the dramatic developments of the plot towards the ultimate founding of a new world order, just as history in Hegel's theory is driven by "passion" towards unforeseen but rational ends. *Id.*, 48. Windell also demonstrates how

Hegel's theory of dialectical negation informs various concepts and musical themes throughout the *Ring*, including the opposition between Alberich, the dark-elf, and Wotan, as the light-elf, and the mirror-image rising and falling musical motif of the god's power and demise. Richard Bell, for his part, notes a number of Hegelian concepts at play in the *Ring*, such as a teleological process and divine sacrifice, while Daniel Foster adopts a more idiosyncratic interpretation based on Hegel's theory of aesthetics, reading the *Ring* as an allegory of the historical evolution and de-evolution of ancient Greek poetry and drama. Corse is the only commentator to date to attempt a thorough-going explication of the work in terms of Hegel's *Phenomenology*. Corse identifies the Hegelian notion of dialectical progress as central to the *Ring*, but her attention is principally directed to the development of individual psychology through love, rather than the progress of the species in historical time. In Hegelian terms, Corse focuses on the development of consciousness in the individual ("shapes of consciousness") as opposed to the growth of Spirit which is a world-historical phenomenon ("shapes of a world"). Georg Wilhelm Friedrich Hegel, *Phenomenology of Spirit*, trans. A.V. Miller (Oxford University Press 1977), 265 (§441); see Frederick C. Beiser, "'Morality' in Hegel's *Phenomenology of Spirit*," in *The Blackwell Guide to Hegel's 'Phenomenology of Spirit,'* ed. Kenneth R. Westphal (Wiley-Blackwell 2009), 209–10: "With spirit we are no longer dealing with the individual but the collective subject, no longer with this or that self but the spirit of a people as a whole." In Corse's interpretation, the apex of the drama is the mutual recognition and love between Siegfried and Brünnhilde, and Brünnhilde's final immolation is read principally as thematically reinforcing that moment and message of love. For Corse, Siegfried is the world-historical hero, while Brünnhilde is the last of the gods, who merely reflects her husband's heroic glory. As will be made clear in the course of this book, this interpretation follows the dialectical program of the *Phenomenology* only so far and thus fails adequately to account for *Götterdämmerung*'s world-historical thesis. Insofar as the theme of history is concerned, Mary Cicora in *Wagner's* Ring *and German Drama: Comparative Studies in Mythology and History in Drama* (Greenwood Press 1999) and Daniel Foster in *Wagner's 'Ring'* pursue fascinating lines of inquiry into how the concepts of history and myth intertwine in the *Ring*.

16 See, e.g., Deryck Cooke, *I Saw the World End* (Oxford University Press 2002), 20: "Shaw's blindness to the significance of the love-element in the drama crippled his interpretation"; Carl Dahlhaus, *Richard Wagner's Music Dramas*, trans. Mary Whittall (Cambridge 1979, repr. 1992), 140–1: "Brünnhilde's love for Siegfried features as the alternative to Wotan's resignation and renunciation of the world and looks forward in hope to reconciliation in the future"; the final theme is an expression of "rapturous love." More recent proponents of the love/compassion thesis are Simon Williams and Roger Scruton. Williams, *Wagner and the Romantic Hero*, 101: "Compassion as a force that changes people and brings about a less destructive world has triumphed and a utopia has come into view in our imagination if not in actuality"; Scruton, *The Ring of Truth*, 223: identifying the "compassion" to which Brünnhilde appeals "in her vindication at the opera's end."

17 While Cooke credits this reading (see Cooke, *I Saw the World End*, 22–3), he never had the opportunity to develop the argument fully in his unfinished analysis of the *Ring* that was published posthumously in 1979. At about the same time (1981), Stewart Spencer took up the torch, reading Brünnhilde's compassion as Schopenhauerian *caritas* and arguing that Wotan's "grand scheme for the regeneration of the world is now condemned to failure, because Wagner wills it so." Stewart Spencer, *"Zieh hin! Ich kann dich nicht halten!," Wagner*, Vol. 2, No. 4 (October 1981), 113–14. The Schopenhauerian theory has been more recently and keenly adopted by Warren Darcy. See, e.g., Warren Darcy, "The Metaphysics of Annihilation: Wagner, Schopenhauer, and the Ending of the 'Ring,'" *Music Theory Spectrum*, Vol. 16, No. 1 (Spring 1994); Warren Darcy, "'The World Belongs to Alberich!' Wagner's Changing Attitude Towards the 'Ring,'" in *Wagner's Ring of the Nibelung: A Companion*, eds. Barry Millington

and Stewart Spencer (Thames and Hudson 1993); Warren Darcy, "'Everything That Is, Ends!': The Genesis and Meaning of the Erda Episode in 'Das Rheingold'," *Musical Times*, Vol. 129, No. 1747 (Sep 1988); Warren Darcy, "The Pessimism of the 'Ring,'" *Opera Quarterly*, Vol. 4, No. 2 (1986). James Treadwell pursues the same theme, writing that "Wagner's revolutionary drama . . . seems to have hurled itself into the abyss between past and future, rather than bridging the gap as do those confidently optimistic first drafts of the story's end." James Treadwell, *Interpreting Wagner* (Yale University Press 2003), 88. Roger Scruton in *The Ring of Truth* is more equivocal in his approach to the *Ring*, seeming to accept as given the philosopher's influence ("Wotan's renunciation of the world recalls Schopenhauer's advocacy of the renunciation of the will," 291, and the cycle "ends in a spirit of resigned acceptance rather than visionary hope," 47) while at the same time finding a life-affirming message in the very act of renunciation ("the absolute value of life and love, revealed in the moment of their annihilation," 302). Emslie also takes the Schopenhauerian model for granted but is more alert to the contradictions inherent in this approach, noting that the "final act of renunciation and redemption not only takes the work onto a higher plane; it also makes nonsense of all the previous striving after power, after possession, even after *worldly* love. Instead, it exposes all these things as matters of lesser worth, as expressions of a lower, untrustworthy reality. . . . At the end the music drama narratively transcends itself . . . Yet at the point where structure and ideology meet, it does more than transcend itself, it contradicts itself." Emslie, *Centrality of Love*, 78–9. Marc Berry more strategically and transparently threads the interpretive needle by introducing two vectors of analysis in the *Ring*, contrasting the themes of Becoming (Hegel) and those of Being (Schopenhauer) which according to his analysis live uncomfortably side by side in the work, creating an "unresolved friction." Mark Berry, *Treacherous Bonds and Laughing Fire: Politics and Religion in Wagner's* Ring (Ashgate 2006); Mark Berry, "The Positive Influence of Wagner Upon Nietzsche," *The Wagner Journal*, Vol. 2, No. 2 (1999). Foster similarly adopts a purposefully ambivalent stance, acknowledging the validity of both interpretative approaches and explaining their tension in terms of Wagner's own manipulation of ambiguity. Foster, *Wagner's 'Ring,'* 236, 249–52. See also Roger Hollinrake, *Nietzsche, Wagner and the Philosophy of Pessimism* (George Allen & Unwin 1982), 75; Leland J. Rather, *The Dream of Self-Destruction: Wagner's Ring and the Modern World* (Louisiana State University Press 1979).

18 Dahlhaus's argument rests on four points: (a) that Wotan's end does not signal the end of the world but only the downfall of the gods; (b) that Wagner eventually rejected the Schopenhauerian approach as evidenced by his letter to Mathilde Wesendonck; (c) that the love of Siegfried and Brünnhilde is destroyed by an outside agency, not from within; and that (d) the final theme is an expression of "rapturous love" rather than resignation. Dahlhaus, *Richard Wagner's Music Dramas*, 103–4.

19 In the 1830s Wagner was introduced to the thought of the Young Germany movement principally through Heinrich Laube and Heinrich Heine and their writings. Hollinrake, "Philosophical Outlook," 143; Millington, *The Sorcerer*, 25; Stewart Spencer, "The 'Romantic Operas' and the Turn to Myth," in *The Cambridge Companion to Wagner*, ed. Thomas Grey (Cambridge University Press 2008), 69. See also Mitchell Cohen, "To the Dresden Barricades: The Genesis of Wagner's Political Ideas," in *The Cambridge Companion to Wagner*, 47; Rudiger Krohn, "The Revolutionary of 1848–49," in *Wagner Handbook*, eds. Ulrich Muller, Peter Wapnewski and trans. John Deathridge (Harvard University Press 1992), 157–8.

20 Pierre-Joseph Proudhon, *What Is Property?* eds. Donald R. Kelley and Bonnie G. Smith (Cambridge University Press 2008), 13–14; Cohen, "To the Dresden Barricades," 51; Krohn, "The Revolutionary," 157–8.

21 Krohn, "The Revolutionary," 157–8: Röckel was "well versed in the relevant political and socialist writings of these turbulent years, and he clearly exerted a lasting

... influence on the composer." Roger Hollinrake, "Epiphany and Apocalypse in the 'Ring'," in *Wagner's Ring of the Nibelung: A Companion*, eds. Stewart Spencer and Barry Millington (Thames and Hudson 1993), 41. Berry, *Treacherous Bonds*, 39: "Röckel studied movements of social reform in France and England."

22   See Corse, *Wagner and the New Consciousness*, 16–19; Foster, *Wagner's 'Ring,'* 6–9. Curt von Westernhagen, *Richard Wagners Dresdener Bibliothek 1842–1849* (Brockhaus 1966), 93: Wagner owned Karl Hegel's second edition of 1840, which is the version I reference throughout the book in the 1988 translation by Leo Rauch.

23   Hollinrake, "Epiphany and Apocalypse," 42; Krohn, "The Revolutionary," 161.

24   Richard Wagner, "Toast on the Tercentenary of the Royal Kapelle at Dresden," in *Pilgrimage to Beethoven and Other Essays*, trans. W. Ashton Ellis (University of Nebraska Press 1994; repr. 1st edn. 1898), 315.

25   Barry Millington, "*Der Ring des Nibelungen*: conception and interpretation," in *The Cambridge Companion to Wagner*.

26   Cohen, "To the Dresden Barricades," 61.

27   Westernhagen, *Richard Wagners Dresdener Bibliothek 1842–1849*, 97–8; Richard Wagner, "Annals," in *The Diary of Richard Wagner: The Brown Book 1865–1882*, trans. George Bird (Cambridge University Press 1980), 98; Richard Wagner, *My Life*, trans. Andrew Gray and ed. Mary Whittal (Cambridge University Press 1983), 420: "entertained myself for a long time with Lamartine's diverting and compelling *Histoire des Girondins*."

28   Hollinrake, "Epiphany and Apocalypse," 42. Wagner's diary notes reflect that in 1850 he read "Much Proudhon: *propriété*." *The Diary of Richard Wagner*, 100; Wagner, *My Life*, 420.

29   Letters to Karl Ritter, 19 Nov. 1849, and August Röckel, 12 Sept. 1852, SL 180 and 270.

30   Kitcher and Schacht assert that Wagner's "revolutionary hopes for a political transformation of Europe that would make Feuerbach's humanistic dreams come true had been dashed by the defeat of the revolutionaries of 1848–49." Kitcher and Schacht, *Finding an Ending*, 23. Berry, for his part, makes cursory reference to Wagner's "disillusionment in Swiss exile" (Mark Berry, "Richard Wagner and the Politics of Music-Drama," *The Historical Journal*, Vol. 47, No. 3 (2004), 663), while Michael Tanner points to Wagner's "more somber outlook" after Dresden (Michael Tanner, *Wagner* (Princeton University Press 1995), 100). But many other scholars dispute this characterization of Wagner's existential attitude in exile. See, e.g., Frank B. Josserand, "Wagner and German Nationalism," in *Penetrating Wagner's Ring: An Anthology*, ed. John DiGaetani (Da Capo Press 1978), 209: "Wagner's post-Dresden view of life was still fundamentally optimistic – after the revolution all would be well"; Spencer, "*Zieh hin!*," 106: "Wagner's revolutionary ardour increased, rather than diminished, after his flight to Switzerland"; Krohn, "The Revolutionary," 165: "There is no doubt that Wagner's convictions during his turbulent Dresden years continued to make their mark on his creative work long after the events of 1848–49"; Deathridge, *Wagner*, 49: "This is not to say, as many still do, that Wagner had a political change of heart [after 1849]. We only need to read his letters to see that he seldom stopped believing in his particular brand of revolutionary idealism . . . ." Wagner wrote to Minna in April of 1850, "you think of the past only with longing and regret, – I abandon it and think only of the future." SL 196. Over a year later, he noted to Theodor Uhlig in a letter of 12 Nov. 1851 that he could conceive of a performance of the *Ring* "only *after the Revolution*." SL 234.

31   Richard Wagner, *The Artwork of the Future*, trans. Emma Warner, in *The Wagner Journal* (2013) (hereafter "AF" in text), 19.

32   In addressing Carlyle's influence, Simon Williams rejects as untimely any "active" influence of Carlyle on the *Ring*, given that the historical record we are left with only shows Wagner first referring to Carlyle in the early 1870s. Williams, *Wagner and the Romantic Hero*, 19. See *Cosima Wagner's Diaries 1869–1883*, trans. and ed. Geoffrey Skelton, 2 vols. (London 1978–80) (hereafter "CT"), i, 299, 320, 339 (24 Nov. 1870; 10 Jan. 1871; 20 Feb. 1871). The work we know Wagner read at that time was Carlyle's biography

of Frederick the Great. But Wagner's library at Wahnfried also contained the *Selected Works of Carlyle*, in a six-volume Leipzig edition of 1855–6, which included *Sartor Resartus* in the fifth volume and the essay "Characteristics" in the second volume. There is also another possible avenue through which Wagner may have become acquainted with Carlyle as early as 1839, and that is his own week-long sojourn in London that year. By 1839, Carlyle had gained celebrity status, having already published *Sartor Resartus* in England (the first edition was printed in the U.S.), as well as *The French Revolution*, and given a series of well-received public lectures which were reported in the national press. Kaplan, *Thomas Carlyle*, 251; John Morrow, *Thomas Carlyle* (London 2006), 22. Wagner was in London again in 1855 for a more extended stay. Ferdinand Praeger, German composer and host to Wagner in London in 1855, notes in his memoir of Wagner that Wagner and Minna reminded him of Thomas and Jane Carlyle: During a two-month visit to Zurich in 1856 he observed that "she is a fitting parallel of Mrs. Carlyle, as Wagner is of Carlyle. Both men were thinkers, aye, and 'original' thinkers. . . . They both elected hard fare, nay, actual deprivation, to submission to the unrealities, and both are educators of our teachers." Ferdinand Praeger, *Wagner as I Knew Him* (reprint 2018), 171. Praeger's obvious familiarity with Carlyle and his work, and his association of Wagner with the British historian, hints at the possibility that he may very well have discussed Carlyle's work with the composer. Another source may have been Wagner's Dresden friend and correspondent August Röckel, who had a profound influence on the composer during the 1840s when they worked together in Dresden. Berry, *Treacherous Bonds*, 38–40. Röckel was immersed in the political and social issues of the day and had studied movements of social reform in England and France. Berry, *Treacherous Bonds*, 38–40; Krohn, "The Revolutionary," 157–8. Röckel lived in London in the early 1830s, during which period Carlyle's seminal essay "Characteristics" was published in the *Edinburgh Review* and *Sartor Resartus* in serial form in *Fraser's Magazine*. Röckel eventually left England but had brothers there with whom he continued to correspond. In the final analysis, whether Wagner read Carlyle or not during the 1840s and 1850s does not prevent us from using Carlyle's contemporary philosophical musings, particularly those developed in "Characteristics" (1831), *Sartor Resartus* (1838), and *The French Revolution* (1837), as a guide to understanding Wagner's own thought during that period. Moreover, Wagner's well-documented encounter with the English writer in the early 1870s means that the musical solution Wagner chose for the conclusion of the *Ring*, if not the text, can plausibly reflect Carlyle's influence.

33 Richard Wagner, *Opera and Drama*, trans. W. Ashton Ellis (University of Nebraska Press 1995; repr. of 1st edn., 1900), 127 (hereafter "OD" in text).

34 Westernhagen, *Richard Wagners Dresdener Bibliothek 1842–1849*, 103.

35 CT, i, 293 (7 Nov. 1870).

36 Frederick Burwich, "Shakespeare and Germany," in *Shakespeare in the Nineteenth Century*, ed. Gail Marshall (Cambridge University Press 2012), 314; Williams, *Wagner and the Romantic Hero*, 73: "By this time [mid-nineteenth century], Shakespeare had become the most widely performed of classic dramatists in the German theatre."

1   Siegfried as historical anomaly

The classic definition of Siegfried is the free man endowed with natural gifts and unfettered by the rule of law – a pristine exemplar of nature's purity and power.[1] These qualities made Siegfried, in Bernard Shaw's view, the very model of a modern English Protestant revolutionary – an activist who could fearlessly break through the falsehoods perpetrated by Church and State and establish the foundations for a new socialist world. The moment when Siegfried cuts through Wotan's spear with his newly forged sword is indeed a compelling symbolic pantomime of the defeat of the *ancien régime* by liberated and free-thinking man. As a result of Shaw, and no less Wagner's own instinct for broad dramatic gestures, the conception of Siegfried as a force of nature has been routinely wedded to a vision of the revolutionary man of action;[2] but these two modalities of Siegfried's character are not logically compatible.

The fundamental dilemma has always been: If Siegfried was to be the heroic progenitor of a new age, why did Wagner subject him to such a crushing demise in *Götterdämmerung*?[3] Shaw did not bother asking that question; he simply ignored the final stage of the cycle. Indeed, as he explained, Wagner's "revision, if carried out strictly, would have involved the cutting out of *Siegfried's Tod*, now become inconsistent and superfluous."[4] But as Wagner worked backwards in drafting the libretto of the *Ring*, he was necessarily conscious of the end point he was to reach – Siegfried not as heroic victor, but as conquered and compromised. Recent commentators have more directly confronted the paradox that the supposed harbinger of the future is not capable of bringing about that future.[5] The result has been a thorough-going indictment of Siegfried's character in an attempt to account for this failure.[6] Kitcher and Schacht have taken a particularly skeptical view of the hero, offering in the process the most damning critique of Siegfried to date.[7] In their interpretation, Siegfried's character is fatally flawed: a "brainless youth" marked by "rashness, pride, crassness, insensitivity." In the end they credit Wagner with describing a "*Heldendämmerung*" as much as a "*Götterdämmerung*."[8] But it is hard to square these critical appraisals of Siegfried with, among other things, the praise heaped on him by none other than Brünnhilde and the nobility accorded him in Wagner's powerful funeral march.[9]

Another challenge to comprehending Siegfried as revolutionary is his obvious lack of self-consciousness, which is not at all consistent with the role of a political firebrand. Berry attempts to shoehorn this inconvenient truth into the Shavian heroic framework by explaining it as the "fatal weakness of the charismatic revolutionary."[10] But how can the charismatic revolutionary be so blind? A revolutionary, by definition, must at least be able to understand and identify what must be destroyed, even as the job of rebuilding may have to be left to another. Berry admits as much when he observes, I think quite rightly, that Siegmund "might even be regarded as a greater hero than Siegfried, for he is not unaware of the laws and customs he is transgressing, nor of the price he might pay."[11] Nor was this notion of the myopic revolutionary at all one familiar to Wagner. Rather, Wagner prescribed:

> [O]nly those who are driven by a desire to break away from the cowardly bonds created by our criminal social and political structures, or from mindless subjection to them – who are revolted by the stale joys of our inhuman culture . . . who are filled with contempt for the self-satisfied sycophants (these most worthless of egoists!) . . . only he . . . can discover the power to rebel, to rise up and attack the oppressor of this same nature.
>
> (AF 85)

Needless to say, this portrait of the rebel disgusted by the hypocrisy of contemporary society is not a description of Siegfried.

In further defense of Siegfried as the revolutionary, many commentators argue that Siegfried is an example of Hegel's world-historical figure.[12] But in light of Siegfried's conceptual limitations, such a view hangs solely on the premise that the world-historical individual has "no consciousness of the Idea at all."[13] That is indeed what Hegel said in his lectures at the University of Berlin, but it is not the whole story. Hegel's discussion states in full:

> These heroic [world-historical] individuals, in fulfilling these aims of theirs, had no consciousness of the Idea at all. . . . *Yet at the same time they were thoughtful men, with insight* into what was needed and what was timely: their insight was the very truth of their time and their world – the next species, so to speak, which was already there in the inner source. It was theirs to know it, this universal concept, the necessary next stage of their world . . .[14]

There can simply be no debate that Siegfried is no "thoughtful man with insight" who has the capacity to grasp "the necessary next stage of the world."

In the final analysis, the gloss on Siegfried as anarchic revolutionary and world-historical hero puts much too much weight on Siegfried as a *dramatis persona*. Clearly Siegfried was not designed to function in this way. In *The Sorcerer of Bayreuth* (2012) Barry Millington intriguingly sketches the outlines of an interpretation that returns to the fundamentals of Siegfried's role as a man of nature and reads him in the context of Rousseau's philosophy of culture.[15] Such an interpretation offers a solution to the seeming conundrum of Siegfried's personality and heroism, and it is time to follow the logic of this thesis.

In attempting to understand the true essence of man and his social organizations, philosophers of the seventeenth and eighteenth centuries looked back to man's most primitive origins in the state of nature. From first principles of primeval time they sought to derive the fundamental truths that would guide humankind forward. The most practical thinkers accepted man for what he was, egoistic and violent. Thus, Thomas Hobbes famously declared in *Leviathan* (1651) that life in nature was "solitary, poor, nasty, brutish and short." In his Berlin lectures, Hegel agreed that "[f]reedom, as the ideal dimension of original nature, does not exist as an original and natural state. . . . [T]he 'state of nature' is not an ideal condition, but a condition of injustice, of violence, of untamed natural drives, inhuman acts, and emotions."[16] In this view, government and laws were necessary to temper man's antisocial instincts and promote civil peace. Eighteenth-century utilitarians such as Bernard Mandeville in *The Fables of the Bees* (1714) and Adam Smith in *The Wealth of Nations* (1776) made a virtue out of this apparent necessity, declaring that society would flourish to the extent that it promoted the pursuit of each man's self-interest.

Jean-Jacques Rousseau, on the other hand, refused to accept man as a selfish given. In fashioning *his* construct of the state of nature in *Discours sur l'origine et les fondements de l'inégalité parmi les hommes* (*A Discourse on the Origins and Foundations of Inequality among Men*; 1755) Rousseau rejected Hobbes's crabbed vision of humankind: "Above all, let us not conclude with Hobbes that man is naturally evil." Rousseau argued instead that the earth's first men were strong and happy. "[W]hat kind of misery can be that of a free being whose heart is at peace and whose body is in health?" Natural man was also essentially good, gifted with moral instincts, among them an "innate repugnance against seeing a fellow creature suffer," which led to "compassion."[17]

Rousseau's radical thesis – which turned the Christian doctrine of original sin and salvation through faith on its head – was that man's natural goodness and strength has been corrupted over time and that centuries of civilization had alienated him from his true self. "[S]ociety no longer offers to the eyes of the philosophers anything more than an assemblage of artificial men and factitious passions which are the products of all men's new relations and which have no true foundation in nature."[18] Placing the two historical prototypes side by side, Rousseau observed that "savage man and civilized man differ so much in the bottom of their hearts and inclinations that that which constitutes the supreme happiness of the one would reduce the other to despair."[19]

Fellow *philosophe* and friend Denis Diderot shared Rousseau's vision of an uncorrupted dawn of time and in his *Supplément au Voyage de Bougainville* (*Reflections on the Voyage of Bougainville*; 1771/1796) applied Rousseau's theoretical musings in the context of real-world history – dramatizing the gulf between natural and civilized man in a dialogue between a Tahitian native and a European explorer. Confronted with the apparent absurdity of European laws and mores, the noble savage is bewildered. In a fervent defense of the state of nature, the Tahitian points out the internal contradictions of eighteenth-century civil society and limns a worldview freed of customary constraints. Commenting on the practice of marriage, for example, the wise Tahitian Orou asserts:

> I find these strange precepts contrary to Nature. . . . . Contrary to Nature, because they assume that a being which feels, thinks and is free may be the property of another being like himself. . . . Such rules are contrary to the general order of things. What could seem more ridiculous than a precept which forbids any change of our affections, which commands that we show a constancy of which we're not capable, which violates the nature and liberty of male and female alike in chaining them to one another for the whole of their lives?[20]

The Tahitian also understands that under the yoke of laws and custom, man becomes at odds with himself: "You will merely breed rascals and wretches, inspired by fear, punishment and remorse, depraving their conscience, corrupting their character. People will no longer know what they should do and what they should avoid. Anxious when innocent, calm only in crime, they will have lost sight of the pole star which should have guided their way." He concludes that "the society whose splendid order your leader acclaims will be nothing but a swarm of hypocrites who secretly trample on the laws . . . "[21]

These *philosophes'* compelling vision of the natural goodness of man and the dangerous impact of civilization resonated with many thinkers in the early nineteenth century, inspiring a program of reform that set its goal on clearing out the Augean stables of contemporary belief systems and disposing of the ancient traditions, laws, and customs that had outlasted their relevance and continued to weigh on man's freedom. By destroying the illusions and falsehoods of the past that hampered man's potential, these thinkers sought to retrieve a measure of his original strength and happiness. Feuerbach, for example, in 1841 decried the burden of ancient modes of thought: "World-old usages, laws, and institutions continue to drag out their existence long after they have lost their true meaning. . . . [W]hat was once good, claims to be good for all times."[22] Likewise John Stuart Mill in his famous series of essays in *The Examiner* in 1831, "The Spirit of the Age," diagnosed the discontents of English society as symptoms of "an age of transition." "Mankind have outgrown old institutions and old doctrines, and have not yet acquired new ones. . . . [T]he same jacket which fitted him then, will not fit him now." The task, therefore, was to better understand the needs of the present so that man could prepare himself appropriately for the challenges of the future. "Society demands, and anticipates, not merely a new machine, but a machine constructed in another manner."[23] Carlyle performed an intricate fantasia on these recurrent themes of cultural reform in his utterly confounding yet brilliant work of didactic fiction, *Sartor Resartus* (1838), first serialized in *Fraser's Magazine* in 1833–34. Consistent with Mill and Feuerbach, Carlyle found society constrained and confounded by inherited norms and traditions, and called on men to liberate themselves by casting off these strictures as just so many outmoded and ill-fitting tweeds: "[T]here is something great in the moment when a man first strips himself of adventitious wrappages; and sees indeed that he is naked."[24]

The principal inherited burden that many nineteenth-century thinkers sought to jettison was Christianity. Edward Gibbon in his magisterial *History of the Decline and Fall of the Roman Empire* (1776–88) had helped open the way to seeing Christianity not as timeless truth but as a historical phenomenon, one that history and time could logically supersede.[25] And in the *Kritik der reinen Vernunft* (*Critique of Pure Reason*; 1781) Kant had conclusively demonstrated that it was impossible to prove the existence of God. As Heinrich Heine wryly remarked, "We must write Dante's words: 'Abandon all hope!' above this section of the *Critique of Pure Reason*."[26] Early nineteenth-century German philosophers set about completing Gibbon's and Kant's work by methodically dismantling the perceived truths of Christian theology. The Young Hegelians led the charge with David Friedrich Strauss's *Das Leben Jesu, kritisch bearbeitet* (*The Life of Jesus, Critically Examined*), published in 1835–36,[27] which sought to prove that the Gospels were myth, not true history. Ludwig Feuerbach was the next to recklessly take up the cause of demystifying and secularizing religious beliefs. As a student Feuerbach had heard Hegel teach, and that scholar's historicist perspective conclusively shattered Feuerbach's faith in biblical revelation.[28] In his highly influential study *Das Wesen des Christentums* (*The Essence of Christianity*; 1841) Feuerbach argued in exhaustive detail – "unhelpful prolixity" in Wagner's view – that the time-honored tenets of the Christian faith were riddled with internal contradictions and that God was simply the objectification of man's best and highest capabilities. "God as a morally perfect being is nothing else than the realized idea, the fulfilled law of morality, the moral nature of man posited as the absolute being" (EC 49). Correcting for centuries of excessive focus on man's spiritual nature, Feuerbach called for a return to man's sensual being.

Members of the Young Germany movement also joined the bandwagon of religious reform. In words that would inspire Nietzsche later in the century, Heinrich Heine wrote in *Zur Geschichte der Religion und Philosophie in Deutschland* (*On the History of Religion and Philosophy in Germany*; 1835) how Christianity had made European man sick. He looked forward to the day when "humanity has again attained its complete health, when peace has again been established between soul and body, and soul and body again mingle in their original harmony – on that day it will hardly be possible to understand the artificial discord which Christianity sowed between the two."[29] Many took this sensualism to its logical socio-political extreme, advocating, like Diderot's Tahitian, for free love and liberation from bourgeois values – themes that Wagner would exploit in *Das Liebesverbot*.

The contemporary aspirations to reconcile body and soul and to restore man to his natural wholeness and integrity were challenges that Wagner himself took seriously, and his post-Dresden writings fully embrace the reformist Rousseauvian agenda as articulated by the Young Hegelian and the Young Germany movements – the need to eradicate the artificial constructs of civilization in order to liberate the true inner core of human strength. In *Art and Revolution*, for example, Wagner echoed Rousseau in denouncing modern culture and society as the "efflorescence of corruption, of a hollow, soulless and unnatural condition of human affairs and human relations."[30] Similarly, in *The Artwork of the Future*, he explained that "all the vice and depravity that sickens you about the masses are nothing but the desperate symptoms of the struggle which true human nature is waging against its brutal oppressor, modern civilization, and that these appalling symptoms, far from being the true face of nature, reflect rather the false grotesque face of your state and police culture" (AF 84). In a succinct summary of Rousseau's thesis Wagner wrote in *Opera and Drama*:

> From this possession grown into an *ownership*, which wondrously enough is looked on as the base of all good order, there issue all the crimes of myth and history. . . . The Thinkers of this State . . . retained these very imperfections as a given thing, as the only thing to fit the 'sinfulness' of human nature, and never went back to the real Man himself, – who from his at first instinctive, but at last erroneous views had called these inequalities into being . . .[31]
>
> (OD 192)

Rather than start fresh from first principles of man's natural goodness, political scientists had accepted man's historically corrupted character as the real thing and had built elaborate but tenuous political structures designed not to foster man's inner goodness but simply to cabin and control his selfish instincts. Reinforcing Rousseau's insights through Carlyle's sartorial metaphor, Wagner wrote that contemporary intellectuals had as a result "taken a soft, pliable garment suited to the easy movement of human bodies and made a rigid, stuffed iron coat of armour, an ornament in a historic armoury" (AF 19).[32]

Following the lead of the Young Hegelian philosophers, Wagner principally condemned the "halo of Christian hypocrisy" and "Christian dogma" which had "set man's goal entirely outside his earthly being," focusing it instead on "an absolute and superhuman God" (AR 42, 49). As a result of Christianity's denial of life, and its preaching of "humility, renunciation, contempt of every earthly thing" (59-60), men were currently slaves, "slaves, whom bankers and manufacturers teach nowadays to seek the goal of Being in manual toil for daily bread" (AR 51). Christianity was also responsible for the critical flaw in civilized society, namely "that egoism which has been the cause of such immeasurable sorrow in the world and of such deplorable mutilation and inauthenticity in art" (AF 28). As egoists, men viewed other men as means, not as ends in themselves: "The horror of the absolute egoist, then, is that he or she sees in others only the natural conditions of his or her own existence, consuming them – in however peculiarly barbaric, effete ways – as fruit and beasts consume nature, giving nothing, only taking" (AF 27). Wagner warned that "as long as these conditions persist, as long as they suck the lifeblood from the wasted strength of the people, as long as they, themselves impotent, sap the potency of the people in their selfish persistence – in these circumstances all meaning, creativity, change, betterment, reform is just willful, pointless, fruitless" (AF 19). The goal of revolution as well as of art, therefore, was to "tear down the web of relationships which creates the conditions for the unnatural to reign" (AF 19). For Wagner, the way to enlightenment was to eradicate cultural artifice – Carlyle's "adventitious wrappages" – and thereby free mankind "from doubt of its own worth to consciousness of its highest godlike might" (AR 65). With a nudge from Feuerbach, then, Rousseau's simple savage had become the focal point of a new religion of man.

Wagner wrote *Siegfried's Tod* while wedded to this *Weltanschauung*, and the work emerged out of his attempt to dramatize these truths about the incompatibility of the natural inner core of humanity with the superficial encrustations of civilization. In *Eine Mittheilung an meine Freunde* (*A Communication to My Friends*; 1851) Wagner explained the process by which he arrived at Siegfried as the choice for his new opera. He "drove step by step into the deeper regions of antiquity, where at last to my delight, and truly in the *utmost* reaches of old time, I was to light upon the fair young form of *Man*, in all the freshness of his force."[33] Wagner's process, therefore, paralleled that of Rousseau and other Enlightenment thinkers to delve deep into human history in order to discern the characteristics of original man. Once again Wagner employed the metaphor of clothing to highlight his theoretical approach of stripping away man's customs and habits, defined by centuries of historical precedent, to find the true character of a human being. "What here I saw, was no longer the Figure of conventional history, whose garment claims our interest more than does the actual shape inside; but the real naked man, in whom I might spy each throbbing of his pulses, each stir within his mighty muscles, in uncramped, freest motion; the type of the true *human being*" (CF 358).[34]

Instead of following the *philosophes* in creating a theoretical construct of the dawn of time to discover his noble savage, Wagner sought the reflection of man's most authentic form in his own primeval myths. Conceived in the earliest stages of man's social development, the Norse myths revealed a truth about man's innate character well before the complications of civilization had buried his natural traits beneath layers of custom, law, and tradition. Carlyle too had been seduced by the Norse myths, the Poetic and Prose Eddas, as well as the ancient Teutonic tales that so enchanted Wagner, and in 1831 published *The Nibelungen Lied*, summarizing for English readers the story of Siegfried, Brunhild, Hagen, and King Gunther. In these traces of pre-history, Carlyle found a "broad simplicity, rusticity," a "homely truthfulness, and rustic strength, a great rude sincerity," "the infant Thought of man opening itself, with awe and wonder, on this ever-stupendous Universe." Carlyle believed that by focusing his contemporaries' attention on the "first beautiful morning-light of our Europe" in these myths, he could inspire a rediscovery of the "[w]onder, hope; infinite radiance of hope and wonder, as of a young child's thoughts, in the hearts of these strong men!"[35]

In developing the character of Siegfried, Wagner reveled in this golden age fantasy of the natural man freed of the fears, anxieties, and ambitions that tormented contemporary members of civil society. The traits associated with Siegfried reflect those that Rousseau assigned to his first men. Siegfried is "robust agile and courageous" and free of the fear of death.[36] He lives at peace in the forest and among the animals there[37] and is all action, moving from challenge to challenge without much if any circumspection. And like Carlyle's original Norseman, Siegfried is a stalwart with a child's heart and naivete. As Wagner wrote to Röckel, "his intense feeling for nature means that he only ever sees things as they are."[38] But with his childlike purity also comes all the impetuousness, braggadocio, and disrespect for social norms that are fundamental to a child's mindset, in other words "the crude aspects of his genuine boyishness," as Heinrich Porges – parroting Wagner – would later record.[39]

Such a figure as Siegfried is defined not only by his callowness but also by his lack of self-consciousness. Man in his savage state, Rousseau opined, "dwells only in the sensation of its present existence, without any idea of the future, however close that might be, and his projects, as limited as his horizons, hardly extend to the end of the day. Such is, even today, the extent of the foresight of a Caribbean Indian: he sells his cotton bed in the morning, and in the evening comes weeping to buy it back, having failed to foresee that he would need for it for the next night."[40] Consistent with his prototype, Siegfried "lives entirely in the present, he is the hero, the finest gift of the will," as Wagner told his wife.[41] Or as he told Röckel, "in Siegfried I have tried to depict what I understand to be the most perfect human being, whose highest consciousness expresses itself in the fact that all consciousness manifests itself solely in the most immediate vitality and action."[42]

Having conceived of the natural man freed from the corrupting effects of civilization – the burdens of history – what did Wagner intend to dramatize? In "A Communication," Wagner explained how his intentions for *Siegfried's Tod* had evolved out of his original plan for a drama based on the reign of the Holy Roman Emperor Friedrich Barbarossa. There he had wanted to show the "giant forces [the hero] strives to master, only to be at last subdued by them" (CF 359). But in struggling to make sense of the historical material for his five-act play, Wagner came to realize that the historical setting was itself an impediment to his dramatic purpose. "[A]s artist, I should have met precisely the same fate in my drama as did its hero: to wit, I should myself have been crushed by the weight of the very *relations* that I fain would master – i.e. portray –, without ever having brought my *purpose* to an understanding" (CF 359-60). In engaging with the complex array of details necessary to portray the historical events in their proper context, Wagner anticipated that he would meet the same fate as the hero he intended to portray – that is, he too would be "crushed by the weight" of those "relations" which he had hoped to master. For Wagner, those "relations" represented "the excrescences of history" that had "at last usurped dominion over Man and ground to dust his freedom" (CF 358).[43] Ultimately Wagner gave up on his historical material as too cumbersome for the stage and turned to the myth of Siegfried to drive home his point. But it is apparent from his discussion that the underlying conception for the drama that would become *Siegfried's Tod* was not about a hero who would triumph over the forces of civilization arrayed against him, but instead would be overcome by them.[44]

As noted, Diderot recognized that there was a historical precedent for such a fable of the clash between natural man and civilization. The history of the New

World was replete with examples of how the societies of the American aborigines had been utterly decimated by conquering Europeans. These native cultures, preserved as it were in a vacuum of time, were no match for the degeneracy of modern man.[45] Diderot was all too aware of the unfair odds. In his *Reflections on the Voyage of Bougainville*, an old Tahitian foresees the danger posed by the European explorers and exhorts his countrymen: "Weep, wretched natives of Tahiti, weep. But let it be for the coming and not the leaving of these ambitious, wicked men. . . . One day they will come back . . . to enslave you, slaughter you, or make you captive to their follies and vices." Recognizing the psychological as well as the physical toll of civilized existence, the Tahitian pleads with the European explorers, "Go back to your own country to agitate and torment yourself as much as you like. But leave us in peace. Do no fill our heads with your factitious needs and illusory virtues."[46]

In the nineteenth century, this chasm between the natural innocence of the man of nature and his corrupted successor, the product of civilization, was brought starkly – and poignantly – into relief in Herman Melville's novel of 1891, *Billy Budd, a Sailor*, left unpublished at his death. Melville's tale attests to the continuing vitality of the Rousseauvian paradigm even late into the century,[47] and his parable of the simple sailor, Budd, and his evil nemesis, Claggart, comes closest, I believe, to capturing Wagner's thesis for *Götterdämmerung*. "[H]appily endowed with the gaiety of high health, youth, and a free heart," Budd is "such a fine specimen of the *genus homo*, who in the nude might have posed for a statue of a young Adam before the Fall."[48] He is a model of the "Handsome Sailor" who "showed in face that humane look of reposeful good nature which the Greek sculptor in some instances gave to his heroic strong man, Hercules."[49] In extolling his hero's virtues Melville alternately draws on Biblical and Hellenic motifs, but it is clear in the end that his character is a child of nature – a noble savage. Melville calls him an "upright barbarian," a "Tahitian, say, of Captain Cook's time or shortly after that time."[50] Melville is quick to clarify that Budd's noble traits of character do not derive from civilized culture but rather from his inherent natural gifts: "[I]t is observable that where certain virtues pristine and unadulterate peculiarly characterize anybody in the external uniform of civilization, they will upon scrutiny seem not to be derived from custom or convention, but rather to be out of keeping with these, as if indeed exceptionally transmitted from a period prior to Cain's city and citified man."[51] Consistent with his innocence, Budd has no capacity to understand the intricacies and duplicity of civilized life. He is a "novice in the complexities of factitious life," and "to deal in double meanings and insinuations of any sort was quite foreign to his nature."[52] Against this paragon of manly simplicity, Melville pits the evil Claggart, who forms a hatred of Budd borne of "envy and antipathy." Melville archly asks "what might eventually befall a nature like that, dropped into a world not without some mantraps and against whose subtleties simple courage lacking experience and address, and without any touch of defensive ugliness, is of little avail."[53] From the formulation of this question it is clear who must win in the end. Budd ultimately kills Claggart – in an instinctive physical response to Claggart's unfounded accusation of treason – but must hang for his murderous act. Melville chillingly summarized the paradox: "Struck dead by an angel of God! Yet the angel must hang!"[54]

Like Melville, Wagner sought to highlight the corruptions of civilized society by pitting man's best nature against his future alienated self, engaging in the same thought experiment of "dropping" a natural man into the middle of corrupt society.[55] Wagner conceived *Siegfried's Tod* as an allegorical tale about the confrontation of man's natural being with the forces of civilization. The "relations" that had come to dominate man's modern life would "crush" even man in his best natural form, and such a spectacle would imbue the audience with the terror and pity necessary to force into recognition the shortcomings of current human existence. As Wagner observed in a later work, *Religion und Kunst* (*Religion and Art*; 1880), "our sympathy belongs not to the victor, but the vanquished hero."[56] Siegfried, armed only with native intuition like Diderot's Tahitian or Melville's "upright barbarian," is no match for Hagen, whose artful cunning and duplicity reflect the skills of civilization developed and honed over millennia of human history. In Wagner's hands, Hagen's selfishness, falsity, and duplicity mark him as the quintessential modern man who displays "the arrogance of hypocrisy, as usury, as robbery of Nature's goods, and egoistic scorn of suffering fellow-men" (AR 60). When it comes to the palace intrigue of the Gibichung Court and the nasty deviousness of Hagen, Siegfried is a complete novice. Siegfried has no capability to discern the evil intentions of Hagen behind the mask of hospitality. He thus all too easily falls into the trap set by the Gibichungs and remains a mere plaything of the schemers until Hagen reopens his eyes on his deathbed. This extraordinary vulnerability is not Siegfried's failing as a human being or even a paradox of the revolutionary mindset. It demonstrates instead Siegfried's natural purity and quality of character that he does not have the means to counter Hagen's highly cultivated form of evil.

Wagner could not possibly have known of Melville's work, but there was another model for this archetypal conflict between heroic forthrightness and duplicitous cunning that would have been very close at hand: Shakespeare's *Othello*.[57] Wagner knew the play well and likely attended a performance in Zurich with the famous American actor Ira Aldridge in the title role in 1857.[58] Wagner was deeply moved by the tragedy. Indeed, it "lay closest to his heart" after *Lear*.[59] One October afternoon in 1879 as he was finishing his smoke and crushing out the light in his cigarette, Wagner's thoughts turned to the fatal smothering of Desdemona. "Beyond words" was how he described the play to Cosima that day.[60] Some years earlier, after seeing the last three acts of the play in November 1870, Cosima herself was left "unutterably moved."[61] The story of *Othello* was already known to Europeans in operatic form through Gioachino Rossini's 1816 setting of a French version of the play. Celebrated for its moving final third act, Rossini's work was regularly performed throughout Europe in the decades after its premiere and was known to Wagner, who praised its music as among Rossini's best.[62] The lyrical lament of the gondolier from Act III – sung to a line from Dante's *Inferno* – was memorialized in Franz Liszt's adaptation of the theme in *Venezie e Napoli* (1840; revised and published in 1859), a set of three piano works supplementing his *Annés des Pélérinages*.[63]

Heinrich Porges, music critic and assistant to Wagner at Bayreuth, described the "cosmic drama" of the *Ring* as one "in which the spirit of antique tragedy and that of Shakespeare seem to have joined hands,"[64] and it is not hard to recognize in the ill-fated encounter between Siegfried and Hagen the iconic conflict of Othello and Iago.[65] Othello, like Siegfried, is a heroic strong man but also an outsider who does not readily fit into the culture of Venice. In words that perfectly capture Siegfried's unique qualities and fate, Shakespeare critic Harold Bloom has described Othello as "an ontological splendor . . . a natural man self-raised to authentic if precarious eminence."[66] Flush with victory, Othello woos and wins the prized Desdemona. But he and Desdemona violate the normal rules of courtship when she runs off with him without first seeking her father's consent. Iago steps in to poison their happiness. Iago is a master of deception who matches Hagen in villainy: "I am not what I am." Othello, on the other hand, for all his exploits on the battlefield, is a naif, and so tragically vulnerable to Iago's manipulation: "The Moor is of a free and open nature/That thinks men honest that but seem to be so."[67] Just so Siegfried. Under the false guise of friendship, Iago and Hagen coopt their heroes to their demonic plans, driving them to acts of violence towards their loved ones.

Harold Bloom has stressed the importance of reading Othello as a "great soul hopelessly outclassed in intellect and drive by Iago,"[68] and that is in fact how many in the nineteenth century viewed him. Among the English critics, William Hazlitt called the Moor "noble, confiding, tender, and generous."[69] Algernon Swinburne, in his *Study* of 1880, called him the "noblest man of man's making."[70] At the end of the century, Andrew Cecil Bradley concluded in his lectures on *Shakespearean Tragedy* (1904) that the character of Othello is "so noble" that he "stirs, I believe, in most readers a passion of mingled love and pity which they feel for no other hero in Shakespeare."[71] As for the Germans, August Wilhelm Schlegel, who commented on the play in his lectures *Über dramatische Kunst und Literatur* (*On Dramatic Art and Literature*; 1809–11), a book that was widely read throughout the nineteenth century and that Wagner maintained in his Wahnfried library in an 1846 Leipzig edition, advanced a more jaundiced interpretation of the central character's motivations. He judged Othello from a racist perspective as a product of "that glowing zone which generates the most ravenous beasts of prey and the most deadly poisons."[72] For Schlegel, Othello was a man divided between his innate savage nature and the cultured morality of his Venetian social world. In this way, he read the universal human tragedy out of the play, choosing instead to see the fate of Othello as driven not by a common "jealousy of the heart," but rather a particular manifestation "of the sensual kind which, in burning climes, has given birth to the disgraceful confinement of women and many other unnatural usages."[73] All the same, he was prepared to concede that the character "is noble, frank, confiding, grateful for the love shown him" and "moreover, a hero who spurns at danger, a worthy leader of an army, a faithful servant of the state."[74] Many contemporaries disagreed with Schlegel's portrait of Othello as a man uniquely vulnerable to an inborn strain of violence.[75] Victor Hugo, for one, in his introduction to his son's translation of the play published in 1860, took direct aim at Schlegel, arguing that Othello's intellectual and moral superiority was the key to the drama: Shakespeare was not just depicting a particular African man who succumbs to jealousy but humanity itself.[76] Later in the century, when responding to a performance of Othello by the celebrated Italian actor Ernesto Rossi, whose interpretation stressed the barbaric nature of the Moor, Henry James protested "how crude it was, how little it expressed the hero's moral side, his depth, his dignity – anything more than his being a creature terrible in mere tantrums."[77] In reviewing the performance that Wagner is believed to have seen in 1857, the poet and revolutionary Georg Herwegh sidestepped (to a degree) the racial element in Schlegel's account, describing Shakespeare's character more generally as a "tiger," hence a powerful being endowed by nature with a capacity for great violence, but all the same a "brave, noble, lovestruck" one.[78]

Nineteenth-century critics, on the other hand, were unanimous in their condemnation of Iago as the embodiment of evil. William Hazlitt described Iago as "an extreme instance of . . . diseased intellectual activity, with an almost perfect indifference to moral good or evil."[79] Schlegel was unequivocal in his condemnation of Iago as "black within."[80] For Hugo, the character combined the hypocrisy of Tartuffe with the skepticism of Don Juan, who, but for his lack of supernatural powers, could properly be called a Mephistopheles. "Lyricism is denied him," Hugo observed.[81] Bradley found the scheming ensign "decidedly cold by temperament" and "thoroughly selfish and unfeeling."[82] Nineteenth-century critics traced Iago's evil to one central character trait: Egoism. Bradley observed that "his creed – for he is no sceptic, he has a definite creed – is that absolute egoism is the only rational and proper attitude."[83] And indeed Iago is perfectly frank with Rodrigo about his motivations: "in following him [Othello], I follow but myself."[84] As Schlegel completed his portrait: "Cool, discontented, and morose, arrogant where he dare be so, but humble and insinuating when it suits his purposes, he is a complete master in the art of dissimulation; accessible only to selfish emotions, he is thoroughly skilled in rousing the passions of others . . ."[85]

This inhuman coldness, duplicity, and monomaniacal egoism – traits Wagner identified as some of the worst vices of modern society – unsurprisingly shape Hagen's portrait as well. Hagen feels no kindred spirit with other men, and Alberich concedes that he "brought up Hagen to feel stubborn hatred" (RN 34). Hagen admits to Siegfried that his blood is "stubborn and cold . . . curdles within me" (RN 298), and in the dream sequence tells his father, "I hate the happy, am never glad!" (RN 309). Alberich's spite and single-minded greed have become entirely Hagen's own. When Alberich urges Hagen to regain the ring, he asks, "Do you swear to it, Hagen, my hero?" Hagen replies, "To *myself* I swear it: silence your care!" (RN 311-12, emphasis added). Hagen also has no difficulty employing the "art of dissimulation" to get his way. "Since his death is bound to afflict her [Gutrune], then let the deed be hid from her," Hagen tells Gunther (RN 330). Wagner permits a joke about Hagen's lack of more lyrical sensibilities when it comes time for him to summon Gunther's vassals to the wedding celebration. Gutrune directs him, "You, Hagen, lovingly call the menfolk to Gibich's garth for the wedding!"

But incapable of doing anything "lovingly," Hagen responds by summoning the vassals with a war cry punctuated by foreboding blasts on his cowhorn: "*Wehe! Wehe! . . . Waffen! Waffen!*" (RN 315).[86] Finally, Hagen's stark manipulation of the dramatic action with his application of the poison and then its antidote is a concrete manifestation of Iago's recognized role as the symbolic playwright.[87]

Siegfried may be the noble soul brought low by evil manipulation, but it is important to acknowledge that he does not suffer the same fate as Shakespeare's character. Wagner does not give his hero a fatal weakness and then let the audience watch in prurient horror as he suffers the psychological damage that it wreaks. To the contrary, Wagner goes to great lengths to preserve Siegfried's moral innocence. The potion is a cumbersome plot device indeed – one not seemingly worthy of Wagner's skills as a dramatist.[88] And yet, it insulates the hero from guilt he has no ability to carry as a pure man of nature. As a result he remains completely untainted by the corruptions around him. By the device of the drug, Wagner ensures that his hero is not compromised in any moral way by the schemes of Hagen and the Gibichungs. His integrity and honor are preserved.[89] Wagner told Cosima in 1873 that "there is a veil over him since winning Brünnhilde for Gunther, he is quite unaware." It is for this reason that Wagner concluded that Siegfried is not a "tragic figure."[90]

Kitcher and Schacht interpret the potion of forgetfulness as a mechanism to reveal or accelerate the purportedly boorish failings in Siegfried's character. "The drink . . . should be understood as a distillation of the debasement to which desire is susceptible in the absence of true inner strength and quality."[91] But this reading is inconsistent with Wagner's dramatic treatment. The Siegfried we have come to respect is the one who finds Brünnhilde and falls in love. Siegfried – the fearless son of the woods – learns fear on encountering his counterpart in nature. And by learning fear and subsequently love, Siegfried embraces his full humanity.[92] When Siegfried arrives at the Gibichung palace his only fault is trustingly accepting a drink of welcome from his hostess. On first quaff, Siegfried succumbs to the poisonous brew and forgets his love for Brünnhilde. To remove Brünnhilde entirely from his psyche is to leave Siegfried with only the callow swagger of his heroic deeds. The softening compassionate lesson of his human embrace is promptly unlearned. A key aspect of his identity is thus eradicated by the potion. As Wagner explained to Röckel, individual freedom is founded on "integrity." "He who is true to himself, i.e. who acts in accord with his own being . . . is *free*; strictly speaking, outward constraint is powerless unless it succeeds in destroying the integrity of its victim, inducing him to dissemble and to persuade himself and others that he is a different person from the one he really is."[93] Since by operation of the potion he is not entirely himself, the complete person he has become through his love of Brünnhilde, Siegfried loses his integrity as a human being and hence his free will.[94] Wagner underscores this point musically by denying Siegfried his characteristic motif during the pendency of the poison.[95]

Kitcher and Schacht, and Berry as well, also note Siegfried's first greeting to Hagen and Gunther as evidence of his lack of moral compass, even before the potion takes effect: "Now fight with me, or be my friend!" (RN 293). As Kitcher and

Schacht scold, "[t]his puerile swaggering seems a poor way of pursuing the venture."[96] This salutation, however, is not Wagner's own but derived from his historical sources.[97] Moreover, consistent with the thesis of Siegfried as man of nature, the statement can just as reasonably be interpreted as an expression of the young man's moral simplicity at his key moment of encounter with the duplicity of civilized culture. Siegfried understands only friends and enemies, interlocutors whose intentions are clear. He has no capacity to discern the malevolence that lies hidden behind Hagen's mask of hospitality. Wagner would later write of mythic heroes such as Herakles and Siegfried that "a lie to them was inconceivable, and a free man meant a truthful man" (RA 278).

Kitcher and Schacht further point to Siegfried's cruel coercion of Brünnhilde on the rock as further evidence of his inherent callousness. "Even if we imagine him as unaware of the vows he has sworn to this woman . . . there still is a shock in what he shows himself to be capable of doing."[98] But it is critical that Siegfried acts in this way only when fully under the power of the tarnhelm, a trophy that originally meant nothing to him and which he only uses at Hagen's urging. By allowing its wearer to defy the laws of time and space, the tarnhelm manufactures miracles. But as Feuerbach made clear in the *Essence of Christianity*, miracles represent a corruption of natural law and a false understanding of the world: "The belief in a special Divine Providence is the characteristic belief of Judaism; belief in Providence is belief in miracle; but belief in miracle exists where Nature is regarded only as an object of arbitrariness, of egoism, which uses Nature only as an instrument of its own will and pleasure. . . . And all these contradictions of Nature happen for the welfare of Israel" (EC 116).[99] Echoing Feuerbach, Wagner himself wrote that "the Judaeo-Christian Wonder tore the connexion of natural phenomena asunder, to allow the Divine Will to appear as standing *over* Nature" (OD 213). As a talisman whose miraculous powers are antithetical to natural law, the tarnhelm encapsulates the worst vices of modern society. By using the tarnhelm to become Gunther, Siegfried dons "the false grotesque face of . . . state and police culture," sacrificing his natural strength in exchange for the hypocrisies and lies of deceitful egotistical civilization. Through its sinister magic Siegfried becomes a master of dissembling, further betraying his true self and his "integrity." And under its malign influence, Siegfried succumbs to the "monstrous sin of the absolute egoist," treating other humans as means, not ends-in-themselves.

Siegfried's unwitting betrayal of Brünnhilde and his unknowingly false oath to Gunther also reflect Wagner's insights about the conflict between the individual and society. In *Opera and Drama*, Wagner dwelt at length on the myth of Oedipus and its significance to the Greek worldview. Wagner criticized the ancient Greeks for judging Oedipus as morally responsible for parricide and incest in spite of the fact that his transgressions were committed without knowledge. While Oedipus may have been a victim of fate, he was not personally guilty of his actions. In Wagner's view, "Oedipus and Jocasta *knew* not, in what social relation they stood to one another: they had acted unconsciously, according to the natural instinct of the purely human Individual" (OD 182). As an ignorant victim of circumstances,

Wagner asserted, Oedipus could not be held individually accountable. But, as Wagner observed, Oedipus is not only condemned by outer society, he internalizes the social condemnation as well. Consumed by guilt he stabs out his eyes and, in doing so, "plunged down to the mangled carcass of the Sphinx, whose riddle he now must know was yet unsolved" (OD 183). By placing Siegfried in the position of Oedipus of unwittingly committing crimes against society, and yet securing his inner integrity and innocence through the device of the potion, Wagner was correcting the errors and "misinterpretations" propounded by Greek mythic drama.[100]

Only in this way, then, can we make sense of Brünnhilde's final observations about Siegfried: "the purest of men it was who betrayed me. . . . Never were oaths more nobly sworn; never were treaties kept more truly; never did any man love more loyally; and yet every oath, every treaty, the truest love – no one betrayed as he did!" (RN 348-49). Brünnhilde recognizes that while Siegfried went through the outward motions of betrayal, he was not inwardly corrupted by them. Othello was actually duped about his wife's fidelity, and thus part of the tragedy is his lack of sense – "one that loved not wisely, but too well."[101] Through Brünnhilde's final speech, Wagner makes clear that he has absolved Siegfried of any guilt. Siegfried betrayed, but unknowingly. His internal nobility is not in any way diminished by broken oaths the external society of the Gibichungs deems criminal. Like Billy Budd, he embodies the paradox of an "angel of God" who must yet "hang."

Siegfried's naivete and inability to pierce the false masks of culture and hypocrisy, to even conceive of the need for revolution, is thus not his failing but his strength. His purpose instead is a didactic one to model for Wagner's audience the unadulterated virtues of a mankind unsullied by the corrupting influences of society. In a passage from the Abbé Guillaume Raynal's *Histoire philosophique et politique des établissements et du commerce des Européens dans les Deux Indes* (*Philosophical and Political History of the Two Indies*; 1772/1774/1780), Diderot upheld the noble savage as a valuable lesson for mankind:

> Without doubt it is important for future generations that they do not lose the accounts of the life and behaviour of primitive men. It is to this knowledge, perhaps, that we owe all the progress which moral philosophy has made among us. . . . This discovery has already brought much enlightenment but it is as yet no more than the dawn of a beautiful day for humanity. . . . That happy prospect should be a consolation for the present generation.[102]

What then did Siegfried, as the noble savage, have to teach? For Wagner, Siegfried modeled a form of human experience that is utterly free and therefore capable of a love that is truly reciprocal. As the "fearless" natural man, Siegfried is the "one who never ceases to *love*," and "only through love . . . do man and woman become human."[103] In Hegelian terms, this is the moment when the isolated individual consciousness recognizes the object as another locus of subjectivity. As Wagner digested this philosophical point for Röckel, "[e]goism, in truth, ceases only when the 'I' is subsumed by the 'you.' . . . [T]he world will not become a complete reality for me until it becomes 'you,' and this is something it can become only in the shape of the individual whom I love."[104] For modern man, however, this form of spiritual engagement was nothing more than an abstraction. Over the course of human history, man's natural strengths had atrophied to such an extent under the accumulated pressures of civilization that he was now a sorry shadow of his former self: "The garment once removed, we were horrified to see nothing but a shriveled, loathly shape, which bore no trace of resemblance to the true man, such as *our thoughts* had pictured in the fulness of his natural essence" (OD 176).[105] As a result, all that civilized man could hope for was "a conceptual, abstract, non-sensuous love." As Wagner told Röckel, "Not only you, but I, too, – like everyone else – now live in circumstances and conditions which force us to depend on surrogate measures and makeshift solutions; for you, no less than for me, the truest, most real life can be only something imaginary, something we long for."[106] Siegfried's immediacy of access to the emotion of love is the stuff of nineteenth-century dreams.

While Siegfried is the "one who never ceases to *love*,"[107] Brünnhilde is more akin to Lohengrin. Wagner wrote, "I remain convinced that my Lohengrin (according to my own conception of it) symbolizes the most profoundly tragic situation of the present day, namely man's desire to descend from the most intellectual heights to the depths of love, the longing to be understood instinctively, a longing which modern reality cannot yet satisfy."[108] Having "descended from the heights" Brünnhilde is initially apprehensive and anxious about giving herself to the exuberant youth. It is no accident that Siegfried must first cut through her outer "wrappage" – an inflexible, constraining "iron coat of armour" – a symbol of the constraints inherited through outdated cultural norms – before Brünnhilde can even contemplate embracing her true womanhood and receiving Siegfried's love. It is this process by which Siegfried and Brünnhilde emerge from the chrysalis of egoism and come to a crucial recognition of the other that Sandra Corse sees as the goalpost of Wagner's philosophical project in the *Ring*. For Corse, Siegfried embodies what she calls "the new consciousness," the highest stage of Hegelian development that will guide the way to the future.[109] In this interpretation, then, Siegfried "is the hope of the new movement of spirit in the world."[110] But Corse admits difficulty squaring this conclusion with the events of *Götterdämmerung*.[111] The difficulty originates, I believe, in the mistaken view that Siegfried represents a form of world-historical hero. But as shown in the beginning of this chapter, his limited frame of reference – as explicitly posited by Wagner and entirely consistent with Rousseau's model of the noble savage – is simply not up to the challenge of self-consciously detecting the movement of Spirit in the world. The "I-Thou" relationship that he achieves may represent a core element of human potential, but it is by no means the end of the dialectical road.[112] Thus while the love that Brünnhilde and Siegfried model on the mountaintop appears to be a solid beacon for the future, an inviting resolution of the problem of modernity, there are several reasons why this cannot be so. The first reason, which we will explore in this chapter, is that while Siegfried is capable of discovering a form of love denied to modern man, implicit in his role as the noble savage is the historical impossibility of his return.

The return of the native?

The historical challenge for Rousseau and his followers had always been to determine whether the innocent state of nature could be restored to humanity, whether man's original unblemished character could be retrieved. Even Rousseau did not believe it possible. Indeed, as he himself recognized, man's true natural gift, the "faculty of self-improvement," carried the seeds of his alienation:

> It would be sad for us to be forced to admit that this distinguishing and almost unlimited faculty of man is the source of all his misfortunes; that it is this faculty which, by the action of time, drags man out of that original condition in which he would pass peaceful and innocent days; that it is this faculty, which, bringing to fruition over the centuries his insights and his errors, his vices and his virtues, makes man in the end a tyrant over himself and over nature.[113]

True to his time, Rousseau put his faith, then, not in turning back the clock of history but in embracing the new science of political and social engineering.[114] In the laboratory of his mind Rousseau envisaged a way of redressing the corruptions of civilization through civil society; if the state of nature could not be recovered, there was a social order that could be constructed that would offer citizens "moral" if not absolute freedom.

The turn of the eighteenth century, however, proved a potent challenge to these sanguine Enlightenment visions of a rationally constructed future. The sanguinary instincts unleashed by the French Revolution, and the meteoric rise and precipitous fall of Napoleon, dashed any hope of facile socio-political solutions. As Carlyle acerbically queried, "What sound mind among the French, for example, now fancies that men can be governed by 'Constitutions'; by the never so cunning mechanising of Self-interests, and all conceivable adjustments of checking and balancing. . . . Were not experiments enough of this kind tried before all Europe, and found wanting, when, in that doomsday of France, the infinite gulf of human Passion shivered asunder the thin rinds of Habit; and burst forth all-devouring, as in seas of Nether Fire?"[115] Hegel too rejected as deeply flawed Rousseau's idealized faith in the "absolute freedom" of the General Will. In the *Phenomenology* he concluded that the end result of such a theory was Robespierre's Terror: "the sole work and deed of universal freedom is therefore *death*, a death too which has no inner significance or filling, for what is negated is the empty point of the absolutely free self. It is thus the coldest and meanest of all deaths, with no more significance than cutting off a head of cabbage or swallowing a mouthful of water."[116]

Hegel's philosophical answer to the social and political catastrophe that was the French Revolution was to seek redemption in the sweep of history. Hegel had no illusions that history as experienced on the quotidian level was anything but a "slaughter bench." But he saw the sufferings of humanity as tending towards a higher purpose. Refusing to dwell in the gory details of daily human misery, Hegel took the long view, seeing history as a glorious process through which the World Spirit becomes increasingly manifest in the form of freedom and reason. "Spirit's consciousness of its freedom, and hence also the actualization of that very freedom," is the "final goal . . . toward which all the world's history has been working. It is this goal to which all the sacrifices have been brought upon the broad altar of the earth in the long flow of time. . . . [T]he events that present such a grim picture for our troubled feeling and thoughtful reflection have to be seen as the *means* for what we claim is the substantial definition, the absolute end-goal or, equally, the true *result* of world history."[117] Thus, for Hegel, the utopia of unfettered freedom which Rousseau had posited in the aboriginal forest was not the beginning of human existence but rather the end goal of human society. "Freedom, as the ideal dimension of original nature, does not exist as an original and natural state. On the contrary, it must first be achieved and won, and indeed won through an endless process involving the discipline of knowledge and will."[118]

What Hegel taught was that a perfect society and government could not simply be constructed from first principles and imposed by logical fiat. Rather, human freedom and civil morality could only be advanced through a continual process of change and accommodation that transpired over centuries of human history and human self-reflection.[119] Hegel's unique insight was to ground his faith in progress in the basic predicate of human nature – self-consciousness. Because humankind is an "apperceptive" species, animals that can think and reason about themselves and their goals, the species is continually seeking to justify its means as ethical ends.[120] And as the species grapples over time with the fundamental questions of social order and morality, the species learns and matures. In the course of history man's collective thinking becomes more refined, and as a result, manifestations of freedom become more apparent in the lived experiences of individual humans. But this process of reasoning towards valid ends takes time and requires multiple failures of iteration. And, most important, each failure is itself a step in the historical learning process and therefore a necessary stage in the road to enlightenment. In dismissing Rousseau's theoretical construct for the social contract, Hegel rejected the whole notion that there was a rational form of government that was true for all time. Instead he recognized a multiplicity of forms of government each characteristic of its historical time frame: "each form of government in the sequence is not a matter of choice, but rather is such as to conform to the Spirit of the people. . . . The forms of government, in which the world-historical peoples have blossomed, are characteristic of those peoples. Thus the various forms do not present one universal basis of government."[121]

For all his stated belief in the "cunning of Reason," Hegel was not a determinist. Although Spirit could be described in abstract terms spinning its arc of freedom, it could only manifest itself in and through the phenomenal world.[122] Spirit was a force of development immanent within human experience, which emerged only as a function of concrete action, conflict, and the consequent education of mind. As Hegel explained in the preface to the *Phenomenology*, "The Truth is the whole. But the whole is nothing other than the essence consummating itself through its development. Of the Absolute it must be said that it is essentially a *result*, that only in the *end* is it what it truly is; and that precisely in this consists its nature, viz. to be actual, subject, the spontaneous becoming of itself."[123]

Hegel's theory thus put a premium on – in Isaiah Berlin's phrase – "change as development."[124] It was the ever-fluid but never-ceasing dialectic of history which carried mankind to ever higher levels of insight. In the context of world history Hegel observed that "[t]his restless succession of individuals and peoples that are here for a time and then disappear suggests one general thought, one category above all, that of universally prevalent *change*. . . . [Spirit] does, indeed, go against itself, and consume its own existence. But in so doing, it reworks that existence, so that whatever went before is the material for what comes after, as its labor elevates it into a new form."[125]

Building on Hegel, intellectuals of the early nineteenth century repeatedly extolled "change" as the natural condition of man and the organic mechanism of progress. In 1831, Mill wrote in *The Examiner* that "the times are pregnant with change."[126] That same year, Carlyle consoled his readers in the *Edinburgh Review*, "[I]n Change, therefore, there is nothing terrible, nothing supernatural: on the contrary, it lies in the very essence of our lot and life in this world. Today is not yesterday: we ourselves change; how can our Works and Thoughts, if they are always to be the fittest, continue always the same? Change, indeed, is painful; yet ever needful; and if Memory have its force and worth, so also has Hope."[127] The American historian George Bancroft reaffirmed this fundamental Hegelian principle a few decades later in his famous 1854 lecture on the "Progress of the Human Race" which he delivered to the New York Historical Society on the occasion of its 50th anniversary. To the distinguished members and officers of the society gathered at Niblo's Saloon in New York City, Bancroft revealed the stunningly modern insight that man's "existence is flowing on in eternal motion, with nothing fixed but the certainty of change."[128]

As the nineteenth century unfolded, therefore, the *philosophes'* mechanistic vision of a clockwork universe, and their prescriptive approach to social structure, gave way to a more organic time-mediated understanding of cultural and political development. Under Hegel's powerful influence, history and historicism became the relativistic touchstone by which nineteenth-century man came to understand the world and himself.[129] For Carlyle in the 1830s, history had emerged as a new form of Scripture, "that divine BOOK OF REVELATIONS, whereof a Chapter is completed from epoch to epoch" (SR 135).[130] Most characteristic of this nineteenth-century mindset was the belief not in a particular given of logically derived truth, but instead in an ineluctable *process* of enlightenment that would ensure a path to truth. Thus Bancroft grounded his faith in progress on the guiding principles of scientific proof. "[The human mind] proceeds from observation to hypothesis, and from hypothesis to observation, progressively gaining clearer perceptions, and more perfectly mastering its stores of accumulated knowledge by generalizations which approximate nearer and nearer to absolute truth."[131] Carlyle recognized the same progressive mechanisms at work in the course of political and religious history: "Paganism give[s] place to Catholicism,

Tyranny to Monarchy, and Feudalism to Representative Government, – where also the process does not stop. Perfection of Practice, like completeness of Opinion, is always approaching, never arrived."[132] For all their optimism, Carlyle and Bancroft had clearly grasped Hegel's basic historical insight: The goal of truth would never be fully attained, but only approximated in ever increasing degrees of purity over the millennia of history.[133]

Hegel's historical change was an entirely cultural and political phenomenon and had no origin in nature. Nature for Hegel was the quintessence of "boredom." "Changes in the world of nature – infinitely varied as these might be – reflect nothing more than an eternally repeated cycle. In nature there is nothing new under the sun. . . ."[134] In spite of Hegel's view, however, many thinkers of the nineteenth century continued to locate the engine of progress in nature's own inherent capacity for development. In the late seventeenth century, Gottfried Wilhelm Leibniz had introduced the notion that the natural world was capable of creative advance. In his treatise *De rerum originatione radicali* (*On the Ultimate Origin of Things*; 1697) Leibniz posited that "every substance must arrive at all the perfection of which it is capable, and which is already found in it, though in an undeveloped form."[135] Almost a century later, Immanuel Kant adopted this principle – the steady maturation of natural traits, including those of man – as a fundamental premise of his theory of human progress. The First Proposition of Kant's essay *Idee zu einer allgemeinen Geschichte in weltbürgerlicher Absicht* (*Idea for a Universal History with a Cosmopolitan Purpose*; 1784) was that "all the natural capacities of a creature are destined sooner or later to be developed completely and in conformity with their end."[136] This idea of inherent but as yet undeveloped traits as potent drivers of progress would continue to have currency after Hegel. Carlyle preached in *Sartor* that "not Mankind only, but all that Mankind does or beholds, is in continual growth, re-genesis and self-perfecting vitality" (SR 31). The highly influential French social theorist Auguste Comte in the *Cours de Philosophie Positive* (*Course on Positive Philosophy*; 1830–42) advanced his theory of a better future with this same evolutionary notion of "the simple spontaneous development, gradually aided by an appropriate cultivation, of the pre-existing fundamental faculties that constitute our nature." Comte posited three stages in the intellectual development of man, the Biological, the Theological, and the final most enlightened state, the Positive. Each of these stages was "the necessary result of the previous one and the indispensable driving force of the next, according to the illuminating axiom of the great Leibniz: the present is pregnant with the future."[137] The faith that evolutionary change necessarily tended in a progressive direction remained secure throughout the nineteenth century. Even Charles Darwin felt compelled to shade the radical implications of his theory with a decidedly Panglossian tint when he wrote in the final pages of *On the Origin of the Species* (1859) that "as natural selection works solely by and for the good of each being, all corporeal and mental endowments will tend to progress towards perfection."[138]

During the late 1840s and early 1850s, as Wagner imbibed the philosophies of Hegel, Feuerbach, Proudhon, and others, he developed his own theory of human progress and potential. Wagner rejected the caricatured view that had turned

Hegel's faith in the logic of historical process into a quasi-religious belief in the unfolding of a providential destiny. Criticizing in *Opera and Drama* the "artistic and scientific barrenness" of the view that a "Necessity" soars above "historic personages" "using them as tools of its transcendent wisdom" (OD 174), Wagner favored instead the contemporary belief in nature and its constant state of restless change as the fundamental impetus for historical progress. For Wagner, nature was a "living Organism;" not "an aimfully constructed Mechanism" as the *philosophes* had envisioned in the clockwork universe, but rather, like Hegel's World Spirit, "the *forever becom-ing*" (OD 217). As he further developed the idea in a letter to Röckel, "the essence of reality lies in its endless *multiplicity*. This inexhaustible multiplicity which incessantly produces and renews itself."[139] Following Leibniz and Kant, Wagner believed that nature's inexorable processes ensured that all living things could and would reach their best inherent potential. In Röckel's revolutionary *Volksblätter* of February 10, 1849, Wagner posited that *"Man's **destiny** is: through the ever higher perfecting of his mental, moral and corporeal faculties to attain an ever higher purer happiness."*[140] Critical to Wagner's thinking, this process of "becoming" was not random or arbitrary. Consistent with contemporary mindsets, Wagner clearly trusted in the purposefulness of natural evolution. In his defense of progress, Kant had recognized that without this insight, "we are faced not with a law-governed nature, but with an aimless, random process, and the dismal reign of chance replaces the guiding principle of reason."[141] Wagner shared the same historico-temporal *horror vacui*, boldly asserting in *Art and Revolution* that "it is impossible that the final state, which this movement shall attain one day, should be other than the direct opposite of the present; else were the whole history of the world a restless zig-zag of cross purposes, and not the ordered movement of a mighty stream; which with all its bends, its deviations, and its floods, yet flows for ever in one steadfast course" (AR 56). The ultimate goal of the orderly flow of this "mighty stream" of history was to free man "from his last heresy, the denial of Nature, – that heresy which has taught him hitherto to look upon himself as a mere instrument to an end which lay outside himself" (AR 57).

This last sentence might appear to suggest a belief that man could return to his original state of one-ness with nature. But Wagner understood as well as Rousseau that it was simply not possible to recover man's first stage of innocence. As he explained in *The Artwork of the Future*, "the moment we humans . . . began to develop as human beings and to break away from our unconscious, animal existence as children of nature to wake to conscious life. . . this was the moment we went astray, error as the first expression of consciousness" (AF 13). Man's very make-up ensured his alienation from nature.[142]

Adopting Romanticism's Rousseauvian agenda, Carlyle had sought to put man back in touch with his intuitive, unconscious nature and to reject the artificial, the mechanical, and other symptoms of "diseased self-consciousness." But Carlyle was quick to reassure his readers that "he was no Adamite, in any sense, and could not, like Rousseau, recommend either bodily or intellectual Nudity, and a return to the savage state" (SR 157). Society for him was as inevitable as it was necessary;

man simply needed to find a new suit of clothes – a new form of faith – that would be suitable to his liberated state. Although he commenced his 1831 essay in the *Edinburgh Review* – "Characteristics" – by praising unconscious intuition, Carlyle concluded that essay with an encomium to the accumulated knowledge of mankind: "So too, Scepticism itself, with its innumerable mischiefs, what is it but the sour fruit of a most blessed increase, that of Knowledge; a fruit too that will not always continue *sour*?"[143]

In the same fashion, Wagner wished for man to return to an unmediated relationship with the instinctive forces of nature. The "insight of nature" was the "acknowledgement of the unconscious, the instinctive and thus the necessary, the true, the sensual" (AF 14). But at the same time he also believed, again like Carlyle, that the means to attain this renewal was a Hegelian process of emergent self-consciousness. As he explained, "out of error knowledge is born and the history of the birth of knowledge out of error is the history of the human species from primitive myth to the present day" (AF 13). This knowledge – fruit of Feuerbach's teachings – would show that nature was not regulated by some "external imaginary power," in short, the "rules predicated on religion, nationality, or state," but was defined rather by its own "necessary," "true," and "sensual" internal forces. Man would therefore become free only "when we become joyfully aware of our relationship with nature." And this joyful *self*-awareness, Wagner recognized, was the end result of scientific inquiry and knowledge. "The path of science is one from error to insight, from hypothesis to reality, from religion to nature" (AF 14).

There is an inherent contradiction in Wagner's (and Carlyle's) celebration of the unconscious instincts of nature and his simultaneous embrace of the dialectical process of self-consciousness as the means to that end. In Wagner's pronouncement that science would ultimately be negated and end "in its pure antithesis" through man's renewed engagement with the natural world, Wagner seems to want to have it both ways. As Mary Cicora has aptly summed up the problem, Wagner believed in a "second Paradise of unconscious consciousness."[144] But critical to Wagner's theory, and evidence of his ultimate trust in the Hegelian dialectic, the new stage of free engagement with nature would not be a mere repetition of a past state of bliss, but a higher level of consciousness. In his pre-revolutionary toast to the Dresden Königliche Kapelle, Wagner told his audience, "Man's purpose is to act usefully, and his activity will be then completely useful, when he lets it operate in unceasing accord with his best and highest faculty."[145] It was not appropriate or "useful" to continue hewing stones when one had acquired the capacity to design "fair edifices." In *Art and Revolution*, in true historicist fashion, Wagner traced the history of art and culture through the centuries, finding that although the great Athenian tragedies of Aeschylus represented some of the highest achievements of human art, the "historical sin" of the Greeks had ensured their political downfall and hand-in-hand with that the demise of true drama (AR 33–5, 50). This historical sin was the same that Hegel had identified in his Berlin lectures, namely the acceptance of slavery among the Greeks. "It was among the Greeks that the consciousness of freedom first arose," Hegel had taught, "but they, and the Romans as well, knew only that *some* persons are free, not the human as such."[146]

Accordingly, Wagner demanded in *Art and Revolution* not a "slavish *Restoration*," but a "*Revolution*" (AR 53). "No, we do not wish to revert to Greekdom; for what the Greeks knew not, and, knowing not, came by their downfall: that know *we*." Man would indeed regain "the Grecian element of life," but now "in vastly higher measure" (AR 54, 57). And he hammered home the point a year later in *Kunst und Klima* (*Art and Climate*; 1850), where he explained that "if, therefore the kernel of the world's history, from the Asiatic down to the close of the Grecian period, was the emanation of the *unit Man* from Nature: so is the kernel of the new European history the resolution of this idea into the actuality of *Men*."[147] The art of ancient Greece reflected "the need of a peculiar people" and therefore "remained hedged about with Egoism." Men of the future – once again guided by Feuerbach's insight that the "realisation of God" was in the "physical verity of the Human Race" – would move beyond the confines of a particular national culture or climate to embrace an all-encompassing "non-national" "*love for Universal Man*" (AC 263-64; AF 23). Arising out of this "new beauty of a nobler Universalism" (AR 53), the artwork of the future would be "moulded by unheard-of manysideness of *felt and living* sense of Beauty" which would put the works of ancient Greek artists to shame and "turn those mouldering remains of Grecian art to unregarded playthings for peevish children" (AC 264).[148]

At one moment, however, in his famous letter to Röckel Wagner indulged in the fantasy that Siegfried, or some form of him, could emerge in later stages of history provided the right conditions were prepared for his return: "Siegfried is the man of the future whom we desire and long for but who cannot be made by us, since he must create himself on the basis of *our own annihilation*."[149] But Wagner's considered theoretical conclusions in his published works of the 1840s and 1850s lead one to question his intellectual commitment to this singular epistolary assertion that Siegfried is the symbol of a future "regenerate type of man."[150] As noted, Wagner at that time clearly did not believe in a mere return to a utopian pre-historic golden age, but understood that the promise of the future would be the product of an evolutionary process of unfolding human potentialities. And his construct of Siegfried as a primitive consciousness – capable of hewing stones – is fully at odds with any coherent notion of a latter-day human being that would ultimately emerge from the historical process – adept at designing fair edifices.[151] Apart from pure theory, Wagner personally did not relish the idea of a return to man's origins in the primeval forest. To Theodor Uhlig, a Dresden musician, friend of Wagner, and illegitimate son of the King of Saxony, he protested in 1850, "Shall we return then to a state of nature, shall we reacquire the human animal's ability to live to be 200 years old? God forbid! Man is a social, all-powerful being only through *culture*. Let us not forget that culture alone grants us the power to enjoy life to the full as only mankind can enjoy it."[152]

But even if we accept the view that the natural man could return, in one form or another, in Wagner's formulation it would only be the end point of a long historical process – the utopian man would have to await the appropriate historical/natural conditions in order to flourish. Referencing the artwork of the future, Wagner wrote: "It is impossible however to evoke a need against nature's will where the conditions are not right. If the need for the artwork is not there then the artwork itself cannot exist; that must arise sometime in the future when life produces the right conditions" (AF 21). Until those right conditions could be achieved, however they might be achieved in the fullness of time, the Siegfried of the future remained every bit a thought experiment as the natural man of Rousseau. "None of us shall see the promised land," Wagner complained to Röckel. "[W]e shall all die in the wilderness."[153]

In the final analysis, then, whether he is conceived as a symbol of the origin of man or his end goal, Siegfried's dramatic role was designed to explore the fundamentals of human bravery, freedom, and love – in short, human integrity – but *not* to solve the problem of history. Siegfried is the alpha – and possibly the omega – of human evolution, but not the means of getting from point A to point B. As the Old World confronted the New, explorers were fascinated by the savages they found in the Americas, not only because of their different mores but even more so because they appeared to be untouched by time. History as Christian Europe had experienced it had completely bypassed them. Natural man was therefore a historical anomaly.[154] Likewise, having walked out of the bright sunshine of eternal myth into the dreary night of human civilization, Siegfried is caught unawares. His tragedy is that he is in the wrong place at the wrong time, historically speaking.

As explored in the next chapter about Brünnhilde, however, there are further deep impurities that cloud the pristine spectacle of a primitive Siegfried and his gift of love. As Wagner reveals in *Götterdämmerung*, even truly reciprocal erotic love is not free of complications, complications that make even Siegfried's newly acquired state of consciousness as lover of Brünnhilde inadequate to handle the demands of history. Through the tragedy of Brünnhilde, Wagner recognized not only that the return of the native is a naive notion, but that even the untarnished *ur-mensch* is riven with inherent contradictions. In the end, it is not Brünnhilde but the Siegfried who "never ceases to love" who represents the utopian construct of love as panacea.

Notes

1 See, e.g., Williams, *Wagner and the Romantic Hero*, 86–7: Siegfried is "boisterous and full of energy, akin to several of the fictional manifestations of Rousseau's 'natural man.'" Roger Hollinrake, "Epiphany and Apocalypse," 41: "Siegfried, the perfect human being . . . guided by instinct and uncorrupted by civilization: a modern protagonist of the messianic religion of nature with which Rousseau had inflamed the imagination of an earlier revolutionary epoch"; Dieter Borchmeyer, *Drama and the World of Richard Wagner*, trans. Daphne Ellis (Princeton University Press 2004), 223: noting an "archaic naivete" in Siegfried's character.

2 See, e.g., Deathridge, *Wagner*, 63–4: "Not least Siegfried is intended as an analogy with the 1848–49 Revolution and its aftermath" and "it is crucial that Siegfried should be a hero of 'nature.'"

3 Warren Darcy has summed up the problem thus: "In short, the hero's actions do not seem to follow logically from premisses established earlier in the cycle and there

appears to be no convincing reason why Wagner's 'man of the future', his symbolic portrait of regenerate humanity, should so decisively crash to his ruin." Darcy, "'The World Belongs to Alberich!,'" in *Wagner's Ring of the Nibelung: A Companion*, 48. See also Deathridge, *Wagner*, 65–6: "If our Nordic superman is the man of the future who leads us with phenomenal strength into a new age of light and social harmony, why is he doomed?" Williams, *Wagner and the Romantic Hero*, 86: "Siegfried fulfills neither the nationalist ambitions nor the high ideals that are placed in him."

4 Shaw, *The Perfect Wagnerite*, 79; Emslie, *The Centrality of Love*, 70: "The *Ring*'s collapse into incoherence is not to be hindered. In fact it couldn't have been hindered unless *Götterdämmerung* had been thoroughly remade."

5 A few examples should suffice. Williams notes that the problem with *Götterdämmerung* lies with Siegfried: "[he] never becomes what he promised to be." Williams, *Wagner and the Romantic Hero*, 95. In the end he generalizes from Siegfried's fate that "human nature is too frail to live up to the high expectations of free heroism." Williams, *Wagner and the Romantic Hero*, 96. Emslie comments that "Siegfried is shortchanged in respect of both [action and knowledge], and thereby inadequate to the greater role Wagner wants him to fulfil," and later notes the "narrative clumsiness and unpleasant consequences that follow from turning to this gauche boy to save the world." Emslie, *The Centrality of Love*, 25, 76. Darcy attributes this disjunction to Wagner's change in focus from Siegfried as "the god's redeemer" to a symbol of fallen humanity: "his actions may be understood as recreating Wotan's mistakes: he embraces power, entangles himself in false treaties and renounces true love." Darcy, "'The World Belongs to Alberich!,'" in *Wagner's Ring of the Nibelung: A Companion*, 52.

6 The question Kitcher and Schacht pose reflects this critical approach: "to what extent do his loss of his memory of Brünnhilde and his sudden ardor for Gutrune correspond to something in his own character?" Kitcher and Schacht, *Finding an Ending*, 167. Kitcher and Schacht contend that Siegfried is "less a paradigm of the heroic than a parody of the stereotypical hero as witless marvel" and that "his heroic virtues are bound up with the serious limitations and liabilities he displays as a human being." Kitcher and Schacht, *Finding an Ending*, 186, 190. Williams likewise points to Siegfried's "inner lack of resilience" and critiques his "shameful career of betrayal, lying, womanizing, and indolence" which render him "the antithesis of the hero." Williams, *Wagner and the Romantic Hero*, 95–6. Treadwell observes that "the *Ring* doesn't put destiny in the hands of aspiring individuals (its greatest hero, Siegfried, is extraordinarily incompetent and thoughtless)." Treadwell, *Interpreting Wagner*, 95. Some commentators, on the other hand, have questioned this interpretive perspective. Geck, for one, asks whether it is "necessary to dismiss the Siegfried of *Götterdämmerung* as an 'idiot'. . . . Nor do we need to take the fashionable view of him as a guileless fool . . . [or] a slovenly dropout." Martin Geck, *Richard Wagner: A Life in Music*, trans. Stewart Spencer (The University of Chicago Press 2002), 294. But Geck does not explain further why the negative assessment is erroneous. Roger Scruton is also less inclined to hold Siegfried responsible for his actions, coming closest to my interpretation when he asserts that Wagner "wanted his hero to fall just as far as he could, while retaining the inner innocence that wells up as he dies, and washes all corruption away." Scruton, *The Ring of Truth*, 277.

7 Even Kitcher and Schacht themselves concede that "much of what we have said about him is dismissive, even harsh." Kitcher and Schacht, *Finding an Ending*, 185.

8 Kitcher and Schacht, *Finding an Ending*, 167–8, 188.

9 Williams agrees that there is a "puzzling gap between Siegfried's character and Brünnhilde's praise of it." Williams, *Wagner and the Romantic Hero*, 97.

10 Berry, *Treacherous Bonds*, 231–2. One recent commentator on the *Ring*, Paul Heise, attempts to reconcile Siegfried's heroism with his lack of consciousness through an intriguing interpretation of the tetralogy as an allegory of Wagner's aesthetics and creative process. Heise's study reads the *Ring* in light of Wagner's later thesis for

Religion and Art of 1880 that "where Religion becomes artificial, it is reserved for Art to save the spirit of religion." According to the allegory, Siegfried is the artist hero who is inspired by the muse of unconscious artistic inspiration, represented by Brünnhilde. In this way, Heise turns on its head the Hegelian approach to the *Ring*, reading the advance of consciousness in human evolution as a malign influence which degrades the unconscious existential sources of inspiration for true art. Thus Alberich and the ring represent the curse of *consciousness*, while Siegfried is the hero who struggles to redeem man's religious impulses through the intuitive power of secular art. While Heise purports to ground his thesis in Feuerbach's philosophical program, he at the same time asserts that "there was little Wagner found in Schopenhauer that was not already implicit in the *Ring* drama." And indeed the final message of bleak futility which Heise identifies in the *Ring* reflects a reading that is more consistent with the Schopenhauerian agenda than with the Young Hegelian. Paul Brian Heise, "The Wound That Will Never Heal," *Wagnerheim.com*.

11 Berry, *Treacherous Bonds*, 228. Williams takes the opposite view of Siegmund, writing that "he is the opposite of a hero. . . . He remains in our imagination as a weak figure, driven more by fear than hope." Williams, *Wagner and the Romantic Hero*, 85.

12 Berry, "The Positive Influence of Wagner on Nietzsche," 19 n.27 (Siegfried as "god of revolution") and 23 ("It is not difficult to see in Siegfried a great deal of the Hegelian world-historical individual"). See also Berry, *Treacherous Bonds*, 210: "the Wagnerian hero would be a world-historical figure"; Darcy, "'The World Belongs to Alberich!,'" in *Wagner's Ring of the Nibelung: A Companion*, 50: "Siegfried comes remarkably close to fulfilling Hegel's concept of the world-historical figure, the hero, who, heeding only inner necessity, unwittingly assists the dialectical process of history"; Corse, *Wagner and the New Consciousness*, 21–4, 162: "the Hegelian idea of the hero, exemplified in Siegfried, as one who expresses spirit better than his contemporaries and therefore is the object of history"; Emslie, *The Centrality of Love*, 125: "the hero [Wagner] sketched . . . has much in common with the world-enhancing individual celebrated for his amoral greatness in the pages of . . . Hegel"; Scruton, *The Ring of Truth*, 20: Wagner first conceived the work as the story of a world-historical hero.

13 Berry, *Treacherous Bonds*, 228; Darcy, "Metaphysics," 4.

14 Georg Wilhelm Friedrich Hegel, *Introduction to the Philosophy of History*, trans. Leo Rauch (Hackett 1988), 33 (emphasis added).

15 Millington, *The Sorcerer*, 105.

16 Hegel, *History*, 43.

17 Jean-Jacques Rousseau, *A Discourse on Inequality*, trans. Maurice Cranston (Penguin 1984), 97–9. Hegel emphatically rejected Rousseau's argument, pointing out that "the assumption is one of those nebulous images necessarily produced by the theory (i.e., the image of the noble savage) to which it ascribes existence, without historical justification." Hegel, *History*, 43.

18 Rousseau, *A Discourse on Inequality*, 135.

19 *Id.*, 135–6.

20 Denis Diderot, "Reflections on the Voyage of Bougainville," in *Political Writings*, eds. and trans. John Hope Mason and Robert Wokler (Cambridge University Press 1992), 50.

21 *Id.*, 52–3.

22 Ludwig Feuerbach, *The Essence of Christianity*, trans. George Eliot (Barnes and Noble Books 2004) (hereafter "EC" in text), 120.

23 J.S. Mill, "The Spirit of the Age," in *The Spirit of the Age: Victorian Essays*, ed. Gertrude Himmelfarb (Yale University Press 2007), 53.

24 Thomas Carlyle, *Sartor Resartus*, eds. Peter Sabor and Kerry McSweeney (Oxford University Press 2008), 45 (hereafter "SR" in text).

25 Wagner owned the work in a German translation by Johann Sporschil (1840). Westernhagen, *Richard Wagners Dresdener Bibliothek 1842–1849*, 90.

26 Heinrich Heine, *On the History of Religion and Philosophy in Germany*, trans. Howard Pollack-Milgate and ed. Terry Pinkard (Cambridge University Press 2007), 84.

27 At Wahnfried Wagner owned an 1864 edition of this work.

28 Kelly, *Discovery of Chance*, 196.

29 Heine, *On the History of Religion*, 13.

30 Richard Wagner, "Art and Revolution," in *The Artwork of the Future and Other Writings*, trans. W. Ashton Ellis (University of Nebraska Press 1993; repr. of 1st edn., 1895), 43 (hereafter "AR" in text).

31 Wagner, *Opera and Drama*, 192.

32 Alexander Herzen would also adopt the sartorial metaphor to explain the incongruities of the age of transition: "Our morality is still in feudal dress, albeit now faded and tattered." As quoted in Kelly, *Discovery of Chance*, 226. Testament to the continuing vitality of this metaphor throughout the nineteenth century, Nietzsche would write in *The Birth of Tragedy* in 1872 that the poet in his search for truth must "discard the mendacious finery of that alleged reality of the man of culture."

33 Richard Wagner, "A Communication to My Friends," in *The Artwork of the Future and Other Writings*, trans. W. Ashton Ellis (University of Nebraska Press 1993; repr. of 1st edn., 1895), 357–8 (hereafter "CF" in text).

34 Treadwell inexplicably condemns any reliance on *Communication to My Friends* as a guide to understanding the character of Siegfried or the *Ring*. He emphatically states that that work "cannot possibly endure now as a principle for determining the meaning of Siegfried – at least not without a self-imposed blindness so willful as to render the whole matter of interpretation completely pointless." James Treadwell, "The Urge to Communicate: The Prose Writings as Theory and Practice," in *The Cambridge Companion to Wagner*, 168. Treadwell gives absolutely no explanation for this categorical rejection of Wagner's contemporary writings as a guide to understanding his intentions at the time he wrote the *Ring* libretto, and, indeed, in the very same breath, he fully contradicts himself when he admits that the passage he quotes from that essay "describes the character's behavior in the eponymous opera rather well." If Treadwell is merely pointing out that the political and social context of 1851 when Wagner composed the text had completely changed by 1876 when he finally performed the work in public, then his point is unremarkable.

35 Carlyle, *On Heroes, Hero-Worship, and the Heroic in History. Six Lectures* (James Fraser 1841), 31, 44.

36 Rousseau, *A Discourse on Inequality*, 89.

37 Sandra Corse rightly points out how, contrary to Rousseau's model, Siegfried is raised in a social context by Mime who carries the corruptions of society with him. Corse, *Wagner and the New Consciousness*, 131. And yet Wagner is at pains to show how Siegfried learns his life lessons from nature and intuitively rejects everything that Mime teaches and stands for. "The idler is skilled in subtle wiles; he ought to admit to being a bungler. . . . Away with the bungler! . . . I'll forge the sword myself!" Richard Wagner, *Wagner's Ring of the Nibelung*, trans. Stewart Spencer, ed. Barry Millington (Thames and Hudson 1993), 220 (hereafter in text "RN").

38 Letter to Röckel, 24 Aug. 1851, SL 228.

39 Heinrich Porges, *Wagner Rehearsing the 'Ring': An Eyewitness Account of the Stage Rehearsals of the First Bayreuth Festival*, trans. Robert L. Jacobs (Cambridge University Press 1983), 81.

40 Rousseau, *A Discourse on Inequality*, 90.

41 CT, i, 466 (12 Mar. 1872).

42 Letter to Röckel, 25/26 Jan. 1854, SL 309. Corse interprets this statement quite differently, choosing to see it as a definition of "highest" consciousness, rather than as a description of the most fundamental stage of consciousness. Corse, *Wagner and the New Consciousness*, 24. This interpretation is not widely shared. See, e.g., Berry, *Treacherous Bonds*, 230–1.

43 As Wagner noted in *Opera and Drama*, "these historic facts upheaped themselves to so huge a mass of recorded incidents and actions that . . . [it must be] pierced to its core . . . in order to unearth from amidst its crushing waste the one thing that might reward such toil, the genuine undisfigured Man in all his nature's verity" (OD 169).

44 See Wagner, *My Life*, 376: Acknowledging the "more powerful attraction exerted upon me by the Nibelungen and Siegfried legends," Wagner explained that it was "their mythic treatment of material that struck me as somewhat similar" to the theme he was exploring for Barbarossa.

45

> The savage was the natural man; savage society, in so far as it existed, was as distant as possible from the hegemonies of kings, republics and priests which provided history with its subject matter; and Diderot was able to join Rousseau in asking whether it had been good to leave the state of nature for the processes of history, but whether that departure once taken was not irreversible. . . . The *Histoire* [*des Deux Indes*, of Abbé Raynal] became a narrative of the encounter of history with nature, and necessarily . . . ends by telling Europeans they must recover their own nature, corrupted by a civil society itself corrupted by empire. . . . [B]ut . . . there is doubt whether humans are not too far committed to history to return to its beginnings.
>
> (J.G.A. Pocock, *Barbarism and Religion, Vol IV: Barbarians, Savages and Empires* (Cambridge University Press 2005), 7)

46 Diderot, *Reflections*, 41–3.

47 See, e.g., Peter Gay, *Schnitzler's Century: The Making of Middle Class Culture 1815–1914* (W.W. Norton 2002), 106: "Rousseau's doctrine that human beings are born pure and that it is society that corrupts them, was to find pervasive resonance across the decades [of the nineteenth century] in the writings of educators."

48 Herman Melville, *Billy Budd, Sailor* in *Billy Budd, Sailor, and Other Stories* (Penguin 1986), 298, 345.

49 *Id.*, 299.

50 *Id.*, 301, 73.

51 *Id.*, 301.

52 *Id.*, 299, 301.

53 A dedicated Rousseauvian, Melville was an ardent critic of contemporary civilization who celebrated the innocence of the noble savage. In his utopian novel *Typee*, Melville rehearsed the already century-old fantasy of the state of nature: "in a primitive state of society, the enjoyments of life, though few and simple, are spread over a great extent, and are unalloyed; but Civilization, for every advantage she imparts, holds a hundred evils in reserve – the heart burnings, the jealousies, the social rivalries, the family dissensions, and the thousand self-inflicted discomforts of refined life, which make up in units the swelling aggregate of human misery, are unknown among these unsophisticated people." Herman Melville, *Typee* (Penguin 1996), 124–5; *See also* Gorman Beauchamp, "Melville and the Tradition of Primitive Utopia," *Journal of General Education*, Vol. 33, No. 1 (Spring 1981).

54 Melville, *Budd*, 352.

55 A nineteenth-century incident which highlighted the tragically irreconcilable gap between the man of nature and civilized society, that Wagner may well have known, has recently been brought to light in a fascinating essay in *The Wagner Journal* about Germany's obsession with the tragic story of Kasper Hauser, a boy raised in the woods with little or no social interaction, who, when introduced to society, was initially forthright, honest, and filled with awe, but ultimately was too vulnerable to survive. Edward A. Bortnichak and Paula M. Bortnichak, "The 'Missing Link' in the Evolution of Wagner's *Siegfried*," *The Wagner Journal*, Vol. 10, No. 2 (2016). Further proof of the relevance of this incident to the Rousseauvian mindset of the time is the fact that Melville

likened Billy Budd to a "Casper Hauser, wandering dazed in any Christian capital of our time." Melville, *Budd*, 302.

56 Richard Wagner, *Religion and Art*, trans. William Ashton Ellis (University of Nebraska Press 1994, repr. of 1st edn., 1897), 246 (hereafter "RA" in text).

57 The play likely served as well as a prototype for Melville's tale. See Harold Bloom, *Shakespeare: The Invention of the Human* (Riverhead Books 1999), 439.

58 Alex Ross, "Othello's Daughter," *The New Yorker*, July 29, 2013. Wagner's friend and fellow German exile, the revolutionary and poet Georg Herwegh, wrote a review of the performance. Georg Herwegh, "Othello – Ira Aldridge," in *Der Freiheit eine Gasse: Aus dem Leben und Werk Georg Herweghs* (Volk und Welt 1948), 298–9.

59 CT, i, 758 (15 May, 1874).

60 CT, ii, 373 (1 Oct., 1879).

61 CT, i, 293 (7 Nov., 1870).

62 Herbert Weinstock, *Rossini: A Biography* (Knopf 1968), 68–9, 118–21. Wagner also commented how the last act of Rossini's *Otello* was full of "feeling." CT, i, 295 (13 Nov. 1870). In April 1876, a chamber music recital at Wagner's home included selections from Wagner's works, *Tristan* and *Meistersinger*; the next day a performance of passages from Rossini's *Otello* (which Cosima, at least, condemned as "that absurdity"). CT, i, 902 (18 Apr. 1876). Hegel heard a performance of the opera in Vienna in September 1824. Weinstock, *Rossini*, 118.

63 Julian Budden, *The Operas of Verdi*, vol. 3 (Oxford University Press 1981), 303.

64 Porges, *Wagner Rehearsing the 'Ring,'* 145.

65 A handful of commentators on the *Ring* have noted in passing a resemblance between Iago and Hagen, but none has developed this connection further. See, e.g., Margaret Inwood, *The Influence of Shakespeare on Richard Wagner* (Edwin Mellen Press 1999), 189; Robert L. Jacobs, "The Shakespearean Element in the 'Ring'," *Wagner*, New Series Vol. 4, No. 1 (Jan. 1983). *Götterdämmerung* has more typically been compared to *King Lear*. See, e.g., Kitcher and Schacht, *Finding an Ending*, 79; Jacobs, "The Shakespearean Element," 4; Deathridge, *Wagner*, 59.

66 Bloom, *Shakespeare*, 446.

67 William Shakespeare, *Othello* (Signet Classics 1998), 5, 28.

68 Bloom stresses the importance of viewing Shakespeare's character as a great soul and thus endeavors to rescue him from much twentieth-century criticism that has sought to cast him – not unlike Siegfried – as a psychologically flawed individual. Bloom, *Shakespeare*, 433, 445–7.

69 William Hazlitt, *Characters of Shakespear's Plays* (C.H. Reynell 1817), 45–6.

70 Algernon Charles Swinburne, *A Study of Shakespeare* (William Heinemann 1920), 177.

71 Andrew Cecil Bradley, "Lecture V: *Othello*," in *Shakespearean Tragedy: Lectures on Hamlet, Othello, King Lear, Macbeth*, 16th Imprint, 2nd edn. (MacMillan and Co. 1922), 191.

72 August Wilhelm Schlegel, *Lectures on Dramatic Art and Literature*, trans. John Black, 2nd edn. (George Bell & Sons 1904), 401.

73 *Id.*, 402.

74 *Id.*

75 James A. Hepokoski, *"Guiseppe Verdi: Otello"*: *Cambridge Opera Handbook* (Cambridge University Press 1987), 164–70.

76 Victor Hugo, "Introduction," to *Oeuvres Complètes de Shakespeare*, Tome V: *Les Jaloux II: Cymbeline et Othello*, trans. Francois-Victor Hugo (Pagnerre 1860), 62. Despite his celebration of Othello as representative of the best that humanity had to offer, Hugo did not entirely avoid the racism inherent in Schlegel's interpretation; his argument rested on the assumption that Shakespeare did not intend to portray a black man, but an Arab. Some years later, moreover, in stark contradiction to his stated

position on Schlegel, Hugo penned another portrait of Othello in his book on *William Shakespeare* (1864) that reverted almost entirely to Schlegel's perspective: "Now, what is Othello? He is night; and immense fatal figure. Night is amorous of day. Darkness loves the dawn. The African adores the white woman. Desdemona is Othello's brightness and frenzy! And then how easy to him is jealousy! He is great . . . this Othello: but he is black. And thus how soon, when jealous, the hero becomes monster, the black becomes the negro! How speedily has night beckoned to death!" Victor Hugo, *William Shakespeare*, trans. Melville B. Anderson, 6th edn. (A.C. McClurg & Co. 1899), 242.

77 As cited in Hepokoski, *"Guiseppe Verdi Otello,"* 167.
78 Herwegh, "Othello – Ira Aldridge," 298–9.
79 Hazlitt, *Characters of Shakespear's Plays*, 55.
80 Schlegel, *Lectures*, 402.
81 Hugo, "Introduction," *Oeuvres de Shakespeare*, Tome V, 67.
82 A.C. Bradley, "Lecture VI: *Othello*," 217.
83 *Id.*, 219.
84 Shakespeare, *Othello*, 5.
85 Schlegel, *Lectures*, 402. Arrigo Boito's portrait of Iago for Verdi's *Otello* likewise captures the rank evil at the heart of Iago's soul, but couches it as a subversive form of pagan atheism. Iago declares "of a vile atom I was born" and then that "death is nothingness," both hallmarks of the philosophy of Lucretius, the tenets of which, set forth in his first-century B.C. poem *De Rerum Natura*, were deemed heresy by the Church. Stephen Greenblatt, *The Swerve: How the World Became Modern* (W.W. Norton & Co. 2011).
86 Scruton also recognizes this confusion of intentions insofar as he notes that "Hagen misuses the call to war in order to gather the vassals for the double wedding." Scruton, *The Ring of Truth*, 144. In light of Hagen's antisocial instincts, some commentators have had no hesitation in identifying him as a Jewish character. Foster, *Wagner's 'Ring,'* 224–8; Emslie, *The Centrality of Love*, 217–18; see also Marc A. Weiner, *Richard Wagner and the Anti-Semitic Imagination* (University of Nebraska Press 1995), 308–25; Michael P. Steinberg, "Music Drama and the End of History," *New German Critique*, No. 69 (1996), 164. If we credit these interpretations, Wagner's joke about the "loving" call to the wedding hints that a sardonic interpretation of Hagen's martial summoning of the vassals is not unwarranted. I proceed further to hazard the theory that Hagen's menacing blasts on his cowhorn is an intentional parody of perceived forms of Jewish music. *Compare* Barry Millington, "Nuremberg Trial: Is There Anti-Semitism in 'Die Meistersinger,'" *Cambridge Opera Journal*, Vol. 3, No. 3 (Nov. 1991); Foster, *Wagner's 'Ring,'* 226–7. Throughout European history, Jewish music was associated with strident and harsh tones. See Ruth HaCohen, *The Music Libel Against the Jews* (Yale University Press 2011), 2, 22–3, 129. Jessica's comment in *The Merchant of Venice* that "I am never merry when I hear sweet music" has been read to reflect the Jews' alleged constitutional indifference to harmony. David Nirenberg, *Anti-Judaism: The Western Tradition* (W.W. Norton & Co. 2013), 296–7. One of the archetypal examples of strident Jewish music for anti-Semitic apologists was the sound of the *shofar* on the occasion of the Jewish New Year. The *shofar* is a ram horn – not markedly different from the cowhorn that Hagen employs – that was associated, along with other "noises" of the synagogue, with wailing, barking, and alarm. HaCohen, *The Music Libel*, 22, 129. Heine articulated one aspect of Christian Europe's common perception of this ritual sound when, in discussing Spinoza's excommunication from the Jewish community, he conjured the image of the "Rabbi of the Amsterdam synagogue, sounding the battle call on the ram's-horn of faith." As he observed, "there must be something terrible [i.e. terrifying] about the *shofar*." Heine, *On the History of Religion*, 51, 59. Hagen's "battle call" on the cowhorn evokes a similar

reaction. Curiously, Karl Gutzkow, a member of the Young Germany movement and advisor to the Dresden Court Theater as of 1847, dramatized a similar story of Jewish apostasy and banishment in Amsterdam in his history play of 1847, *Uriel Acosta*, which Wagner knew. See Cohen, "Dresden Barricades," 57. In that play, Act II, scene ii, when Acosta is summoned to the Synagogue to disavow his apostasy, Gutzkow calls for ram horns to sound.

87 Foster describes Hagen as a "conjurer, an artist skilled in the work of making appearances seem real, in other words, a dramatist," Foster, *Wagner's 'Ring,'* 213, which is exactly how Shakespearean scholars view Iago. See Bloom, *Shakespeare*, 453–4: noting Iago's "improvisatory genius" and the fact that the "plot of *Othello* essentially is Iago's plot."

88 See Thomas S. Grey, "Leitmotif, Temporality, and Musical Design in the *Ring*," in *The Cambridge Companion to Wagner*, 111: the potion characterized as one of the "most egregious contrivances of the *Ring* plot."

89 Borchmeyer is one of the few commentators to assert that the potion is designed to ensure that "no moral opprobrium attaches to him." Borchmeyer, *Drama and the World of Richard Wagner*, 225.

90 CT, i, 653 (4 July 1873).

91 Kitcher and Schacht, *Finding an Ending*, 168; See Williams, *Wagner and the Romantic Hero*, 95: The drink "does nothing more than indicate Siegfried's present state of mind when he meets Gutrune. His surrender to her charms displays an inner lack of resilience."

92 As Scruton notes, "[t]he grown-up Siegfried who emerges from Brünnhilde's cave . . . is someone who has matured through love, and not through trickery. This is the most important aspect of him, since it is the foundation for Brünnhilde's trust." Scruton, *The Ring of Truth*, 279.

93 Letter to Röckel, 25/26 Jan. 1854, SL 301.

94 It has been suggested that the potion represents Siegfried's lack of consciousness, and his ability only to live in the present. Dahlhaus, *Richard Wagner's Music Dramas*, 91. The potion, however, is so selective in its effects that it does not support this conclusion. The potion does not erase all Siegfried's memory of the past, but only some part of it so as to further Hagen's plot. Other theories of the potion also seem to miss the sinister implications of Hagen's drought. Cooke, for one, curiously interprets the potion as exaggerating Siegfried's natural instincts by making him simply too indiscriminate in his loving. Cooke, *I Saw the World End*, 18: Siegfried "eventually meets his end through loving human beings too indiscriminately." Corse takes this interpretation one (implausible) step further, arguing that the potion turns Siegfried into "the abstraction of love. As an abstraction (or spiritualization) of love, he forms love relationships with everyone around him." Corse, *Wagner and the New Consciousness*, 175.

95 Grey, "Leitmotif, Temporality, and Musical Design in the *Ring*," 96–7.

96 Kitcher and Schacht, *Finding an Ending*, 167; see also Berry, "Nietzsche," 16 ("comic strip heroism of his arrival at the Hall of the Gibichungs").

97 Elizabeth Magee, *Richard Wagner and the Nibelungs* (Clarendon Press 1990), 91.

98 Kitcher and Schacht, *Finding an Ending*, 170.

99 Likewise, Strauss remarked that "we have outgrown the notion, that the divine omnipotence is more completely manifested in the interruption of the order of nature, than in its preservation." Strauss, *The Life of Jesus*, as excerpted in Stepelevich, *Young Hegelians*, 51.

100 Scruton appears to disregard the impact of the poison when he argues that Siegfried is the "true transgressor," "the one who, by failing to understand the meaning of promises, contracts and laws, brings about his own and others' destruction." Scruton, *The Ring of Truth*, 193.

101 Shakespeare, *Othello*, 127.

102 Denis Diderot, "Extracts from the *Histoire des Deux Indes*," in *Political Writings*, eds. and trans. John Hope Mason and Robert Wokler (Cambridge University Press 1992), 192–3.
103 Letter to Röckel, 25/26 Jan. 1854, SL 303, 307.
104 *Id.*, 304.
105 Carlyle was even more graphic in his portrayal of modern man's decline: "How much among us might be liked to a whited sepulchre; outwardly all pomp and strength; but inwardly full of horror and despair and dead-men's bones!" Carlyle, "Characteristics," 336.
106 Letter to Röckel, 25/26 Jan. 1854, SL 304–5.
107 *Id.*, 307.
108 *Id.*, 306.
109 Corse, *Wagner and the New Consciousness*, 25. Scruton pursues this same thesis when he writes "In the two stories of Brünnhilde and Siegfried, which are one story only by moments, we see the way in which the sacred and the ideal are captured by the personal – through the forging of self-identity, and through love offered unconditionally in the heights of erotic desire." Scruton, *The Ring of Truth*, 293, 306 ("this [sacred] aura arises spontaneously in the experience of the self-conscious being, and is inseparable from the I to You encounter that shapes the *Lebenswelt*").
110 Corse, *Wagner and the New Consciousness*, 24, 26–7: "Siegfried was intended to embody Hegel's notion of consciousness at its highest individual stage."
111 Corse, *Wagner and the New Consciousness*, 32–8.
112 Scruton recognizes this gap when he explains that "Siegfried as Everyman has passed stage 2 of *Selbstbestimmung*, the encounter with the Other . . . as lover (Brünnhilde). He now must move on, according to the rules of the dialectic, to stage 3, which is the stage of self-knowledge. . . . But it is just this that Siegfried cannot do." Scruton, *The Ring of Truth*, 280.
113 Rousseau, *A Discourse on Inequality*, 88.
114 Frank M. Turner, *European Intellectual History from Rousseau to Nietzsche* (Yale University Press 2014), 14.
115 Carlyle, "Characteristics," 354.
116 Hegel, *Phenomenology*, 360 (§590).
117 Hegel, *History*, 22–4.
118 *Id.*, 43.
119 Krasnoff, *Hegel*, 58:

> [T]he Absolute must be conceived of not as any sort of preestablished harmony between ourselves and the world . . . but only as "a result," the end of a process of historical development. . . . A free and realized individual, Hegel argued, is one who has emerged from such a process of historical development to achieve a kind of unity or identification with his or her social world and the norms that govern it. . . . This realized condition, the Absolute, the end or goal of both philosophy and history, Hegel called "Spirit's self-realization." To Rousseau's question of when and how human beings can be said to be free even as they live under social norms, Hegel's answer is: when Spirit has come to know itself.

Smith, "Hegel," 245: "Instead of setting out, as the empiricists do, by positing rights in some hypothetical state of nature or, as the formalists do, as part of the transcendental structure of consciousness, Hegel regarded rights as part of the dynamic structure of history. Rights claims are not static but are part of a long and arduous historical process leading men gradually, but inexorably, toward an awareness of their own freedom." Kelly, *Discovery of Chance*, 190: Hegel advocated a drastic change in philosophy's approach to the nature of truth, making clear that it could only fulfill its role by "abandoning the search for eternal and universal values and truths in favor of a historicist approach to philosophical doctrines as the products of human thought in specific cultural contexts"; 193: "Hegel stresses the difference between his historicist approach and conventional opinion on the nature of truth – the 'formal' thinking that holds that truth can be formulated in fixed propositions of eternal validity."

120 Terry Pinkard, *Does History Make Sense?* (Harvard University Press 2017), 11, 20–38.
121 Hegel, *History*, 49–50.
122

> [S]pirit arises from and becomes real only in and through human subjects and their concrete experiences with the world. Self-consciousness is necessarily mediated through the actual forms of life of individual thinking subjects, because without this 'real-life' mediation there is no self-consciousness: the advent of spirit requires encountering what is initially beyond consciousness, comprehending it and incorporating it into one's self understanding. . . . Such mediation is thus a condition of the self-realization of spirit and also the very mode of its constitution.
>
> (Marina F. Bykova, "Spirit and Concrete Subjectivity
> in Hegel's *Phenomenology of Spirit*," in *The Blackwell Guide
> to Hegel's 'Phenomenology of Spirit,'* 274)

As Hegel stated, "Only through [human activity in general] is the concept (along with its implicit determinations) realized, actualized – for these aims and principals are not immediately valid in and of themselves. The activity which puts them into operation and into existence is that which stems from human need, drive, inclination, and passion." Hegel, *History*, 25.

123 Hegel, *Phenomenology*, 11 (§20). Contrary to the common understanding of Hegel's system, then, Hegel's "Spirit," in the words of one academic, "is not something that descends upon the world from without; it is something which develops within the world, and only through our own efforts." Bykova, "Spirit and Concrete Subjectivity," 274. See also Smith, "Hegel," 259: "The end is not brought about by a superintending providence operating outside of history but through conscious human will and activity working in and through history. Consequently it is never enough to wait patiently for the end; it is necessary to force the end, to act as if the end were already immanent in our deeds." As Kelly explains, "Hegel admitted the role of contingency in history, distinguishing in the preface between mathematical truths . . . and historical truths, which concern 'particular existence and the accidental and arbitrary.'" Kelly, *Discovery of Chance*, 194–5. And yet, as many intellectual historians concede, Kelly included, Kelly, *Discovery of Chance*, 191, there is a tension in Hegel's statements on this point, arising from assertions such as, "Spirit does not toss itself about in the external play of chance occurrences; on the contrary, it is that which determines history absolutely, and it stands firm against the chance occurrences which it dominates and exploits for its own purpose." Hegel, *History*, 58.
124 "Regarding change as development, in other words the gradual actualisation of potential, the coming into being according to laws intelligible to reason of something which had from the beginning been 'potentially' present in the circumstances which is changing" was a fundamental insight first articulated in the modern era by Gianbattista Vico and taken up by Hegel, who "combined these elements into a vast unitary system." Isaiah Berlin, *Political Ideas in the Romantic Age*, ed. Henry Hardy (Princeton University Press 2014), 297. See also Corse, *Wagner and the New Consciousness*, 21: "for Hegel, 'the real world exists precisely as continual change, *constant* change.'"
125 Hegel, *History*, 76. As George Windell has noted, "Reality [in Hegel's philosophy] ceased to be something given and therefore unchanging, as in the Christian tradition; it became dynamic, always evolving." Windell, "Hegel, Feuerbach and Wagner's *Ring*," 41.
126 Mill, "The Spirit of the Age," 52.
127 Carlyle, "Characteristics," 352.

128 George Bancroft, *The Necessity, the Reality, and the Promise of the Progress of the Human Race* (Kessinger Legacy Reprints; repr. of 1854 edn. of Bancroft's lecture), 8, 10.
129 Bell, "Teleology, Providence," 38–9.
130 John D. Rosenberg, *Carlyle and the Burden of History* (Harvard University Press 1985), 49–50.
131 Bancroft, *Progress of the Human Race*, 32.
132 Carlyle, "Characteristics," 351.
133 Pinkard, *Does History Make Sense?*, 41–3, 102.
134 Hegel, *History*, 57.
135 As quoted in Rotenstreich, "The Idea of Historical Progress and Its Assumptions," 208.
136 Immanuel Kant, "Idea for a Universal History with a Cosmopolitan Purpose," in *Political Writings*, ed. H.S. Reiss (Cambridge University Press 1991), 42.
137 Vincent Guillin, "Comte and Social Science," in *Love, Order and Progress: The Science, Philosophy and Politics of August Comte* (University of Pittsburgh Press 2018), 134–50: "Comtean historicism considered historical development as the natural and spontaneous result of dispositions or potentialities inherent in human nature, which required some historical maturation to manifest themselves."
138 Kelly, *Discovery of Chance*, 343–6. See Sander Gliboff, *H.G. Bronn, Ernst Haeckel, and the Origins of German Darwinism* (MIT Press 2008), 140–2. Wagner owned at Wahnfried the third German edition of 1867, translated by Heinrich G. Bronn, and "updated and corrected" by J. Victor Carus.
139 Letter to Röckel, 25/26 Jan. 1854, SL 302.
140 Richard Wagner, "Man and Established Society," in *Jesus of Nazareth and Other Writings*, trans. W. Ashton Ellis (University of Nebraska Press 1995; repr. of 1st edn., 1899), 228.
141 Kant, *Political Writings*, 42.
142 As the philosopher Slavoj Zizek and Wagner commentator has expressed this point, "once we are in negativity, we never quit it and regain the lost innocence of Origins." Slavoj Zizek, "Afterword: Wagner, Anti-Semitism and 'German Ideology,'" in *Five Lessons on Wagner*, ed. Alain Badiou and trans. Susan Spitzer (Verso 2010), 217.
143 Carlyle, "Characteristics," 353.
144 Mary A. Cicora, *Mythology as Metaphor: Romantic Irony, Critical Theory and Wagner's* Ring (Greenwood Press 1998), 71.
145 Wagner, "Toast," 316.
146 Hegel, *History*, 21.
147 Richard Wagner, "Art and Climate," in *The Art-Work of the Future and Other Works*, trans. W. Ashton Ellis (University of Nebraska Press 1993; repr. of 1st edn., 1895), 261 (hereafter "AC" in text).
148 Equally illustrative is Wagner's letter of 1870 to Nietzsche regarding Plato and Socrates: "And what high hopes and aspirations may we then cherish for ourselves, when we feel deeply and clearly that we can, and must, achieve something that was denied to them!" (Letter to Nietzsche, 4 Feb. 1870, SL 771). Wagner was also highly critical of any attempts to revive Greek tragedy itself, labeling such "antiquarian fidelity" as "a clumsy artistic fib" (OD 150); see Cicora, *Wagner's* Ring *and German Drama*, 2: "Wagner never advocated a simple return to the form of Greek tragedy. He felt that it needed to be redefined for the modern age"; see also Mark Berry, "Richard Wagner and the Politics of Music Drama," *The Historical Journal*, Vol. 47, No. 3 (2004), 666, 675: "He aimed not at a restoration of tragedy, but at its renewal."
149 Letter to Röckel, 25/26 Jan. 1854, SL 308.
150 Some commentators accept this premise as the essence of Wagner's theory, among them Deathridge, who explains how the future of man is "to become at the same time his 'fundamental origin' (*Ursprung*)." Deathridge, *Wagner*, 65; Darcy, "'The World Belongs to Alberich!,'" in *Wagner's Ring of the Nibelung*: 48: Siegfried described as "Wagner's 'man of the future,' his symbolic portrait of regenerate humanity"; Cooke,

I Saw the World End, 26; Tanner, *Wagner*, 33–4: Wagner conceived of Siegfried as "the man of the future" and "sole representative of the new order." But as Cooke himself concedes, "there is always the awkward fact that Siegfried, even as a *symbolic* projection of regenerate man, is a very curious figure." Cooke, *I Saw the World End*, 26. See also Hollinrake, *Nietzsche*, 45, noting "obstacles" to reconciling Rousseau's natural man as a precursor to the *übermensch*.

151 Any attempt to conclusively pin Wagner down on this evolutionary point is further complicated by the fact that Wagner was still flirting with Rousseauvian utopianism and the myth of a regenerate man in his final years of life. In *Religion and Art* of 1880, he returned to the dream of restoring human nature to its original state, calling for a regeneration of a "gentler manhood" through universal adoption of vegetarianism. Not content simply to ground this insight in a forward-looking implementation of Schopenhauer's ethics of *caritas*, Wagner struggled to find this model for future humanity in the historical *ur-mensch*. "Many a hint from observation of the natural man, as also dim half-legendary memories, had made them guess the primal *nature* of this man, and that his present state is therefore a degeneration" (RA 231). Tellingly, however, Wagner did not blame this degeneration on some congenital flaw in man's design, but hypothesized instead that it was a series of natural cataclysms that "overtook primeval man while yet all unprepared" and drove humankind to a state of hunger and homelessness that forced him to hunt animals for his livelihood (RA 238–39). By positing "overpowering *outward* influences, against which pre-historic man could not defend himself through inexperience" as the cause of this degeneration, and not some trait "unconditionally inherent in his nature" (RA 237), Wagner committed himself even more intently to the touchstones of Hegelian progress: the role of change and development of consciousness through history as the engines of man's ultimate renewal and control over his future: "Whoever rightly weighs these aptitudes of the human race . . . must come to the conclusion that the giant force which shaped this world by testing every means of self-appeasement, from destruction to re-fashioning, had reached its goal in bringing forth this Man; for in him it became conscious of itself as *Will*, and, with that knowledge, could thenceforth rule its destiny" (RA 244). And further, Wagner justified his utopian thesis of a cycle of innocence, corruption, and regeneration by relying on the latest findings of modern science! Thus, "[I]ndefinite though be the results of our Scientific Research . . . yet one hypothesis of our geologists appears established beyond cavil: namely that the youngest offspring of the animal population of this earth, the human race . . . has survived . . . a violent transformation of the surface of our planet" (RA 237).

152 Letter to Uhlig, 22 Oct. 1850, SL 219. Some months earlier, in a July 1850 letter to Herwegh, the Russian essayist and journalist Alexander Herzen expressed a similar concession to the intellectual comforts of modern man: "Don't we belong despite ourselves to this world which we hate, with its vices, its virtues, its passions, and its habits? What would we do in virgin lands – we who can't spend a morning without devouring a dozen newspapers? It must be admitted, we would make poor Crusoes." As quoted in Kelly, *Discovery of Chance*, 313. In many notable ways, Herzen's intellectual development parallels that of Wagner. Steeped in Hegel, Feuerbach, and Proudhon before the revolutions of 1848–9, friend and associate of Herwegh in exile after the revolution, and intellectual correspondent with Thomas Carlyle, Herzen, like Wagner, was deeply disappointed by the failure of 1848. But he emerged from the despair with a newfound faith in history and man's role in it. While Herzen took a much more cautious view of mankind's power to shape history, informed by a deep appreciation for the contingencies of human experience, he still trusted in the accumulated wisdom of generations to propel man to higher stages of evolutionary development. Kelly, *Discovery of Chance*, 354. Wagner knew of Herzen through Herwegh and took note in his diary of the affair between Herwegh and Herzen's wife. Wagner, "Annals," 101: "(Herwegh-Herzen scandal)." What is tantalizing about this diary

entry from 1852 is that the confrontation between Herzen and Herwegh had actually taken place a year earlier in 1851, with news spreading to Switzerland already in July of that year. Kelly, *Discovery of Chance*, 332–3. Herwegh, a "remarkably handsome man with the aura of a martyr in the fight for freedom," spread the word in Geneva that Herzen was a "tyrannical husband denying his wife the freedom to rejoin her lover." *Id.*, 332–3. Wagner likely heard about the incident in 1851 yet does not mention it in his diary until mid-1852 when he was in the process of drafting the libretto for *Die Walküre*. Then Wagner mentions the two events in conjunction with one another: "Valkyrie written. – (Herwegh. – Herzen scandal)." "Annals," 101. Clearly, then, Wagner associated Herzen's marital scandal with his story of Siegmund and Sieglinde. Through his friendship with Herwegh, Wagner may have imbibed some of Herzen's thought, of course as distilled by Herwegh.

153 Letter to Röckel, 25/26 Jan. 1854, SL 311. Thinkers and theorists of the early nineteenth century, as survivors of a recent world-historical cataclysm, were all too conscious of their precarious place in world history. Hegel conceded in the Preface to his *Phenomenology* that "ours is a birth-time and a period of transition to a new era. Spirit has broken with the world it has hitherto inhabited and imagined, and is of a mind to submerge it in the past. . . . But this new world is no more a complete actuality than is a new-born child." Hegel, *Phenomenology*, 6–7 (§§11–12). This maxim was rehearsed throughout the century as a comforting mantra. In his articles in *The Examiner* in 1831, Mill called his time "an age of transition." Mill, "The Spirit of the Age," 53. Thomas Carlyle reached the same conclusion in his article of the same year in the *Edinburgh Review*, although expressed in a far more prophetic style. "The doom of the Old has long been pronounced, and irrevocable; the Old has passed away: but, alas, the New appears not in its stead; the Time is still in pangs of travail with the New." Carlyle, "Characteristics," 361. Herzen opened his series of essays entitled *Dilettantism in Science* (1843) with the acknowledgement that "[w]e live on the border between two worlds." As quoted in Kelly, *Discovery of Chance*, 205. See also Gay, *Schnitzler's Century*, 142–3. But like Wagner, Herzen concluded in one of his *Letters from Avenue Marigny* (1851) that he was not fit for the new era he heralded: "The death of the world that has outlived its time will engulf us too: there is no escape, our damaged lungs can only breathe infected air. . . . But . . . [we] will joyfully welcome the new world – which will not be our world – with the words: 'We who are about to die, salute you, Caesar!'" As quoted in Kelly, *Discovery of Chance*, 336.

154 See Pocock, *Barbarism and Religion*, 7.

2 Brünnhilde and the tragedy of jealousy

Driven by the vision of Brünnhilde as a paradigm of virtue, most interpreters of the *Ring* completely ignore or at best quickly pass over Brünnhilde's own frailties. But Wagner did not view Brünnhilde in *Götterdämmerung* as a saintly eternal feminine, as Shaw would have it, or more recently Barry Emslie and Roger Scruton,[1] but as a real flesh and blood woman subject to all-engrossing human passions – passions that lead to tragic consequences: it is not the curse of the ring, but Brünnhilde's uncontrollable outburst of jealousy, that dooms Siegfried as well as her.

Siegfried falls directly into Hagen's snares at their first encounter, and through the operation of the potion Wagner insulates Siegfried from moral responsibility for his actions. Siegfried is therefore unknowing in his betrayal of Brünnhilde. Brünnhilde, on the other hand, more tragically falls into Hagen's trap. Seeing Siegfried in Gutrune's embrace, she is overcome with emotion, and in a jealous rage worthy of Medea conspires with Hagen and Gunther to have Siegfried killed. Wagner is explicit in his stage directions about the emotional torment that Brünnhilde experiences. When Brünnhilde first sees Siegfried after her abduction from the mountain top, she is thrown into a state of intense confusion. "*Scarcely able to control herself*" she faints in Siegfried's arms. She then sees her ring on his finger. "*Forcibly restraining the most terrible agitation*," she demands to know how he acquired it. Realizing that it was Siegfried, not Gunther, who stole the ring from her finger on the mountain, she cries out "*in the most terrible anguish*" accusing him of "[m]ost shameful deceit! Betrayal! Betrayal!" (RN 319-21). In her emotional turmoil, her ancient wisdom is rendered obsolete: "Where now is my wisdom against this bewilderment? Where are my runes against this riddle?" (RN 326). At the height of her distress she vows revenge and reveals to Hagen the secret of Siegfried's singular physical vulnerability. Wagner directed Amalie Materna, his first Brünnhilde, that "[a]fter a fearful inner struggle with the uncontrollable forces taking possession of her," she must cry out revenge "with clenched fists."[2] It is Brünnhilde's moment of sexual jealousy that leads to the tragic demise of the hero.

Musically, the scene in which Brünnhilde recognizes Siegfried's betrayal has been described by Geck as "one of the most shocking in any of Wagner's music dramas, making it hard to believe that it was written by a composer who claimed to be weary of emotional outbursts."[3] And Wagner was particularly exacting in his demands for the performance of this scene and the following. Porges observed of

Brünnhilde's lines just preceding the oath trio that "[o]nly by straining her physical and mental faculties to the limit did the Brünnhilde eventually succeed in realizing Wagner's intention."[4] Yet despite the musical and textual "display of brute force," and the importance that Wagner attached to these scenes, Brünnhilde's emotional turmoil and her homicidal disclosure have received insufficient attention from commentators.[5] Brünnhilde's outburst of jealousy warrants further investigation.

Rousseau saw sexual jealousy as "a terrible passion which braves all dangers, defies all obstacles, and which in its fury seems liable to destroy the very human race it is meant to preserve. What must become of men, who are prey to this unrestrained and brutal rage, without shame, without modesty, fighting every day over their loves at the cost of their blood?" As a result he was at pains to exclude it from his natural utopia. "[I]t is only in society that even love, together with all the other passions, has acquired that impetuous ardour which so often renders it fatal to men." To bolster his theoretical conclusion, Rousseau drew support from the anthropological evidence of the Caribs "who of all peoples existing today have least departed from the state of nature" and are the "least subject to jealousy."[6] In his *Reflections*, Diderot imagined in prurient detail the pleasures of sex in a prehistorical world liberated from jealousy. When the chaplain of the European ship is assigned to stay with the family of Orou: "they undressed the chaplain, washed his face, hands and feet, and served him a wholesome and frugal meal. When he was about to go to bed, Orou . . . reappeared, presented him with his wife and three daughters, each of them naked, and said. . . . 'Here is my wife; here are my daughters. Choose whomever you prefer.'"[7]

For Wagner, however, jealousy could not be so easily erased from the Arcadian landscape. In dismissing *Götterdämmerung* as merely a form of grand opera, Shaw accused Wagner of "Lohengrinizing." He could not have been more accurate in his assessment, even as he missed the philosophical import of the connection. In *Lohengrin*, Elsa is driven to ask Lohengrin's name – a forbidden condition of their marriage vows – and thus drives him away forever. In "A Communication," Wagner described his moment of insight in developing the character of Elsa: "I grew to find her so justified in the final outburst of her jealousy, that from this very outburst I learnt first to thoroughly understand the purely-human element of love." Wagner attributed Elsa's forbidden question to jealousy, and in his view, her inquiry revealed the true essence of love, the authentic expression of a core human emotion. "This woman . . . who, by the very outburst of her jealousy, wakes first from out the thrill of worship into the full reality of Love, and by her wreck reveals its essence to him who had not fathomed it as yet" (CF 347). As Wagner came to the realization that the depth of Elsa's love paradoxically undermined the very foundation of that love, he "suffered deep and actual grief – often welling into bitter tears – as I saw the tragical necessity of the parting, the unavoidable undoing of this pair of lovers." Jealousy, then, for Wagner, was not an incidental or adventitious calamity but a fundamental aspect of human attachment. *Et in Arcadia ego.*[8]

But whereas in *Lohengrin*, jealousy merely separated the lovers, in *Götterdämmerung*, Wagner – following the lead of his favorite playwright – took a step closer to the abyss and showed how a more dangerous strain of the same emotion – sexual jealousy – leads to murder.

Once again *Othello* becomes a relevant touchstone for understanding the conflicts in *Götterdämmerung*. For who had more effectively captured the destructive force of jealousy than Shakespeare in his tragedy of the Moor of Venice? Moses Mendelsohn noted that "Shakespeare has realized the causes, consequences, and effects of jealousy in a splendid play, better, more accurately and more completely than such material has been treated in all schools of worldly wisdom."[9] Later, at the turn of the nineteenth century, the great Shakespeare critic A.C. Bradley eloquently and passionately summarized the human predicament at the heart of the play:

> Such jealousy as Othello's converts human nature into chaos, and liberates the beast in man; and it does this in relation to one of the most intense and also the most ideal of human feelings. What spectacle can be more painful than that of this feeling turned into a tortured mixture of longing and loathing, the "golden purity" of passion split by poison into fragments, the animal in man forcing itself into his consciousness in naked grossness, and he writhing before it but powerless to deny it entrance, gasping inarticulate images of pollution, and finding relief only in a bestial thirst for blood? This is what we have to witness in one who was indeed "great of heart" and no less pure and tender than he was great.[10]

Wagner altered the Shakespearean model by having Brünnhilde, not Siegfried, become jealousy's tragic victim. In the confusion over Siegfried's possession of the ring, Wagner mimics the dramatic handling of the handkerchief in *Othello*. Woven "with magic in the web of it," the handkerchief is given by Othello to Desdemona as a love token. When found in the possession of Cassio, the handkerchief becomes "ocular proof" of Desdemona's alleged adultery. Just so, the mysterious ring of the Nibelung exchanged between Siegfried and Brünnhilde as a seal of their love becomes evidence of Siegfried's betrayal. The talisman of love in the wrong hands triggers the call for murderous revenge. Just as Othello kneels with Iago to swear an oath to ensure Cassio's death and Desdemona's demise, so Brünnhilde joins with Hagen and Gunther in a pledge to have her beloved Siegfried stabbed in the back on the hunt: "So shall it be! May Siegfried fall: let him purge the shame that he caused me!" (RN 330).

Brünnhilde thus does not sail through the *Ring*'s last opera as a goddess of compassion, showering eternal feminine grace on a corrupted world. She too is tragically marked by the destructive forces of erotic love. And Wagner did not spare her the pains of this awful recognition. She calls on the gods, "[d]irect your gaze on my burgeoning grief [*blühendes Leid*]" (RN 349). Far from an icon of purity or a "privileged, wondrous maid," as Emslie dubs her,[11] then, Brünnhilde is an all too fragile human being. As Wagner celebrated the natural beauty and strength of man in Siegfried who is free to love, he also showed the dark side of that same force, ironically not through his paradigmatic natural man, but through the newly-minted human Brünnhilde. As Bloom observes of *Othello*, "Desdemona's murder is the crossing point between the overflowing cosmos of *Hamlet* and the cosmological emptiness of *Lear* and of *Macbeth*."[12] The story of Othello teaches that even the most vaunted hero, raised to the greatest heights of prestige and glory, can be brought low by the elemental force of the raw human emotions of jealousy and revenge. Thus while one may wonder with Hamlet at "what a piece of work is a man," one must simultaneously acknowledge along with Macbeth that human life is a "tale told by an idiot, full of sound and fury, signifying nothing."

Feuerbach proclaimed that "the *summum bonum* of philosophy is human *being*."[13] But if mankind is to be the center of attention, the philosopher must recognize that man's violent emotions drive his life as much as his natural goodness and compassion, and that even as love is cultivated it carries within it the inner potential for its own destruction. Dahlhaus does not credit Wagner with any insight into the destructive forces inherent in love, preferring to argue that for Siegfried and Brünnhilde "the nature of their love . . . does *not* destroy itself in the very effort to become reality . . . ; it is destroyed by an outside agency and falls victim to a world in opposition to it."[14] But in confronting Elsa's jealousy, Wagner did not condemn it or explain it away as the byproduct of external evil forces; rather, he embraced it as an expression of her core humanity. And he wept at the realization. As Wagner admitted later in "A Communication," it was Elsa and her brush with the authentic essence of love that led him to unearth the natural man Siegfried from ancient myth (CF 375). Love was glorious yet equally capable of bringing deep sorrow and pain. In leading Brünnhilde from the ecstatic heights of communion with Siegfried on the top of the rock, to the depths of despair in the Gibichung palace by the Rhine, Wagner mapped the tragic trajectory of erotic love.

Nietzsche would later criticize Wagner for purportedly failing to understand this fundamental, indeed natural, essence of love. In *Der Fall Wagner* (*The Case of Wagner*; 1888) Nietzsche upheld Georges Bizet's *Carmen* (1875) as the model of operatic truth, privileging it over Wagner's works:

> Finally, love – love translated back into nature. Not the love of a "higher virgin"! No Senta-sentimentality! But love as *fatum*, as fatality, cynical, innocent, cruel – and precisely in this a piece of nature. That love which is war in its means, and at bottom the deadly hatred of the sexes! – I know no case where the tragic joke that constitutes the essence of love is expressed so strictly, translated with equal terror into a formula, as in Don José's last cry, which concludes the work: "*Yes. I have killed her, I – my adored Carmen!*"[15]

Nietzsche may have been right about *Der Fliegende Holländer*, or *Tannhäuser* for that matter, but he was certainly wrong about *Götterdämmerung*. For in his portrait of Brünnhilde, Wagner tapped into the very same emotional contradictions that made the story of *Carmen* so compelling to Nietzsche. "My poem," Wagner boasted to Röckel, ". . . shows nature in all its undistorted truth and essential contradictions, contradictions which in their infinitely varied manifestations embrace even what is mutually repellent."[16]

Brünnhilde's Shakespearean agony borne of love was not a new concept for German thinkers of the early nineteenth century. In *Die Leiden des jungen Werthers* (*The Sorrows of Young Werther*; 1774) Goethe had vividly portrayed the devastating effects of sexual attraction on the human psyche, how, in Bradley's words, "the golden purity of passion" could so readily "split into fragments." Tormented by his unrequited love of Charlotte, Werther ultimately takes his own life, dying a painful death. Goethe understood that the same passion that could ennoble man could also lead into the dark night of the soul. "My heart's immense and ardent feeling for living Nature, which overwhelmed me with so great a joy and made the world about me a very paradise, has now became an unbearable torment, a demon that goes with me everywhere, torturing me."[17] Heaven and Hell are facets of the same human emotion. Some decades later, the Austrian playwright Franz Grillparzer in his dramatic trilogy *Das goldene Vlies* (*The Golden Fleece*; 1821) brought to the stage Medea's Hellenic explosion of jealous rage. In the final drama of the cycle, Medea, revenging herself on her unfaithful and callous husband, Jason, sets fire to the palace, kills her two sons by Jason, and disposes of Jason's lover, Creusa, the daughter of King Creon.[18] As she contemplates her bloody deeds, Medea muses, "Tomorrow, when the sun shall rise, then shall I be alone, the world a desert waste for me, my babes, my husband – gone! A wanderer I, with weary feet all torn and bleeding sore, and bound for exile!"[19]

These vivid and devastating portraits of man and woman's vulnerability to the torments of passion were not favored images for those thinkers with a more meliorative agenda for the nineteenth century. To many, these artists' arresting evocations of love's despair represented a destructive philosophy. In 1842 in the pages of the *Deutsche Jarhbücher*, Arnold Ruge, the Young Hegelian, decried "[t]he absurdities of the caprices of love, from Wertherlike suicides to those stolen from the ancient examples, and the demand which lies behind these inferior interests, i.e., that humanity never gets beyond possessions and enjoyment."[20] Thomas Carlyle also bristled at Goethe's apparent endorsement of suicide in *Werther* and sought throughout his career to counter the damaging corrosion of despair that Goethe had so vividly portrayed in his early work.[21] In the "Sorrows of Young Teufelsdröckh" section of *Sartor Resartus*, Carlyle parodied *Werther*, driving his anti-hero Teufelsdröckh to extravagant heights of misery at the sight of his beloved Blumine passing by in a carriage with her new husband, but ultimately saving his poor Clothes Philosopher from the ravages of unrequited love.

In calling for an end to traditional religious constructs, many nineteenth-century thinkers were optimistic that the eradication of Christian morality and its denigration of human carnality would allow man to find a new equilibrium. As previously noted, Heine looked forward to the day when the sick society of Europe would be healed and humanity "has again attained its complete health, when peace has again been established between soul and body, and soul and body again mingle in their original harmony."[22] Feuerbach was likewise confident that by making its focus "the *real* and the *whole being of man*" the philosophy of the future would "lay[] the foundation of a rational unity of head and heart, of thought and life."[23]

But not everyone was so convinced that the dismantling of religious guideposts alone would have such salubrious effects, or that the transition from a world of faith to a secular society could be accomplished without psychic pain.[24] Carlyle, for one, astutely recognized that the eradication of traditional modes of faith from contemporary society threatened to leave a dangerous spiritual vacuum. Carlyle's agenda in "Characteristics" and then *Sartor* was therefore not just a practical legal and cultural one of advising his readers to adapt their laws and customs to the times, but a spiritual one of trying to solve the urgent moral question about the state of man's soul in a post-theological world. Christianity may have outlived its usefulness, but some form of faith was still a critical requisite for man's composure. Carlyle rejected the legacy of the Enlightenment which promoted a mechanistic, utilitarian vision of man. Materialism and system-building had left man spiritually empty. Logic was not the answer to man's ills. "[T]he sum of man's misery is even this, that he feel himself crushed under the Juggernaut wheels, and know that Juggernaut is no divinity, but a dead mechanical idol," he bluntly told his readers in his 1831 essay "Characteristics." "The God-like has vanished from the world" he mourned.[25] Man needed a receptivity to wonder and mystery in order to flourish.

Carlyle was not naive about the challenge. He recognized that man was caught between two opposing forces of body and soul that were not so readily reconciled. Just as man sought to aspire to the sublime – his "Promethean, Prophetic Character" – he was dragged down to earth by the ridiculous – "the clay-given mandate, *Eat thou and be filled. . . .*" (SR 140).[26] But Carlyle was not satisfied with simply allowing the "clay-given mandate" to hold sway as he believed Goethe had done in *Werther*. For Carlyle, the suicidal pangs of unrequited love and the loss of spiritual guidance were two sides of the same coin, his Teufelsdröckh's emotional pain at the loss of his Blumine the symptom of a larger spiritual absence that could not be filled simply by eradication of religious dogma and an embrace of sensualism. Carlyle offered a spiritual answer to the despair borne of love, promoting, in theology's place, a transcendental spirituality. "The healthy Understanding, we should say, is not the Logical, argumentative, but the Intuitive." From the "abysses of mystery and miracle," Carlyle preached, "all wonders, all Poesies, and Religions, and Social Systems have proceeded."[27] Unlike Goethe, then, Carlyle did not leave his anti-hero to die, but compassionately drew his lovelorn spiritual pilgrim out of the abyss of the Inferno, the "Everlasting No," leading him through the "Centre of Indifference" into the paradisiacal sunlight of the "Everlasting Yea."

Wagner's own wrenching portrayal of jealousy and the destruction it wreaks also threatened to undermine the theoretical foundation for any true reconciliation of heart and mind. But in the end, Wagner grafted a Carlylean parable of faith onto an age-old tale of human jealousy and by doing so strove for a metaphysical solution to the timeless conundrum of the human heart.

Brünnhilde's spiritual crisis

Brünnhilde's despair of love is part and parcel of a spiritual crisis. In Act III of *Die Walküre*, Brünnhilde, facing punishment by Wotan, pleads with her father to spare her the ignominy of becoming the possession of the first man to find her on the rock. As she lays out the arguments for mercy, she tries to revive Wotan's faith in his plan: "you fathered a noble race," "Sieglinde nurtures the holiest seed," "She safeguards the sword" (RN 188). By proposing that she be awakened only by Siegfried, Brünnhilde demonstrates her sustained commitment to Wotan's vision and strives to convince her father to continue to put some renewed hope in his failing enterprise. In the end, she succeeds. In a singular moment of compassionate empathy Wotan promises Brünnhilde that it will only be the freest and bravest of heroes who will liberate her, and sets Loge's fire as a pledge of his promise. When Brünnhilde awakes in the presence of Siegfried, she embraces Siegfried not only as the great hero, but also as the fulfillment of her father's promise and his cosmic destiny. The covenant she made with Wotan that she would be protected from the vagaries and shame of male lust has been honored. Her spiritual worldview, defined by a confidence in a protective paternal god who watches over his human charges, is thereby confirmed. When Waltraute appears to her in Act I, scene iii, of *Götterdämmerung*, Brünnhilde continues to acknowledge and honor her father's authority. She greets Waltraute with surprise – "you've dared to break War-Father's ban?" – and then anxiously looks for signs of absolution from him: "Might Wotan's heart have relented towards me?" She credits his wisdom for her present happiness: "he granted my timid entreaty. . . . So his punishment made me thrice-blessed" (RN 301). Scruton names the musical material that accompanies these expressions of faith as "Brünnhilde's longing to be reconciled with Wotan."[28] And indeed she continues to believe that she is furthering his ultimate plan for the world: "When I shielded Siegmund against the God, erring – I know – I fulfilled his wish none the less" (RN 301). That her human loyalty to Siegfried proves in the end stronger than her duty to the gods does not detract from the fact that the divine power structure is still a vivid reality for her and that the Siegfried she reveres is Wotan's creation and the instrument of his great plan.

Wagner reinforces this conception of Brünnhilde's spiritual mindset through the musical themes he marshals to define Brünnhilde and Siegfried's love. In the third act of *Siegfried*, Wotan's sweeping World Inheritance motif, which captures Wotan's joyous recognition of Siegfried as his heir, is fully appropriated by the lovers. In the Prologue of *Götterdämmerung*, Wagner continues with the same program. The World Inheritance motif sounds again alongside several new themes intended to reflect the deepening trust and love between the heroic pair. One theme in particular has traditionally been identified as marking Brünnhilde's new status as a mortal woman (the "Mortal Brünnhilde" theme).[29] (See Figure 2.1.)

While this theme is clearly associated with Brünnhilde, there is more to its associative power. The Mortal Brünnhilde theme first emerges in the brief orchestral interlude between scenes i and ii of the Prologue, where its roulades are exploited to rapturous effect to evoke the rising sun. It then shapes Brünnhilde's first words to the hero: her exhortation to Siegfried to fulfill his destiny with "new deeds": "*zu neuen Taten*," with "*Taten*" falling on the descending minor seventh. Just as the theme conjures the sunrise, so Brünnhilde's faith in a redemptive hero dawns. A number of commentators have noted, Cooke and Darcy included, that this theme bears a number of similarities with the musical phrase that Sieglinde had

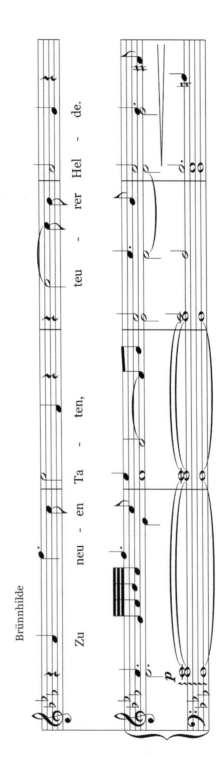

Figure 2.1 Brünnhilde's Faith in Siegfried theme

previously intoned in the third act of *Die Walküre*, variously known as Transformation, Redemption of Love, or Glorification of Brünnhilde. We will return to this important motif later, but for now suffice it to say that this theme is first introduced when Sieglinde learns that she is to bear Siegmund's son and joyously cries out "*O hehrstes Wunder! Herrliche Maid!*" Both musical phrases share a clear diatonic color, a melodic turn, and interval leaps of a fourth and minor seventh. (See Figure 2.2.)

The wonder that Sieglinde had expressed at the miracle of birth, and the prospect of a heroic heir, is now adapted to reflect Brünnhilde's trust in that particular heir. Both are motifs of anticipation – Sieglinde looked forward to the birth of the hero; Brünnhilde now anticipates the hero's deeds. For this reason, the new Brünnhilde motif can just as legitimately be labeled "Brünnhilde's Faith in Siegfried."

But this faith, as we learn, is misplaced, and Siegfried emphatically fails to live up to the destiny envisioned for him. Having drunk Hagen's potion, Siegfried forgets his loving bond with Brünnhilde and becomes not an instrument of Wotan's cosmic plan, as Brünnhilde has come to expect, but rather the blind puppet of Hagen's Machiavellian manipulations. In the encounter with Waltraute, Brünnhilde forcefully defends her love for Siegfried, but the audience, by then privy to the plot of Hagen, already understands that in the scheme of world-historical developments, her argument is specious and naive. Brünnhilde is invoking love as panacea, but the drugged Siegfried is about to prove her assumptions completely wrong. Wagner wanted the audience to "shudder" at this irony[30] and ensured this emotional effect by having Brünnhilde blithely sing the words "I shall never relinquish love" to a musical phrase that signifies the very opposite – the Renunciation of Love.

It is only when Siegfried pierces the wall of fire a second time, now in the false guise of Gunther, that Brünnhilde's faith and her worldview begin to fall apart. This sinister parody of Siegfried's first approach to the mountaintop demonstrates the harsh cruelty of a world suddenly made barren of divine protection. On seeing the stranger within her protected magic circle, Brünnhilde is overwhelmed not only with fear, but also anger. She cries out, "Wotan, grim hearted, pitiless god! Alas! Now I see the sense of my sentence: to scorn and sorrow you hound me

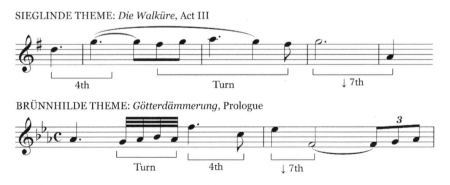

SIEGLINDE THEME: *Die Walküre*, Act III

BRÜNNHILDE THEME: *Götterdämmerung*, Prologue

Figure 2.2 Comparison of Sieglinde and Brünnhilde themes

hence" (RN 307). Wotan's covenant has been broken, and he now shows himself in an entirely new and menacing guise. Brünnhilde's first reaction is to conclude that Wotan has cruelly tricked her and is in truth a vengeful god. Later, she will come to realize that Wotan's power has dissipated and that his promises simply have no force anymore.[31]

Wagner chided Röckel for failing to understand this key moment of the drama. "The terrible and daemonic nature of this whole scene has escaped you entirely: a 'stranger' passes – effortlessly – through the fire which, in accord with his destiny and our own experience, none but Siegfried should or could traverse: everything collapses at Br[ünnhilde]'s feet, everything is out of joint; she is overpowered in a terrible struggle, she is '*God-forsaken*.'"[32] Just as the spectator of the *Ring* experiences the symbolic drama of the passing of the god's hegemony, so Brünnhilde must confront that epochal transition as a personal psychological trauma. The loss of her spiritual moorings, therefore, is crucial to understanding Brünnhilde's outburst of jealousy and homicidal rage. When she extolled the virtues of love to her sister, she remained safe in the knowledge that Wotan singled her out for good fortune; now left spiritually adrift, she is about to experience the deepest confusion, sorrow, and rage from that love. Brünnhilde no longer has any workable framework to evaluate what is happening to her. Her ancient wisdom becomes worthless as she falls into the undertow of human emotions: "where now is my wisdom against this bewilderment? Where are my runes against this riddle?" (RN 326). In her mind, Brünnhilde has not only been betrayed by Siegfried, but also by her father, Wotan. Thus, in conspiring to kill Siegfried, Brünnhilde is not only taking revenge on her faithless lover but destroying Wotan's creation and his dream; her act of jealous revenge strikes at Wotan himself. Brünnhilde has experienced the pain of betrayal not only as a lover but as a believer. It is only through a version of Teufelsdröckh's existential reckoning that she can rise to a higher consciousness.

Wagner poignantly communicates this experience of lost faith and betrayal in his treatment of the Mortal Brünnhilde theme in the last scene of Act I. Just after Siegfried, in the guise of Gunther, subdues Brünnhilde, her "*gaze unconsciously meets Siegfried's*" (RN 308). At this moment the Mortal Brünnhilde theme sounds again on the English horn. But this time a chromaticism has insinuated itself into the phrase, rendering the interval of the fourth a tritone. In the moment of intuitive recognition Brünnhilde's trust is shaken, and the music subtly expresses this sense of betrayal with an interval already associated with Hagen.

Wagner carries the point even further in the final passages of Siegfried's Funeral March. After reaching a noble culmination in triumphant reiterations of the Sword, Siegfried, and Heroic Love motifs, the march dies away in a somber mood as the Brünnhilde theme emerges out of the orchestral reverberations, sounding on the plaintive English horn and clarinet, at a slower tempo, against a diminished harmony; the roulade which had so energized it now takes on a ruminative mien. The theme is followed by the stabbing *marcato* beats that opened the threnody, and then sounds a second time, corroded once again by the acidic tritone. (See Figure 2.3.) The glorious celebration of the Wälsung legacy thus crumbles on a recollection of Siegfried's basest treachery, powerfully anticipating in music the paradox that

Figure 2.3 Brunnhilde's Faith in Siegfried theme in the final measures of Siegfried's Funeral March

Brünnhilde will articulate later in words: "the purest of men it was who betrayed me!" (RN 348). And these elegiac manifestations of her own once exultant theme palpably evoke what has been most tragically lost: Brünnhilde's belief in Siegfried as the heroic heir to Wotan. The theme that had formerly heralded the rising sun now mirrors a somber moonlight. Following on, the sour themes of the Ring's Power, the Ring, and the Curse return as signals of the unfinished business left on Siegfried's death. The sense of loss is further marked in the next few bars as Gutrune frets over Siegfried's absence and looks for Brünnhilde in her room. As she listens at Brünnhilde's door, we once more catch the sound of the Brünnhilde theme, now *piano* on the clarinet and more *a tempo* but still carrying the tritone. Gutrune calls out "Brünnhild'! Are you awake?" and a *fermata* marks the silence as she peers "timidly" into the chamber. Wagner told his orchestra during the 1876 *Ring* rehearsal that this *fermata* "must be lengthened so that the effect of the silence is uncanny."[33] The altered theme then sounds a second time, *pianissimo*. A theme which had celebrated Brünnhilde's new status on the mountaintop as well as her secure religious faith now marks her absence, as ever fainter echoes of the person she no longer is: the vulnerable mortal still enthralled with her father's worldview. What she has become will become clear moments later when she reappears on the stage.

Wagner's fellow artists typically chose to let the dismal facts of life and love speak for themselves. In the final scene of *Othello*, Shakespeare ends with a pile of corpses – the "tragic loading of this bed." Goethe leaves the reader at the graveside of Werther.[34] Bizet concludes his opera with the minor key sequence of the fate motif insistently ringing out as Don José confesses his crime – "Yes, I have killed her." Their audiences are left to ponder the shattering pain of passion borne of love – but no cosmic solutions. These are true Schopenhauerian dramas that unapologetically present the terrors of human existence without any spiritual leavening.[35] Wagner, however, was not satisfied to end his opera where other dramatists had been content to rest their pens; he went further to offer a Hegelian way out of the labyrinth of despair. Enter Brünnhilde in the final scene of the drama.[36]

Beyond tragedy

After the murder of Siegfried is accomplished and his body returned to the Gibichung palace, Brünnhilde reemerges on the stage with a newfound authority – and a clear agenda. No longer driven (indeed blinded) by the force of erotic love she first experienced on the mountaintop, she now calmly takes the measure of the catastrophe that has unfolded along the banks of the Rhine. Brünnhilde calls on Gutrune to "silence your grief's exultant clamour!" (RN 347). Or as Carlyle had urged his fellow students of the French Revolution, "O shrieking beloved brother blockheads of Mankind, let us close those wide mouths or ours; let us cease shrieking and begin considering!"[37] Exercising her powers of reflection, Brünnhilde steps out of time, without denying its force, to observe from a distance the meaning of history.[38]

In his essays *Über die ästhetische Erziehung des Menschen* (*On the Aesthetic Education of Man*; 1801) Friedrich Schiller praised the heightened stage of insight that can be achieved once the soul is freed of the confusion of emotion:

> Contemplation (reflection) is Man's first free relation to the universe which surrounds him. If desire directly apprehends its object, contemplation thrusts its object into the distance, thereby turning it into its true and inalienable possession and thus securing it from passion. The necessity of Nature which governed him with undivided power in the condition of mere sensation, abandons him when reflection begins; an instantaneous calm ensues in the senses; time itself, the eternally moving, stands still while the dispersed rays of consciousness are gathered together, and *form*, an image of the infinite, is

reflected upon the transient foundation. . . . [T]hought . . . triumphs over the laws of time .[39]

Brünnhilde "triumphs over time" with powerful new insight, announcing that "it was I whom the purest man had to betray, that a woman might grow wise. . . . All things, all things . . . all is clear to me now!" (RN 349). Critically, Brünnhilde's tragic rage has not destroyed her but has allowed her to reach a new state of enlightenment. Immersed in a painful psychological and spiritual struggle, she has emerged the wiser for it.

Hegel's historical thesis did not disregard human passions and self-interest; rather he saw them as necessary fuel for the evolution of Spirit. "[I]t is the passions, the aims of particular interests, the satisfaction of selfish desire that are the most forceful things. . . . We must assert as a general proposition that *nothing great* has been accomplished in the world *without passion*."[40] Hegel believed that "[t]his imponderable mass of wills, interests, and activities – these are the tools and means of the World Spirit for achieving its goal, to elevate it to consciousness and to actualize it."[41] Only by fully engaging in the desires and dangers of life, by experiencing the scalding heat of battle, could men achieve the actualization so necessary to the progress of the historical dialectic and, for some, a deeper understanding of their world. Hegel acknowledged the painful course of human affairs: "When we look at this drama of human passions, and observe the consequences of their violence and of the unreason that is linked not only to them but also (and especially) to good intentions and rightful aims; when we see arising from them all the evil, the wickedness, the decline of the most flourishing nations mankind has produced, we can only be filled with grief for all that has come to nothing."[42] But this sorrow served as an intellectual goad. Hegel urged his students to recognize that "the events that present such a grim picture for our troubled feeling and thoughtful reflection have to be seen as the *means* for what we claim is the substantial definition, the absolute end-goal or, equally, the true *result* of world history."[43] Lamartine captured this pragmatic and engaged approach to history in two vividly graphic epigrams that closed his account of the Revolution: "Ideas vegetate from human blood. Revelations descend from scaffolds."[44]

Following Hegel and Lamartine, Wagner also recognized that passion and the sorrows that accompany its expression could constructively be re-deployed as the engine of historical consciousness. On April 13, 1853, Wagner wrote to Liszt:

[T]o acquire this knowledge [of love] by active striving is the task of world history. . . . The state of lovelessness is the state of suffering for the human race: an abundance of suffering now envelops us . . . but you see, it is precisely here that we *recognize* the glorious necessity of love . . . a force of love which would not be possible were it not for this painful recognition; and so, in this way, we acquire a strength of which natural man had no inkling, and this strength – increased to embrace the whole of humanity – will one day lay the foundations for a state on earth when no one need yearn for the other world . . .[45]

Pain and sorrow are the grist for the mill of progress. Only through suffering does man reach a state of self-consciousness and moral vigor that impels him to recognize true need, envision a better future, and actively seek out that future.[46] Suffering, then, at the time he completed the poem of the *Ring*, was not for Wagner the meaningless end and purpose of life, but instead, in true Hegelian sense, the catalyst for progress – a progress which, as Wagner made clear, brings man to a state of evolved consciousness far distant from that of the first natural man.[47] "*Experience* is everything," Wagner told Röckel.[48]

Barry Emslie has argued that if we concede Brünnhilde's human frailty and the depth of her suffering, we undercut her redemptive credibility. In this view, shared by Scruton and others, Brünnhilde is not "just any woman" but a "privileged, wondrous maid" who already understands the world and has access to Wotan's wisdom.[49] But Wagner did not intend for Brünnhilde simply to carry on the program and wisdom of the gods. Not only is her ancient runic knowledge insufficient to navigate the traps of human civilization, but whatever guiding power they had is lost in the groundswell of genuine human emotion. In the process of this upheaval – "the fearful inner struggle with the uncontrollable forces taking possession of her" – Brünnhilde discovers something new that is uniquely human. A vulnerable mortal now bereft of divine protection, Brünnhilde must confront the harsh reality of human life and the truth about love. And she bravely accepts her pain: "Hear my lament." Her vulnerability, then, becomes her strength. Her ultimate claim to know "*Alles*" is certainly arrogant, but she now knows enough to end the reign of the gods – something that her ancient runes certainly could not teach her. While dramatically she mirrors the function of a *dea ex machina*,[50] thematically she is not a return of godhead. Viewed through a Hegelian lens, Brünnhilde's power and heroism lie instead in her ability *as a human* to overcome her pain and transform her devastating experience of sorrow and death into a constructive insight not just for herself but for all humanity. From the scaffold she descends with revelations.

One of the first steps that Brünnhilde takes is to call for a "worthy lament befitting the greatest of heroes" (RN 347) and to direct that a funeral pyre be built to honor Siegfried's memory. Memory was a critical component of Hegel's theory of historical consciousness.[51] Through memory, man makes sense of the historical process and himself, and harnesses the hidden power of the ever-receding and evaporating past to propel him into the future. In the closing paragraphs of the *Phenomenology*, Hegel identified "recollection (*Erinnerung*)" as integral to the struggle towards Absolute Knowing. History passes by, in each era creating a "new existence, a new world and a new shape of Spirit." But nothing remains of the past, except the memory of it. Memory, by "inwardizing" the lived experience, "has preserved it and is the inner being, and in fact the higher form of the substance."[52] This inwardizing process, of recollection, reflection, and analysis, is the means by which the Spirit fully comes to know itself and hence the means to promote the process of becoming. Recalling history and telling of it – and, in doing so, making sense of it – is spiritual renewal and growth at work.

Proudhon came to the same conclusion about the power of recollection in *What Is Property?*: "it is our strength of memory and penetration of judgement which enable us to multiply and combine the acts that are inspired by our social instinct and that teach us how to render them more effective." From the "savage sacrificing everything for a trinket, and then repenting and weeping" – an image adapted from Rousseau – Proudhon traced the "progressive and painful education of our instincts, this slow and imperceptible transformation of our spontaneous perceptions into reflective knowledge."[53] It is this power of reflective memory which Proudhon, following the findings of the naturalist Frédéric Cuvier, recognized as the unique capacity that distinguished man from the animals and secured the promise of his future. Carlyle likewise extolled recollection as the foundation for optimism: "Change, indeed, is painful; yet ever needful; and if Memory have its force and worth, so also has Hope." Comte made memorialization of the great deeds of famous men the centerpiece of his new scientific cult of man. In calling for a yearly Day of All the Dead, and Temples of Humanity, Comte prescribed how his utopian positivist society would honor the memories of past benefactors of mankind.[54]

Building on memory and historical reflection, knowledge and understanding become critical formative factors in the historical process. In his lectures on the philosophy of history Hegel made clear that freedom could be "achieved and won" only "through an endless process involving the discipline of knowledge and will."[55] In keeping with his Hegelian frame of mind at mid-century, Wagner also privileged knowledge as vital to historical progress. In February 1849, just months before the Dresden uprising, Wagner warned the revolutionary readers of Röckel's radical-left *Volksblätter*, "unworthy were it of reason-dowered Man, to give himself resistless, like the beasts, to the will of the waves." Instead, man's "task, his duty bids him do with *consciousness* what the age demands of him. As thinking men, our earnest aim must therefore be to attain this consciousness, this knowledge of what *we* have to do."[56] Reason, thought, consciousness, knowledge, these, then, are the tools of the revolution. Even after the abortive revolt Wagner continued to privilege knowledge as the key to progress. In *Opera and Drama*, he exclaimed, "[e]ven now, it is only knowledge that can prosper us; whilst ignorance but holds us to a joyless, divided, hypochondriacal, scarcely will-ing and never can-ning make believe of Art, whereby we stay unsatisfied within, unsatisfying without" (OD 372). "[I]t was *from thinking*, that there first arose the force to withstand the State" (OD 197). Thus, in the final scene of the *Ring*, passion, so critical to the education of Spirit, cedes control to reflection and thought which comprehend the universal. "All human passions extinguished, [Brünnhilde] is now a pure eye of knowledge," Wagner told Porges in 1876.[57] In *Götterdämmerung*, the twilight that marks the passing of the gods is the same twilight when the Owl of Minerva emerges and philosophy can take the measure of what has passed.

But Brünnhilde does not simply dwell in the past – she harnesses it to carry her forward into a future she has envisioned. Hegel left it to those precious few "world historical individuals" – "those whose aims embody a universal concept" – to perceive at least some measure of the true course of history and help advance it towards its ultimate goal. For these great historical individuals their "own particular aims contain the substantial will that is the will of the World Spirit. The[y] can be called *heroes*."[58] Hegel defined these heroes as "thoughtful men, with insight into what was needed and what was timely: their insight was the very truth of their time and their world. . . . It was theirs to know it, this universal concept, the necessary next stage of their world."[59] World-historical persons are thus the "insightful ones," the "seers," of their age.[60] When Brünnhilde reenters on stage she has inherited her mother Erda's prophetic mantle. Wagner described her at this moment as an "ancient German prophetess" and reinforced this association by recalling the rising and falling motifs of birth and death that accompanied Erda's first appearance in *Rheingold*.[61] (See Figure 2.4.)

But Brünnhilde assumes her new role on strictly human terms; the power of divination is not lost with the fall of the idols. As John Rosenberg has explained, "History as Carlyle understood and practiced it is prophecy."[62] Building on a metaphor of organic growth, J.S. Mill consoled his readers in 1831 that "since every age contains in itself the germ of all future ages as surely as the acorn contains the future forest, a knowledge of our age is the fountain of prophecy – the only key to the history of posterity. It is only in the present that we can know the future, it is only through the present that it is in our power to influence that which is to come."[63] In 1854 Bancroft predicted that "the great mind of collective man may, one day, so improve in self-consciousness, as to interpret the present and foretell the future."[64]

Having become wise and all-knowing through suffering, Brünnhilde is no longer the blind subject of time and history; she has become its author for future generations, dispatching the ravens to Valhalla "with anxiously longed-for tidings." The world-historical individual, in Isaiah Berlin's words, is that person "whose genius consists in . . . discerning the difference between what is dying and what is to come, and who thereby automatically bring[s] the future nearer."[65] Self-consciousness, this uniquely human capacity for self-comprehension, is the engine of progress because it demands reasons and explanations, thereby ensuring that man will always be driven to challenge his held beliefs and set out along new paths of inquiry.[66] Human history thus becomes a self-reinforcing feedback loop. The insights that emerge out of the human struggle and that reveal with ever increasing clarity the forces at work in human development in turn help structure, guide, and accelerate future progress.[67] Thus, essential to an understanding of *Götterdämmerung* is that Wagner not only trusted in the inherent potential of every living thing to become fully manifest over time (as explored in the last chapter), but believed with Hegel that world-historical individuals had critical roles to play in shaping the course of human development and advancing the agenda of freedom. In his collection of philosophical essays *From the Other Shore* (1855) Alexander Herzen observed that "[w]e must be proud of not being needles and threads in the hands of fate as it sews the motley cloth of history. . . . [W]e *can change the pattern of the carpet*."[68] Wagner similarly recognized man's power to change the future. In his Toast to the Königliche Kapelle, he assured his

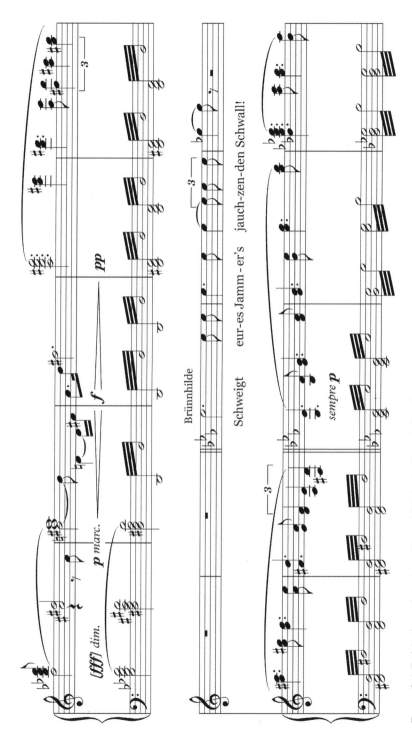

Figure 2.4 Erda's theme introduces Brunnhilde in the Immolation Scene

audience that they were living in "the period of the human spirit's evolution to ever more distinct self-consciousness: in it that spirit has sought with surer tools to grasp its destiny."[69] He further extemporized that "the child of the Present is the Future, and the clearer and more steadily man looks towards that, the more purposefully will he employ the present."[70] It is equally telling that when in 1871–72 Wagner came to republish certain works of his Dresden and early Zurich years in his *Gesammelte Schriften und Dichtungen* (*Collected Writings and Poems*) he chose to introduce volumes iii and iv of that collection with a passage from Carlyle's *Frederick the Great* – calling on sage leaders to hasten the arrival of a better world – to summarize his mindset of the time. A quotation from the closing passages of *What Is Property?*, which Wagner was reading in the years before and after the Dresden uprising, could equally have sufficed to make the same compelling point about man's increasing power over historical progress: "Let me see from my obscurity the people at last instructed: let noble teachers enlighten them; let generous spirits guide them. Make shorter, if possible, the time of our trial."[71]

Brünnhilde conquers tragic despair and sets the future in motion with two momentous deeds on behalf of mankind. Her first metaphysical step is to end the reign of the gods. Having experienced firsthand Wotan's impotence and inability to honor the covenant he made with her, Brünnhilde recognizes that the gods have forfeited their authority to rule the world. Siegfried's sword had sent Wotan running back to Valhalla, but did not conclusively end his reign. Wotan, wrought with anxiety, still searches for a solution to his dilemma, continuing to nurture a shred of hope that the ring's return to the Rhine will free him from the curse. As Waltraute reports of Wotan "[s]ighing deeply, he closed his eye and, as in a dream, whispered the words: 'if she gave back the ring to the deep Rhine's daughters, from the weight of the curse both god and world would be freed'" (RN 303-04). Röckel was confused that the ultimate return of the ring to the Rhine did not automatically save the gods – and it may very well be true that the ring's release would have redeemed them – but *Brünnhilde* will not have it so. She recognizes that the gods' time has come and undertakes to seal their fate – irrespective of what happens to the ring. Just as Wotan had laid Brünnhilde to rest on the rock protected by the ring of fire, now it is Brünnhilde's turn to lull Wotan to sleep along with the other deities and ignite the pyre that will engulf them forever. By recognizing Brünnhilde's affirmative choice to end the reign of the gods – an act she undertakes *before* returning the ring to the Rhinemaidens – we can resolve Röckel's confusion.[72] Brünnhilde has introduced human agency into history, and fate and the curse have thus been superseded.[73] Brünnhilde does not just set things right; she changes the pattern of the carpet.

Her next main act is to return the ring to the Rhine. Having already broken the curse and its endless cycle of destruction through her own affirmative acts of willing historical change and, as we shall explore in the next chapter, her act of forgiveness, the release of the ring amounts in the end almost to a mere gesture. But the gesture is critical not only symbolically, but also in marking Brünnhilde's newly acquired state of self-conscious insight into the workings of Spirit. Initially Brünnhilde would not relinquish the ring to her sister Waltraute, even if the world depended on it. Emslie complains that this blindness to the ring's historical significance is nonsensical insofar as Brünnhilde was privy to Wotan's struggle to regain the golden band. But Emslie discounts the import of Brünnhilde's transformation into a human being and her experience for the first time of erotic love. Whatever stirrings of compassion she had for Siegmund's fate in her guise as an immortal, that state of mind cannot compare in any way to the depth of libidinal attachment she forms with Siegfried once incarnated in the form of a human being.[74] Wagner explained to Röckel that after her awakening "she has no longer any other knowledge save that of love."[75] Having emerged into a new state of being for which there is no model or guide, Brünnhilde must learn the truths of human existence from square one. She first clings to love, and the ring, as panacea. Only once she has gone through the terrifying trials of jealousy does she come to understand and appreciate the broader world-historical implications of the ring's (perceived) power and, privileging the world's universal need over her individual sentimentalism, learn to let the ring go. At the same time she appreciates that her love for Siegfried has no further need of contractual consideration, as it were; she adopts a deeper perspective on love which does not require the selfish possession of a trinket from which to derive its meaning.[76]

It is for these reasons that we must reject Sandra Corse's argument that the Feuerbachian I-Thou relationship "is the organizing principle of the *Ring* cycle" and that sensual love, for Wagner, is the end game of the dialectical process. This thesis, like Shaw's (but for a different reason), stops at the glorious heights of *Siegfried's* final scene and fails to account for the harsh lessons of *Götterdämmerung*. Through Brünnhilde's struggle, Wagner implicitly criticizes Feuerbach's notion that the I-Thou relationship provides a clear road to universalism. The love relationship between Brünnhilde and Siegfried becomes compromised by its own egoistic demands and fuels a volatile passion that can ignite at any moment into violence.[77] As Wagner acknowledged, "man's love for woman, in its most natural form, is a fundamentally selfish, hedonistic love in which, while finding satisfaction in a certain physical pleasure, he is incapable of resolving himself in his whole being" (AF 64). Individual recognition of the other, therefore, is insufficient to accomplish the goal of Spirit in history. Wagner made this clear to Cosima in September 1871 during an evening drive through the countryside when he commented that "the love between Siegfried and Brünnhilde . . . achieves no universal deed of redemption, produces no Fidi [the pet name for their son Siegfried]."[78] It is only through the pain, sorrow, and loss of love that Brünnhilde gains her deeper insight and transforms her parochial erotic attachment to Siegfried into a broader universal love of mankind as a whole.[79] "Siegfried . . . as a man, committed entirely to deeds, . . . knows nothing, he must fall in order that Brünnhilde may rise to the heights of perception," Wagner told Cosima that evening. For Wagner, then, Brünnhilde and Siegfried's blessed oasis of love in the final act of *Siegfried* is not the culmination of a Hegelian process but only a step along the way.

By the same token, Siegfried's failure of memory not only signifies his historical innocence, but his inadequacy to the demands of historical progress. The real work of mankind is accomplished in the pain of daily human life and love and the sorrowful moments of self-conscious reflection that succeed that pain. Wagner's belief in the power of reflection, thought, and knowledge to alter the course of history is clearly evident in Brünnhilde's newfound equanimity as well as her bold assertion of wisdom and insight. In the final scene, she does not react in the heat of the moment, but her actions rationally proceed from dispassionate understanding. In this way, Brünnhilde embodies the unique destiny of Germany. In confronting the bold iconoclasms of the French Revolution, Germans, entrenched in medieval political structures, were entranced and envious. They consoled themselves, however, that they had achieved the same impact on human history through their philosophy and religion. From their perspective, German ideas were the true foundation of modernity.[80] German scholars thus looked to Martin Luther's Reformation as the first critical step out of the Middle Ages, and then to Kant. In his lively treatise *On the History of Religion and Philosophy in Germany* Heine heartily endorsed this thesis of German exceptionalism, trumpeting the intellectual accomplishments of German culture in a playful one-upmanship with French political history. Immanuel Kant was the "great destroyer in the realm of thought" who "far surpassed Maximilien Robespierre in terrorism."[81] Referring to the famous nineteenth-century historians of the French Revolution, Heine opined – flattering himself no doubt – that "if at some point, like the French Revolution, Germany philosophy finds its Thiers and Mignet, its history will be just as fascinating reading; the German will read it with pride, the Frenchman with admiration."[82] Heine clearly had prejudged the answer when he asked rhetorically: "Only our most distant descendants will be able to decide whether we should be praised or reproached for first working out our philosophy before working out our revolution."[83] Wagner clearly agreed with Heine when he wrote in the preface to the re-published *Art and Revolution* that Germany's "own completed *Reformation* would seem to have spared it from the need of any share in the Revolution" (AR 29).

The greatest proponent of the Young Hegelian *Philosophie der Tat*[84] therefore is not the instinctive, physical Siegfried – "the man committed entirely to deeds" – who acts without understanding by way of the sword.[85] As Wagner makes clear, Nothung is *Wotan's* great idea. Instead, it is Brünnhilde who gains insight from passion *and pain* and uses this *knowledge* to take the momentous historical step of annihilating the regime of the gods and purging the curse of the ring. Brünnhilde has the capacity to see beyond the intellectual confines of the theological worldview. Her trust in Siegfried had been bound up with a trust in her father's foresight and power. Once Siegfried betrays that trust, she initially continues to preserve the theological framework, concluding that she had misperceived the nature of Wotan's rule – that instead of a compassionate father, he is a mercurial vengeful god. But she does not maintain this theological *Weltanschauung* for long, ultimately choosing instead to construct a completely new schema for the world order. In the end, she is not tragically defeated by Siegfried's betrayal and violence; rather, she accepts the cognitive dissonance – the dialectically driven negation of his love and heroism – as a pathway to insight. She directly confronts the paradox of the "purest of men" who yet commits the worst betrayal, and perceives the necessity of a paradigm shift to resolve that tension. She concludes that it is not Siegfried who has failed her, but the immortal, all powerful gods. "[N]o one betrayed as he did! Do you know why that was so? Oh you, eternal guardian of oaths! . . . [B]ehold your eternal guilt!" (RN 348-49). Wotan's world must therefore be scrapped entirely, along with Carlyle's other "adventitious wrappages," to make way for a new phase of human development.

It thus was never Siegfried who embodied the world-historical hero, but Brünnhilde who *becomes* one in the final scene of the drama through her deeds borne of conscious suffering and memory.[86] The *Ring* thus makes clear that one is not born great, nor is it enough to have greatness thrust upon one; rather, one must achieve greatness through an arduous process of spiritual awakening.

Notes

1 Emslie asserts that Brünnhilde "isn't just any woman," but a "privileged, wondrous maid." Emslie, *The Centrality of Love*, 90–5. Scruton agrees that Brünnhilde's insights are unique to her status as a former immortal, calling her "an *ideal* woman . . . the incarnation of a femininity prepared in the realm of pure ideals" and the "Christ figure, become mortal through pity"; "From now on [since Brünnhilde's punishment] she is to represent the *Ewig-weibliche* in the realm of mortals." According to Scruton, "[o]nly the former goddess can win through to a proper understanding." Scruton, *The Ring of Truth*, 221, 223, 293, 295. In this regard Scruton characterizes her wisdom as "intuitive." *Id.*, 30. See also Richard H. Bell, "Teleology, Providence," 42: "when she appears in the final scene of *Götterdämmerung* there are signs that she is transfigured and is in the process of regaining her divinity. . . . As in Christian theology the crucified Christ's spirit fills the universe, so in the *Ring* it is Brünnhilde's which flows through the whole re-created order"; Brünnhilde "is the true divine figure, not Wotan"; Corse, *Wagner and the New Consciousness*, 186: describing Brünnhilde "as the last god herself, seeing to the death of all the gods."
2 Porges, *Wagner Rehearsing the 'Ring,'* 132.
3 Geck, *Richard Wagner*, 302.
4 Porges, *Wagner Rehearsing the 'Ring,'* 136.
5 Kitcher and Schacht briefly acknowledge this dramatic moment, but in an oddly neutral tone: "Not content merely to invoke laws and contracts and to appeal for justice, Brünnhilde is moved to action, providing Hagen with the all-important secret to the killing of Siegfried." And that is virtually all they say on the subject. Kitcher and Schacht, *Finding an Ending*, 176. Berry at least confronts the awful reality of her act, recognizing that Brünnhilde is guilty of a "betrayal every inch as foul as Siegfried's perfidy," but he too declines to dwell on these disturbing circumstances. Berry, *Treacherous Bonds*, 237. Scruton briefly references Brünnhilde's complicity in Siegfried's death but quickly tries to explain it away as the act of a "zombie-like replica." Scruton, *The Ring of Truth*, 134. Deathridge similarly discounts the episode as a "schizophrenic leap into the character of an evil, scheming villainess." Deathridge, *Wagner*, 72.
6 Rousseau, *A Discourse on Inequality*, 102–3.
7 Diderot, "Reflections on the Voyage of Bougainville," 47.
8 Magee argues that the plot of *Götterdämmerung* represents an insight about the human condition that is at odds with Wagner's original utopian intentions for the *Ring*, Magee, *Tristan Chord*, 180, but this interpretation sets up a false dichotomy. Wagner was not nearly as utopian in his thinking as Magee suggests, and "all you need is love," Magee, *Tristan Chord*, 122, is not the theme of the Feuerbach ending, as I explain further herein.

9 Moses Mendelssohn, Review of Robert Lowth's "*De Sacra Poesi Hebraeorum; Praelectiones Academicae Oxonii Habitae (Lectures on the Sacred Poetry of the Hebrews)* (1753)," in *Auseinandersetzung mit Shakespeare*, ed. Wolfgang Stellmacher (Akademie-Verlag 1976), 58.

10 A.C. Bradley, "Lecture V," 178.

11 Emslie, *The Centrality of Love*, 90.

12 Bloom, *Shakespeare*, 452.

13 Feuerbach, "Towards a Critique of Hegel's Philosophy," as excerpted in Stepelevich, ed. *The Young Hegelians*, 127.

14 Dahlhaus, *Richard Wagner's Music Dramas*, 104.

15 Friedrich Nietzsche, *The Case of Wagner*, trans. Walter Kaufmann (Vintage Books 1967), 158–9.

16 Letter to Röckel, 25/26 Jan. 1854, SL 307.

17 Goethe, *Werther*, 65.

18 There are a number of interesting parallels between Grillparzer's trilogy and Wagner's poem. Jason, the hero, braves a dragon to retrieve the Golden Fleece and then wins the heart of the wild sorceress Medea. The fleece is cursed, however, and Jason's love for his bride grows cold, driving her into a destructive jealous rage, during which she kills her children and burns down the royal palace.

19 Frank Grillparzer, *Medea* in *German Classics of the Nineteenth and Twentieth Centuries*, trans. Theodore A. Miller (German Publication Society 1914), vol. vi.

20 Arnold Ruge, "Hegel's 'Philosophy of Right' and the Politics of our Times," as excerpted in Stepelevich, ed. *The Young Hegelians*, 214; Mary Cicora, *Wagner's* Ring *and German Drama*, at 17: "The proponents of Young Germany had criticized Goethe."

21 In an essay on Goethe Carlyle praised the poet's novel *Wilhelm Meisters Lehrjahre* (*Wilhelm Meister's Apprenticeship*; 1795–6) as deserving

> our best attention: for the problem which had been stated in *Werther*, with despair of its solution, is here solved. The lofty enthusiasm . . . has here reached its appointed home: and lives in harmony with what long appeared to threaten it with annihilation. Anarchy has now become Peace; the once gloomy and perturbed spirit is now serene. . . . Here the ardent high-aspiring youth has grown into the calmest man, yet with increase and not loss of ardor, and with aspirations higher as well as clearer. For he has conquered his unbelief; the Ideal has been built on the Actual.

Thomas Carlyle, "Goethe" (1828) in *Critical and Miscellaneous Essays* (Houghton, Mifflin and Company 1881), 204–64.

22 Heine, *History*, 13.

23 Ludwig Feuerbach, *Principles of the Philosophy of the Future* in *The Fiery Brook: Selected Writings of Ludwig Feuerbach*, trans. Zawar Hanfi (Anchor Books 1972), 241–4 (§§50, 57). Friedrich Schiller sought to resolve the conflict within man through an appeal to aesthetics. In his essay *On the Aesthetic Education of Man*, Schiller correctly diagnosed the problem in this way: "It is in fact peculiar to Man to combine the highest and the lowest in his nature." Friedrich Schiller, *On the Aesthetic Education of Man*, trans. Reginald Snell (Angelico Press 2014), 91. But Schiller also warned that "if his *dignity* depends on a rigid distinction between the two, his *happiness* depends upon a skilful removal of the distinction." Man could not progress simply by ignoring or denigrating his passionate self. It was here to stay. The dilemma, therefore, was how to find a means to reconcile the two. "So culture, which is to reconcile his dignity with his happiness, will have to provide for the utmost purity of both these principles in their most intimate combination." *Id.*

24 As Scruton observes, "in destroying the gods, we destroy a large part of ourselves. In liberating ourselves from religion, therefore, we expose ourselves to another kind of spiritual disorder." Scruton, *The Ring of Truth*, 193. See Emslie, *The Centrality of Love*, 100: "many pre-Nietzsche philosophers, who, while happy to have got rid of

the doctrinal, commandment-heavy mumbo-jumbo God of their forefathers, were not always comfortable with a world without the divine and were not always sure how you could have one without the other." See also Gay, *Schnitzler's Century*, 166–74: "The classic autobiography of . . . Edmund Gosse, *Father and Son*, published in 1907, is often rightly cited as a lucid, touching demonstration just how painful it could be to free oneself from one's parents' piety."

25 Carlyle, "Characteristics," 343, 345.

26 Hegel captured this idea in his image of man as an "amphibious animal." Pinkard, *Does History Make Sense?*, 12.

27 Carlyle, "Characteristics," 323, 343, 345, 353.

28 Scruton, *Ring of Truth*, 128, 350 (Motif No. 167).

29 Darcy, "Metaphysics," 8–9 (Brünnhilde's "personal motive"). See also Deryck Cooke's thematic analysis in *An Introduction to "Der Ring des Nibelungen"* (Decca 2CD 443 581–2, 1967): themes 148 and 149; Ernest Newman, *The Wagner Operas* (Princeton University Press 1991), 594 (Theme No. 158: "a new Brynhilde"); Robert Donington, *Wagner's "Ring" and Its Symbols: The Music and the Myth* (St. Martin's Press 1969), 291 ("Brünnhilde as a loving woman"); Scruton, *The Ring of Truth*, 346 (Motif No. 150: "Brünnhilde's Womanhood"; N.B. The musical notation of the theme contains an error: the last 32nd note in the turn should be an E-flat).

30 Letter to Röckel, 25/26 Jan. 1854, SL 310.

31 Siegmund is the first to see the emptiness of Wotan's power and his betrayal: "Ha, shame upon him who sent me the sword if he now decrees not conquest but shame!" (RN 162).

32 Letter to Röckel, 25/26 Jan. 1854, SL 310 (emphasis added). It is for these reasons that I cannot join Berry in his conclusion that upon her loss of divinity "Brünnhilde will no longer be constrained by 'faith.'" Berry, *Treacherous Bonds*, 190.

33 Porges, *Wagner Rehearsing the 'Ring,'* 142.

34 Goethe's English biographer G.H. Lewes noted that Goethe's intention was to "paint scenes of life, without comment." As quoted in Rosemary Ashton, "Carlyle's Apprenticeship: His Early German Criticism and His Relationship with Goethe (1822–1832)," *The Modern Language Review*, Vol. 100 (2005), 18. In November 1881, Wagner remarked to Cosima, the "one thing Shakespeare always shows us – the terrible state of the world. In that sense one can regard him as the greatest pessimist of all." CT, ii, 751 (21 Nov. 1881). Porges praised Wagner's gift which "he shares with Shakespeare and Goethe of presenting the tragic with a frightening objectivity bearing no trace of sentimentality." Porges, *Wagner Rehearsing the 'Ring,'* 140.

35 Schopenhauer defined tragedy as "the description of the terrible side of life. The unspeakable pain, the wretchedness and misery of mankind, the triumph of wickedness, the scornful mastery of chance, and the irretrievable fall of the just and the innocent are all here presented to us." Arthur Schopenhauer, *The World as Will and Representation*, trans. E.F.J. Payne (Dover 1969), i, 252–3.

36 Berry, in a typical moment of interpretive dualism, acknowledges, in stark contradiction to the Schopenhauerian thesis, that "[i]t is distorting to claim that Wagner came to believe social progress to be mere illusion, that mankind would simply repeat its past errors." Berry, *Treacherous Bonds*, 235. But Berry locates the source of such a faith in progress in Siegfried's martyrdom, not in Brünnhilde's affirmative acts of historical insight, which he interprets, instead, in light of renunciation. *Id.*, 265, 268–9. Scruton and Deathridge place similar thematic importance on Siegfried's sacrifice. Deathridge, *Wagner*, 71–5; Scruton, *The Ring of Truth*, 283–6.

37 Carlyle, *French Revolution*, 545.

38 As Nietzsche would write in *The Birth of Tragedy*: "Concerned but not disconsolate, we stand aside a little while, contemplative men to whom it has been granted to be witnesses of these tremendous struggles and transitions. Alas, it is the magic of these struggles that those who behold them must also take part and fight." Nietzsche, *The Birth of Tragedy*, 98.

39 Schiller, *On the Aesthetic Education of Man*, 94–5. A list prepared by Minna Wagner reflects that in Dresden Wagner owned Schiller's Complete Works in 12 volumes (1838). Westernhagen, *Richard Wagners Dresdener Bibliothek 1842–1849*, 103.

40 Hegel, *History*, 23, 26.

41 *Id.*, 28.

42 *Id.*, 23–4.

43 *Id.*, 24.

44 Alphonse De Lamartine, *History of the Girondists; or, Personal Memoirs of the Patriots of the French Revolution*, trans. H. T. Ryde, 3 vols. (George Bell & Sons 1905), iii, 546. See in the original French, Alphonse de Lamartine, *Histoire des Girondins* (Meline, Cans et Compagnie 1847), 928.

45 Letter to Liszt, 13 Apr. 1853, SL 284–5.

46 Carlyle wrote, "Suffering, contradiction, error, have their quite perennial, and even indispensable abode in this Earth. . . . Ever must Pain urge us to Labour; and only in free Effort can any blessedness be imagined for us." Carlyle, "Characteristics," 343. Kant made a similar point:

> Man wishes concord, but nature, knowing better what is good for his species, wishes discord. Man wishes to live comfortably and pleasantly, but nature intends that he should abandon idleness and inactive self-sufficiency and plunge instead into labour and hardships, so that he may by his own adroitness find means of liberating himself from them in turn. The natural impulses which make this possible, the sources of the very unsociableness and continual resistance which cause so many evils, at the same time encourage man towards new exertions of his powers and thus towards further development of his natural capacities.

Kant, *Political Writings*, 45.

47 "This lovelessness . . . must inevitably lead us away from our state of natural unawareness towards a *knowledge* of the uniquely beautiful necessity of love." Letter to Lizst, 13 Apr. 1853, SL 284.

48 Letter to Röckel, 25/26 Jan. 1854, SL 307.

49 See *infra* note 1.

50 Foster, *Wagner's 'Ring,'* 245.

51 Joshua Foa Dienstag, "Building the Temple of Memory: Hegel's Aesthetic Narrative of History," *The Review of Politics*, Vol. 56, No. 4 (1994).

52 Hegel, *Phenomenology*, 493 (§808).

53 Proudhon, *What Is Property?*, 180, 191–2.

54 Andrew Wernick, "The Religion of Humanity and Positive Morality," in *Love, Order and Progress*, 228–30.

55 Hegel, *History*, 43.

56 Wagner, "Man and Established Society," 228.

57 Porges, *Wagner Rehearsing the 'Ring,'* 143.

58 Hegel, *History*, 32.

59 *Id.*, 33 (emphasis added). Wagner could also have derived this principle from Feuerbach, who in his *Thoughts on Death and Immortality* (1830) wrote:

> It is granted to only a few to see the end of the present, to be raised beyond its boundaries, and to feel through the hard skin and crust of the currently secure maxims and principles to the eternally bubbling spring of everlasting life. It is granted to only a few to go beyond the superficies that everywhere presents the appearance of something that is unchangeable and self-identical, to press into the depths and to perceive the pulsebeat of the creative new time.

Ludwig Feuerbach, *Thoughts on Death and Immortality*, trans. James A. Massey (University of California Press 1980), 16.

60 Hegel, *History*, 33. See Robert Hartman's translation which reads *"Einsichtigen"* as "seers." Georg Wilhelm Friedrich Hegel, *Reason in History: A General Introduction to the Philosophy of History*, trans. Robert S. Hartman (Macmillan 1985), 40.

61 It is for this reason that the true beginning of Brünnhilde's peroration is not when she calls upon the Gibichung vassals to build a pyre but when she first reemerges to the strains of Erda's prophetic vision from *Rheingold*. See Carolyn Abbate, *Unsung Voices: Opera and Musical Narrative in the Nineteenth Century* (Princeton University Press 1991), 220: "the *Götterdämmerung* motif enters with [Brünnhilde] as her escort, a musical gesture that links her with other sybilline singers (her mother Erda . . .)." See Darcy, "Metaphysics," 19, for further musical correspondences between Brünnhilde and Erda.

62 Rosenberg, *Carlyle and the Burden of History*, 49.

63 Mill, "The Spirit of the Age," 52.

64 Bancroft, *Progress*, 15.

65 Berlin, *Political Ideas*, 305.

66 Pinkard, *Does History Make Sense?*, 103.

67 Rotenstreich, "The Idea of Historical Progress and Its Assumptions," 209; Smith, "Hegel and the French Revolution," 260: "Progress has little to do with millennial faith in a transcendent deity but much to do with 'human self-assertion' and the desire to take control over one's own destiny." Berlin, *Political Ideas*, 304: "These ends [of history] are impenetrable to all but the philosopher, who, because he understands himself and the progress of history, is therefore automatically an agent in its self-fulfillment, for increase in understanding *is* progress."

68 As quoted in Kelly, *Discovery of Chance*, 424–5.

69 Wagner, "Toast," 315.

70 *Id.*, 316.

71 Proudhon, *What Is Property?*, 217. Even as late as *Religion and Art*, steeped as it is in Schopenhauer's ethical teachings, Wagner was still extolling the capacity of mankind to become "conscious of itself as *Will*" and deriving from "that knowledge" the power to "thenceforth *rule its destiny*" (RA 244) (emphasis added). Testament to his continuing faith in the Kantian principle of a creative advance inherent in nature, he asserted that the human species' "aptitude for Conscious Suffering" was the "last step reached by Nature in the ascending series of her fashionings" (RA 280).

72 Darcy proposes to resolve Röckel's conundrum in a different way by explaining that even if the gods are destined irrevocably to pass away, they can still be *spiritually*, if not physically, redeemed and absolved of their guilt through the return of the ring. In my reading, however, the only meaningful absolution for the gods is provided directly by Brünnhilde herself in her final forgiving farewell to Wotan, not by the physical return of the ring itself.

73 As Steven Smith has explained in his discussion of Hegel's philosophy of history, "the end is not brought about by a superintending providence operating outside of history but through conscious human will and activity working in and through history." Smith, "Hegel and the French Revolution," 259–60.

74 Emslie attempts to undercut this emotional distinction by characterizing the *Todesverkündigung* scene as "a crucial step towards [Brünnhilde's] own *sexual* awakening as woman as opposed to Goddess." Emslie, *The Centrality of Love*, 85. But while Brünnhilde's moment of compassion represents the first stirrings of her humanity, it is not an emotion that falls on the erotic spectrum. See Kitcher and Schacht, *Finding an Ending*, 149–51, noting different forms of love (benevolent, empathic and erotic).

75 Letter to Röckel, 25/26 Jan. 1854, SL 309.

76 See Berry's excellent discussion of the paradox of Siegfried and Brünnhilde's marriage "contract" and the "selfish myopia that prevents channelling of love outside the confines of the sexual union." Berry, *Treacherous Bonds*, 206.

77 Kitcher and Schacht, *Finding an Ending*, 177–8: "Exclusive erotic love can neither turn away, . . . nor can it prevail and triumph over the contagious corruption of the world." Scruton, *The Ring of Truth*, 250: "erotic love is jealous . . . and can turn to hatred when betrayed." Or as Köhler rightly notes, the love of Brünnhilde and Siegfried "represents not the solution, but the problem." Köhler, *Wagner*, 387.

78 CT, i, 410 (6 Sept. 1871).

79 Michael Ewans is one of the few to acknowledge Brünnhilde's "learning through suffering." Michael Ewans, *Wagner and Aeschylus: The Ring and the Oresteia* (Faber and Faber 1982), 231.

80 See Conway, *Mourning Sickness*, 1–7; Harold Mah, "The French Revolution and the Problem of German Modernity: Hegel, Heine and Marx," *New German Critique*, No. 50 (1990).

81 Heine, *On the History of Religion*, 79.

82 *Id.*, 89.

83 *Id.*, 115.

84 The *Philosophie der Tat*, as conceived by August von Cieszkowski in his *Prolegomena zur Historiosophie* (1838), represents a future-oriented philosophy of praxis whereby the divisions in human consciousness are expected to be overcome by a synthesis of thought with action. Kelly, *Discovery of Chance*, 149–53; see also Berry, *Treacherous Bonds*, 32 (referencing also the work of the proto-communist Young Hegelian Moses Hess, *The European Triarchy* (1841)).

85 See, by contrast, Berry, "Nietzsche," 17.

86 While most commentators acknowledge Brünnhilde's important role in the drama, they do not as a general rule recognize it as world historical in its impact or implications. Williams, for one, identifies Brünnhilde as a hero, but declines to label her heroism, calling it simply "a heroism of a different constitution." Williams, *Wagner and the Romantic Hero*, 17–19, 98. Windell is the only commentator of whom I am aware who directly acknowledges this key dramatic truth about Brünnhilde's role. Windell, "Hegel, Feuerbach and Wagner's *Ring*," 46.

3   Brünnhilde's immolation

Dramatizing species consciousness

What remains for Brünnhilde? She has fallen into despair and given herself up to the "Everlasting No." Now, in the final scene of the drama she joins Siegfried on the funeral pyre and extinguishes her own life. But this self-immolation is not an act of renunciation consistent with a despairing view of life's meaninglessness; it represents a symbolic embrace of Carlyle's "Everlasting Yea."

Nineteenth-century thinkers recognized that the human race could realize its destiny not in the span of an individual life but only through the accumulated wisdom of successive generations of man.[1] Kant had made clear that one individual's life was woefully insufficient to achieve mankind's full potential. His essay *Idea for a Universal History with a Cosmopolitan Purpose* (1784) observed:

> [E]very individual man would have to live for a vast length of time if he were to learn how to make complete use of all his natural capacities; or if nature has fixed only a short term for each man's life (as is in fact the case), then it will require a long, perhaps incalculable series of generations, each passing on its enlightenment to the next, before the germs implanted by nature in our species can be developed to that degree which corresponds to nature's original intention.[2]

Thus the philosopher interested in understanding and promoting the full inherent potential of mankind had to focus his attention not on individual achievements, but on the broad panorama of history. The plenitude of man's capabilities was only apparent in the life of the species. And the species only existed in time. "God as the totality of all realities and perfections," Feuerbach taught, "is nothing other than the totality of the qualities of the species compendiously put together in him for the benefit of the limited individual, but actually dispersed among men and realising themselves in the course of world history."[3] Ten years later, in the United States, Bancroft summarized these principles in his mid-century review of the state of progress:

> The life of an individual is but a breath; it comes forth like a flower, and flees like a shadow. . . . But as every man partakes of the same faculties and is consubstantial with all, it follows that the race also has an existence of

its own; and this existence becomes richer, more varied, free and complete, as time advances. . . . The many are wiser than the few; the multitude than the philosopher; the race than the individual; and each successive generation than its predecessor.[4]

The Young Hegelians turned the concept of the species life into the principal article of faith of their new humanism. The central purpose of Feuerbach's *Essence of Christianity* was to establish that all the virtues traditionally attributed to God were merely projections of the attributes of the species. "[T]his perfect being, free from the limits of the individual, is nothing else than the species" (EC 160).[5] In place of God, the species would become "the ultimate measure of truth" (EC 161). Species consciousness thus pointed the way to a new form of spiritual redemption.[6] Whatever the frailties, errors, and misdeeds of the individual, these could be overcome, superseded, and perfected in the life of the species.[7] "[W]hat one man cannot accomplish and does not know," Feuerbach wrote, "can be accomplished and known by all men collectively."[8] Or as Carlyle developed the point in "Characteristics": "The true Past departs not. . . . [N]othing is lost; it is but the superficial, as it were the *body* only, that grows obsolete and dies; under the mortal body lies a *soul* which is immortal; which anew incarnates itself in fairer revelation; and the Present is the living sum-total of the whole Past."[9] Individuals come and go, but the immortal soul of mankind lives on through successive generations. This was a concept that was worthy of worship. As Strauss proclaimed, "by the kindling within him of the idea of Humanity, the individual man participates in the divinely human life of the species . . . the sole way to true spiritual life."[10] Redemption could thus be found in history. "Humanity is the sinless one because the course of its development is blameless," Strauss argued. "Pollution cleaves to the individual only; in the human species and its history, pollution is sublated."[11] Comte gave further credence and legitimacy to this new form of theology in his four-volume *Système de politique positive* (*System of Positive Polity*) published between 1851 and 1854, in which he posited the Great Being of humankind as the focus of a secular religion purged of doctrinal cant.[12]

Building on these insights, the Young Hegelians rejected the Christian tenet of immortality of the soul after death and in its place enshrined human futurity as the determinant of meaning in a secular world. In the moving poem that concludes his *Gedanken über Tod und Unsterblichkeit* (*Thoughts on Death and Immortality*; 1830), Feuerbach wrote:

You call out in your distress,
"Give me consolation for death";
Yet behold the mild face of truth
And the sweet light of a new consolation:
Truth does not give you the rust of old fables;
It consoles you with *humans*,
With dear, better, other natures,
Who are because you have been,

With the angelic spirits of precious children,
The future masters of the present masters;
These call you away from life
And whisper you into a peaceful grave.[13]

The fear of death had generated the need for the Christian myth of immortality of the soul. But this "old fable" was false. Man had to confront instead the cold truth that death was not simply an "*appearance*" but "an actual and real death."[14] In the verses quoted here, Feuerbach taught that the spiritual palliative for this blunt realism was not the immortality of the individual soul, but the beautiful prospect of continued human species life, an ever-renewing human futurity incarnated in the "precious children" who will become the "future masters of the present masters." Carlyle likewise recognized species consciousness as a balm for the individual soul in existential torment. In the face of the anxieties and disappointments of human life Carlyle sought consolation – not in the afterlife – but in the march of human history. "On the roaring billows of Time, thou art not engulphed, but borne aloft into the azure of Eternity" (SR 146).

Wagner shared this vision of human spiritual redemption through the species life. In his mid-century writings, he measured the success of man not in the efforts of any one individual but in the united strength of the human species as it developed the full flowering of its potential through the course of time. "The human only find[s] understanding, *redemption* and satisfaction in a higher element," he declared in *The Artwork of the Future*, "and this higher element is the *human species* [*menschliche Gattung*], the community of humans, for there is only one thing higher than the human, and that is humankind" (AF 27, emphases added). In *Man and Established Society*, he reaffirmed Kant's first principle of progress, namely that "[w]e see that man is of himself unable to attain his destiny, that in himself he has no strength to unfold the innate germ that marks him from the beasts. That force which we miss in *man*, however, we find in endless fulness in the *aggregate of men*."[15] In a letter to Liszt in April 1853, Wagner adapted from Feuerbach his own secular vision of a "hereafter" vouchsafed by the promise of successive generations of man: "*Now* we suffer, *now* we must lose heart and go mad without any faith in the hereafter: I too believe in a hereafter: – I have just shown you this hereafter [i.e. 'the future of the human race' 'where no one need yearn for the other world']: though it lies beyond *my life*, it does not lie beyond the limits of all that I can feel, think, grasp and comprehend, for I believe in *humanity* and – have need of naught else!"[16]

The means to achieve this transcendental perspective, Carlyle preached, was to disregard the "Self in thee." With the parable of Teufelsdröckh's romantic and existential crisis, he taught his readers to discard their egoism and their individualistic search for ephemeral happiness and adopt instead the broadened and broadening perspective of man as a species being in time. The way forward according to Carlyle was to take the "preliminary moral Act, Annihilation of Self (*Selbsttödtung*)" (SR 142). This call to "self-annihilation," however, was for Carlyle not an embrace of spiritual or ascetic renunciation but the rejection of egoism in favor of universalism.[17] The focus must be on man writ large, the species being, and the species' course through history; this for the Eminent Victorian was the "EVER-LASTING YEA, wherein all contradiction is solved" (SR 146). Wagner derived the same important ethical insight from this conception of man as species. In *The Artwork of the Future* Wagner rejected "[t]hat egoism which has been the cause of such immeasurable sorrow in the world" (AF 28) and in its place sought "redemption through communism" which embraced "purely human universalism" (AF 63). In the search for meaning, man must not strive simply to improve his own personal circumstances, but to favor the future prospects of humanity: The only answer to life, Wagner told Röckel in 1854, was "a frank admission of the truth, even if there be no other personal gain to be had from this than the pride of knowing the truth, and, ultimately, the will and the endeavor to pass on that knowledge to the rest of mankind and thus set them on the path that will lead to their redemption."[18] Faced with the sorrows and disappointments of his individual life, man could find a secular form of consolation and meaning in the prospect that future generations would be able to reap the benefits of his struggles. Invoking the Young Hegelian's humanist faith, Wagner looked forward, in *Art and Revolution*, to the moment when "Knowledge of all men will find at last its religious utterance in the one effective Knowledge of free *united manhood*" (AR 58, emphasis added).

In *The Artwork of the Future*, Wagner adopted this Young Hegelian form of redemption as the central ethical message of the drama of the future. Through the death of the hero in such a drama, the audience would learn the fundamental truth of humankind: "From the essence of this one human being, revealed in that death, we can grasp the full breadth of all human essence [*menschliches Wesens*]" (AF 79). The spectacle of the hero's sacrifice would make visually and emotionally comprehensible the abstract notion of species values. In tragedy "the last, most complete externalization of [the hero's] personal egoism, the presentation of his complete sublation into the universal is announced by his death, and no arbitrary death but rather a necessary one, one that is determined by his actions from the full force of his being" (AF 79). For Wagner, then, the death of the hero represents not a denial of life or the will, but an affirmation of the universal – a compelling representation in microcosm of nature's macrocosmic process: not a symbol of individual renunciation, but of a transubstantiation into the new spiritual reality – the eternal life of the species.

Brünnhilde's final scene enacts just this form of redemptive immersion in the universal that Wagner prescribed at the time that he wrote the *Ring* libretto as the proper subject matter for the music drama of the future. When Brünnhilde relinquishes the ring which had meant everything to her personally she does not perform this act to promote a personal agenda but as a "world-redeeming deed" that responds to the urgent pleas of the Rhinemaidens. She no longer acts for herself but in the service of the good of humanity. By submitting to the funeral pyre, she ensures that the fire will have a purifying effect. "Let the fire that consumes me cleanse the ring of its curse" (RN 350). Her self-immolation thus serves a dual purpose, simultaneously destructive and freeing – destructive of the individual, but freeing mankind as a whole to pursue its collective destiny. By her death, "one that is determined from the full force of her being," Brünnhilde signals that the struggles of the individual life have little meaning except as they relate to the life of the species as it unfolds in time. Brünnhilde's self-annihilation thus becomes a beacon for humanity, teaching a world-historical lesson that is straight out of Feuerbach's playbook: "the necessary turning-point in history is therefore the open confession, that the consciousness of God is nothing else than the consciousness of the species; that man can and should raise himself only above the limits of his individuality, and not above the laws, the positive essential conditions of his species" (EC 272). Brünnhilde enacts just this historical turning point. In her final "open confession" she rejects traditional theology – the "consciousness of God" – and in its place embraces humanism – but a humanism not geared to the individual and her egotistical wants and needs, but the broader species aspirations. In her moment of metaphysical insight, Brünnhilde transcends her individual identity to embrace the life of mankind as a whole. Having tasted of true love with Siegfried, Brünnhilde was able successfully to break through the confines of her individuality. Now through the unique human power of reflection and thought, she has learned to take that insight beyond just the "I" and "Thou" to the whole of humankind, its species being: "the individual human can only satisfy his or her need for love by giving, indeed by giving him or herself to others and *at the highest level* to humankind" (AF 27, emphasis added). Love of the other is thus superseded "at the highest level" by an all-embracing love of humanity as a whole. Individual self-consciousness gives way to a new plane of existence – the realization of the World Spirit in Hegel's system or the Great Being in Comte's.[19]

In analyzing Wagner's philosophical mindset at the time he wrote the *Ring* libretto, it is important to recognize that there are structural similarities between Young Hegelian theories and those of Schopenhauer. Both philosophies keenly sought a way for man to overcome the spiritual confines of his individuality. Schopenhauer, for his part, called on man to escape the strait jacket of the false *principium individuationis* and recognize the truth of the universal will. Consequently, Schopenhauer highlighted the same species consciousness that so appealed to the Young Hegelians: "It is not the individual that nature cares for, but only the species."[20] But the spiritual import of this insight for both philosophies was entirely different. For Schopenhauer, this expanded notion of mankind as species reinforced the categorical illusoriness of the phenomenal world and of the individual mindset, and the truth of the undifferentiated will. For the Young Hegelians, on the other hand, the wide-angle view of the species in time was a means to celebrate the godlike destiny of humankind. This parallel in thematic material explains in part Theodor Adorno's puzzlement with Wagner's presumed Schopenhauerian agenda in the *Ring* and other works. Adorno's book, *Versuch über Wagner* (*In Search of Wagner*; 1952), points out the contradiction that for Wagner "the Will itself, in other words the essence of the undirected social process, continues to be accepted in a spirit of compliant admiration"; "Wagner obediently submits to it, worshipping it as the sublime order of nature beyond mortal comprehension."[21] But Wagner's attitude of awe towards the vast incomprehensible forces of nature is a logical product of his Young Hegelian worldview, not a mis-interpretation or deliberate misconstruction of Schopenhauer's teachings. Further complicating the effort to distinguish among Wagner's various philosophical pronouncements is the fact that both philosophies cultivated a morality based on love that rejected the selfish dictates of egoism.[22] According to Schopenhauer, *caritas*, or compassion, taught man to see beyond the illusion of his limited individual perspective and find a qualified transcendence in the universal. By the same token, love in Feuerbach's philosophy was not simply an emotional state that reflected the vibrancy of sensual man, but represented a path from blinkered egoism to the truth of the species being. (Of course, Feuerbach's form of love was sensual; Schopenhauer's a more chaste form of pity.) "Love is nothing else than the self-consciousness of the species as evolved within the difference of sex," Feuerbach wrote. "In love, the reality of the species, which otherwise is only a thing of reason, an object of mere thought, becomes a matter of feeling, a truth of feeling; for in love, man declares himself unsatisfied in his individuality taken by itself . . .; he reckons another as part of his own being; he declares the life which he has through love to be the truly human life, corresponding to the idea of man, *i.e.* of the species" (EC 159).[23] Accordingly, when Wagner speaks in the early 1850s in terms of breaking through the limits of egoism, annihilating the self, and embracing universalism, one need not conclude that he is speaking in Schopenhauerian terms of the pre-rational undivided force of the will and the call to renunciation. That said, the parallels and dichotomies identified here did not escape Wagner's own notice, and once he had become fully acquainted with Schopenhauer's teachings he started to search for a way to reconcile renunciation with sensualism and the notion of the will with the Young Hegelian conception of the species. It was in Venice, in December 1858, that Wagner thought he had solved the philosophical puzzle and boasted to Mathilde Wesendonck in a grandiose letter that "[t]he result . . . will inevitably be very important, and fill in the gaps in Schopenhauer's system in a thorough and satisfactory fashion."[24]

Yielding to history

Reading the *Ring* in light of contemporary theories of progress and species values, it further becomes clear that Brünnhilde's act of self-annihilation is not simply a dramatization of a philosophical, and psychological, insight into the universal – it also responds to a concrete historical demand. "Once their goal is achieved," Hegel wrote of the world-historical individuals, "they fall away like empty shells from the kernel."[25] In embracing her own annihilation, Brünnhilde is recognizing that her purpose on earth has been fulfilled. In *Opera and Drama*, Wagner explained that the "Going-under of the State," the dissolution of the political apparatus that had constrained man for centuries, reflected on a political level the love the parent bears towards his children. "Now, by Love the father knows that he has not as yet experienced enough, but that by the experiences of his child, which in love toward it he makes his own, he may endlessly enrich his being. In the aptitude for rejoicing at the deeds of others . . . consists the beauty of reposeful age. . . . It is the giving space to the activity of youth in an element of Love." As Wagner developed the theme: "we are *older* men and *younger*: let the elder not think of himself, but love the younger for the sake of the bequest he sinks into his heart for new increasing, – the day will come when that heirloom shall be opened for the weal of brother Men throughout the world!" (OD 205, 375). The older generation must learn to relinquish its power structures and ways of thought – its selfish needs – and devote itself instead to cultivating the newly emerging ranks of the young. As Andrew Wernick astutely observes in his analysis of Comte's theory of the Great Being, "to love Humanity is not just to love Humanity in the present, in solidarity with living contemporaries. It is to embrace the past and the future as well. Toward past generations, that love takes the form of veneration and gratitude for the long and ever-accumulating gifts they have bestowed; toward the future, that love is solicitous benevolence as for one's children."[26] Brünnhilde has served her role in seeing through the illusion of the gods' power. Now it is time for the next generation to take that insight – that "heirloom" – and develop it further – free from gods and the burdens of defunct belief systems. In his 1854 letter to Röckel, Wagner not only recognized the need to "acknowledge change" but also to "*to yield* to that necessity."[27] Brünnhilde's immolation thus reflects and responds to the highest principles of progress. She willingly withdraws from the stage of history to make way for the new. And, understood as an act of deference to the next generation, the "yielding" or "giving space" to the young, Brünnhilde's death acquires the poignancy of Hans Sachs's blessing on Eva and Walter in *Die Meistersinger* (1868)[28] or for that matter the Marschallin's final exit in Richard Strauss's *Der Rosenkavalier* (1911).

Wagner defined Wotan's role in the drama in the same fashion: "Wodan rises to the tragic heights of *willing* his own destruction. This is all that we need to learn from the history of mankind: *to will what is necessary* and to bring it about ourselves. The final creative product of this supreme, self-destructive will is a *fearless* human being, one who never ceases to *love*: Siegfried. – That is all."[29] Critically, Wotan's self-destruction represented for Wagner *a lesson of history* that points the way to a higher stage of human development.[30] Wotan's demise is not the end of the world, but in Wagner's own words a *creative* act that makes way for a new paradigm of human development.[31] Wagner contemplated incorporating this theme more explicitly in the *Ring* while he was working on the prose draft of *Die Walküre* in May 1852. In the margin he explored the possibility that Wotan would exclaim: "O could I compress all godhead into a seed out of which a free man would sprout! In this way I could annihilate godhead."[32] In this metaphor, annihilation is inextricably tied to germination. Wagner ultimately telegraphed this message of a Hegelian dynamic of death and renewal in Wotan's exuberant recognition of Siegfried as his heir, which was designed to communicate – in similar fashion – "the fusion of a movingly tragic act of heroic resignation with an exalted sense of the joy of life."[33] Of course, as the drama ultimately works itself out, and as shall be discussed further in the next chapters, Wotan is never able fully to enact the yielding withdrawal demanded of him. That task is left to Brünnhilde to accomplish.

Carlyle had recognized that the great tragedy of the French Revolution was the failure of the seigneurial class to read the signs of the times. "No man would listen, each went his thoughtless way; – and Time and Destiny also travelled on. The Government by Blindman's-buff, stumbling along, has reached the precipice inevitable for it."[34] Truth would inevitably have its due. "For long years and generations, it lasted; but the time came. Featherbrain, whom no reasoning and no pleading could touch, the glare of the firebrand had to illuminate." Thus, for Carlyle, the French Revolution was a cautionary tale about the inexorable forces of history. Unless acknowledged, the juggernaut would crush man. "O most fearful is *such* an ending." Carlyle hoped that by recognizing the force of change and grasping its power, man could better weather the future storms of time. "Let those, to whom God, in his great mercy, has granted time and space, prepare another and milder [ending]."[35] The events in France in late February 1848 – a mere ten years after Carlyle's book – lent credence to this new enlightened approach to history. Once the insurgency had erupted in the streets of Paris, King Louis Philippe refused to follow Adolphe Thiers's advice to crush the opposition with military force. When one of the main access routes to the Tuileries palace was breached by the mob, the king, recognizing the inevitable, abdicated his throne. Dressed in bourgeois suit and tie, he slipped into a carriage bound for Honfleur, and so, decisively, if furtively, exited the stage of history.[36] Further bloodshed had been averted, and Lamartine – whose account of the 1789 revolution would so entrance Wagner a year later – announced the establishment of the Second Republic the next morning from the balcony of the Hôtel de Ville. Most monarchs of Europe of that time would not be so polite, as Wagner was soon to learn on the streets of Dresden.

In his portrait of Wotan, and of Brünnhilde, Wagner created great historical seers who not only can envision a better future and strive to reach the goal, but have the additional form of courage, tragic as it is, ultimately to see their purpose in history fulfilled and the need for them to step aside. In this way, they spare mankind the perpetual conflicts and clashes of competing systems of thought and instead allow cultures to leapfrog over stages of struggle, thereby accelerating the end of history.[37] Brünnhilde's sacrifice and Wotan's withdrawal are therefore not just symbolic but performative. They do not simply communicate an ethical message but enact a historical need. It is for this reason that the Sartrian existentialism that Scruton and Kitcher and Schacht read into the *Ring*, *avant la lettre*, is inapposite.[38] Wagner conceived of Brünnhilde's final act of sacrifice not as an affirmation of her individuality and freedom in a world "engulfed by the ambient nothingness,"[39] but rather as an act, indeed of freedom and bravery, but in the service of a universalism which would ensure the future redemption of the species as a historical whole.

Brünnhilde's actions not only transform the world of the stage, but hold out the promise for contemporary German society. Wagner believed in the power of art itself to accelerate the process of historical renovation, explaining to Röckel:

I must now feel urged to do if I and the rest of mankind are to draw nearer the goal which I know has been set for mankind – but from which I, as an individual, must necessarily remain cut off as long as others continue to cut themselves off from it – without having recourse to means of which I can no longer avail myself. This is where my art must come to the rescue.[40]

By limning the dream of a future untainted by the corruptions of egoism, Wagner was serving the purpose of the revolution and Hegelian progress. If current society could not attain the promised land, at least Wagner could hold out the hope for it in his art and thereby force into consciousness the historical need that was required to bring about that future in real life. Like the world-historical individual, "the artist has the power of seeing beforehand a yet unshapen world, of tasting beforehand the joys of a world as yet unborn, through the stress of his desire for Growth" (OD 375). The *Ring*, then, is not simply a concrete dramatization of historic transcendence but a historic deed made manifest in music – an affirmative step in bringing Spirit to consciousness in the here and now. Brünnhilde's peroration and self-immolation not only communicate the truth to the astonished onlookers of the music drama, but critically direct these insights to the theater spectators as well.

The Feuerbach ending reconsidered

Wagner's final text for *Götterdämmerung* in 1852 incorporated the so-called Feuerbach ending. This was the text Wagner chose for his private 1853 printing, as well as for his later 1863 publication of the poem. This ending clarifies that the philosophical message Wagner originally intended the *Ring* to communicate was his Hegelian faith in history, and that the foundation of Brünnhilde's transcendence was not love as panacea, but principles of progress and species values.

The Feuerbach ending has always been characterized as a simplistic celebration of love;[41] this is not the case. In the first place, while Feuerbach trumpeted a philosophy of love, he was not oblivious to the darker side of life. In *Thoughts on Death and Immortality*, Feuerbach wrote, "Only where there are conflict and suffering,/Where pain clouds the clarity of soul,/Only there is my true fatherland;/ Pain is the pledge of Spirit."[42] Later, in the *Essence of Christianity* he recognized further that "the heart is the source, the centre of all suffering. A being without suffering is a being without a heart" (EC 65). Moreover, as noted, Feuerbach's celebration of love was part and parcel of his main philosophical program of materialism which was to reorient man's attention to the natural and temporal as opposed to the divine and immortal, and to locate man in his true context as part of a species whole. Love, for Feuerbach, therefore was not simply a sensual end in itself but the means to access the critical truths of universalism and species being.

In his completed poem Wagner also did not embrace erotic love simply as a cure-all. As we have seen, Brünnhilde does not emerge unscathed from her encounter with sensualism. To the contrary she calls upon the gods to "direct your gaze on my burgeoning grief [*blühendes Leid*]." And indeed, the last line of the Feuerbach ending does not naively wipe the slate clean but states *in full*: "blessed in joy *and sorrow* love alone can be [*selig in Lust und Leid/lässt – die Lieb nur sein*]" (RN 363, emphasis added). For Wagner, as he was at pains to dramatize in Brünnhilde's tragic story, the two aspects of love – joy and sorrow – are indivisible. In *Opera and Drama*, Wagner used a version of this very phrase to demonstrate how music could amplify the meaning of poetry by creating more complex nuanced concepts.

> [I]f we take a verse of mixed emotion, such as: "*die Liebe bringt Lust und Leid*," then here, where the Stabreim combines two opposite emotions, the musician would feel incited to pass across from the key first struck in keeping with the first emotion, to another key in keeping with the second emotion. . . . In this attitude toward one another, "*Lust und Leid*" would become the manifestment of a specific emotion, whose idiosyncrasy would lie precisely in the point where two opposite emotions displayed themselves as conditioning one the other, and thus as necessarily belonging together, as actually akin; and this manifestment is possible alone to Music, in her faculty of harmonic Modulation.
>
> (OD 292)

Music could thus achieve the conceptual synthesis that the words side by side, even in an alliterative *stabreim* format, could not effectively accomplish by themselves. In this way, we can understand Wagner's phrase "*Lust und Lied*" not simply as reflecting two alternative states of mind but an integrated concept that captures the complexity and contradictions inherent in love. As Wagner explained, the artwork of the future will celebrate "the glorious Tragedy of Man. The Tragedy will be the feast of all mankind; in it, – set free from each conventional etiquette, – free, strong, and beauteous man will celebrate the *dolour and delight* of all his love [*die Wonnen und Schmerzen seiner Liebe*], and consecrate in lofty worth the great Love-offering of his Death" (AR 58, emphasis added). Love for Wagner was not a saving grace panacea but part and parcel of the tragedy of life.

It is too much to say, therefore, as Magee does, that Wagner in his Feuerbachian phase expected the world to be perfect.[43] Hegel had concluded that "world history is not the place for happiness. Periods of happiness are empty pages in history."[44] Indeed, world-historical individuals "attained no calm enjoyment, their entire life was toil and trouble; their entire nature was nothing but their master-passion."[45] Likewise, Carlyle's Teufelsdröckh inquires "What Act of Legislature was there that *thou* shouldst be Happy? A little while ago thou hadst no right to *be* at all" (SR 146). Happiness was a myth of the utilitarians. "Foolish Word-monger, and Motive-grinder, that in thy Logic-mill hast an earthly mechanism for the Godlike itself, and wouldst fain grind me out Virtue from the husks of Pleasure. . . . If what thou namest Happiness be our true aim, then are we all astray" (SR 124–5).[46] In similar fashion, Wagner did not view mere equanimity as the proper goal of man, but associated the cult of happiness with false gods. Describing the decline of Greek culture in *The Artwork of the Future*, Wagner deplored how "Pluto, that solitary purveyor of happiness, that god of wealth" had become an object of worship and "ordered [man] to build the idolatrous temple of egoism" (AF 59).

Thus, whatever message Wagner distilled from his philosophical inquiries in the early 1850s, it was not a rose-tinted vision of eternal contentment. Following Feuerbach, Wagner's focus was on man as a complete sensuous being, and as such man carried with him all the intensity and concomitant sorrows of his passions. "[T]o be consumed by truth is to abandon oneself as a sentient human being to total reality," Wagner wrote in 1854, "to experience procreation, growth, bloom – withering and decay, to apprehend them unreservedly, in joy and in sorrow [*mit Wonne und Trauer*], and to choose to live – and die – a life of happiness and suffering [*Lust und Leid*]."[47] The phrase *Lust und Leid* as it appears in the Feuerbach ending, then, represents the poetic synopsis of this sober, clear-eyed perspective on life.

But the sorrow and joy of love is not the sole message of the Feuerbach ending. Notably, in the first section of the passage in question Brünnhilde states:

> You, blossoming life's [*blühenden Lebens*] enduring race:
> heed well what I tell you now! --
> . . . Though the race of gods passed away like a breath,
> though I leave behind me a world without rulers,
> I now bequeath to that world my most sacred wisdom's hoard. . . .
>
> (RN 362)

Against Brünnhilde's despairing "*blühendes Leid*," her burgeoning grief, Wagner poetically opposes her promise of "*blühenden Lebens*," or "blossoming life."[48] Directly addressing future humanity – "you, blossoming life's enduring race" – Brünnhilde consciously makes way for following generations to thrive in a world that she has bettered – a world freed from the gods. Brünnhilde, her life's purpose now at an end, "bequeaths" her wisdom to succeeding generations. Clearly, then, the world was not intended to vanish on Brünnhilde's pyre.[49] Instead, it will continue to "blossom" and "endure" – as a "world without rulers." Just as important as the message of love, therefore, is the acknowledgement of a human futurity and the building of a store of collective knowledge that will serve the development of the species.[50] The golden hoard of the Nibelung has now become abstracted or sublated in true Hegelian fashion into a hoard of sacred wisdom. For progress to be achieved, the species must grow in insight from generation to generation. As each generation cedes place to the next, it bequeaths its knowledge to successive eras of man in order that they may rise to new heights. As Proudhon wrote in his *Système des contradictions économiques, ou Philosophie de la misère* (*System of Economic Contradictions, or the Philosophy of Poverty*; 1846), "[h]owever excellent the future condition of humanity may be, it will be nonetheless the natural continuation, the necessary consequence, of what has gone before."[51] He made a similar point in *What Is Property?*: "In developing his intelligence, man profits not only from his own observations but also from those of others. He keeps an account of his experience and preserves the record, so that there is progress of intelligence in the race as well as in the individual."[52]

Or as Wagner would write to Röckel, "every step is necessary" in the "prodigious efforts of the human race."[53]

As a result of his intellectual inheritance, nineteenth-century man wielded vast powers. In 1831 Carlyle wrote: "Behind us, behind each one of us, lie Six Thousand Years of human effort, human conquest: before us is the boundless Time, with its as yet uncreated and unconquered Continents and Eldorados, which we, even we, have to conquer, to create; and from the bosom of Eternity there shine for us celestial guiding stars."[54] Herzen gave the same idea metaphoric heft: "At our backs, as behind the wave on the shore, is felt the pressure of the whole ocean – of the history of all the world; the thought of all the centuries is in our brain at this moment; there is no thought except in the brain, and with that thought we can be a power."[55]

The shell and the kernel

Again and again we see, in his letters to Röckel and Lizst in the early 1850s, in his speech to the Königliche Kapelle in 1848, and in the full Feuerbach ending of 1852, Wagner looking to the future and making the critical conceptual link between the search for knowledge and truth and the advancement of the species. And yet commentators on the *Ring* reflexively assume that whenever Wagner wrote of "annihilation" prior to 1854 he was speaking in proto-Schopenhauerian terms of renunciation.[56] Berry, for one, writes that for Wagner the concept of annihilation "could take on very different emphases, such as Proudhonesque abolition of private property, Schopenhauerian, Buddhist-tinged renunciation of the Will, and pyromania *à la* Bakunin."[57] But renunciation of the will and the futility of human endeavor had no place in Wagner's worldview of the early 1850s when he completed the poem of the *Ring*. Instead, annihilation had an entirely different philosophical meaning to Wagner at the time.

We have already addressed how the term "self-annihilation" was used by Carlyle to express the suppression of egoism in favor of universalism. Annihilation also signaled a necessary step in the Hegelian dialectic. Under Hegel's system, in order for the creative synthesis to emerge, the theses and antitheses must be overcome and destroyed.[58] In an evocative nut-cracking metaphor Hegel captured the process of historical regeneration: "This source [of the world-historical hero's aims] is the inner Spirit that is as yet hidden beneath the surface; it knocks at the outer world as though that were a shell, and *shatters* it because that inner Spirit is a kernel that is different from the kernel in the outer world's shell."[59] Destruction is thus fundamental to the historical dialectic. Beliefs, cultures, religions are superseded only by breaking through and shattering their constructs. Only through annihilation, elimination, annulment, going under, can the historical process clear the way for the new.[60] In the context of world history, "[Spirit] does, indeed, go against itself, and consume its own existence. But in so doing, it reworks that existence, so that whatever went before is the material for what comes after, as its labor elevates it into a new form."[61]

Hegel's insight that death and destruction made way for new stages of life became a fundamental organizing structure of thought for nineteenth-century thinkers. Arnold Ruge, the prophet of Hegelian progress and editor of the Young Hegelian mouthpiece published in Dresden, the *Deutsche Jahrbücher*, made clear in 1842 that "the fulfillment of our time will be the death of the *present* legalism and theology" and that "it will be necessary to burn up our Alexandrine time and much of its dead wood."[62] Mikhail Bakunin declared in the same journal in 1842 that "[t]he urge to destroy is a creative urge!"[63] Destruction is not an end in itself, but clears the way for new human endeavors. Carlyle expressly used the term "annihilation" to capture the same dialectical principle. "Innumerable 'Philosophies of Man,' contending in boundless hubbub, must annihilate each other, before an inspired Poesy and Faith for Man can fashion itself together."[64] In the first of his lectures, *On Heroes, Hero-Worship, and the Heroic in History* (1841) Carlyle directly correlated this chief principle of Hegelian development with the Norse myth of the Ragnarok, the "Twilight of the Gods": "'twilight' sinking into darkness, swallows the created Universe. The old Universe with its Gods is sunk; but it is not final death: there is to be a new Heaven and a new Earth; a higher supreme God, and Justice to reign among men. . . . [T]hough all dies, and even gods die, yet all death is but a Phoenix fire-death, and new-birth into the Greater and the Better!"[65] In *Sartor* he turned to zoological images of maturation and transformation to capture the same concept of death and renewal as the mechanism for historical progress: "Society . . . is not dead: that Carcass, which you call dead Society, is but her mortal coil which she has shuffled off, to assume a nobler; she herself, through perpetual metamorphoses, in fairer and fairer developement, has to live till Time also merge in Eternity" (SR 179).[66]

It is this pervasive construct of destruction as the means to renewal which may explain in part the late eighteenth and early nineteenth centuries' fascination with ruins and ruination. The eighteenth century's celebration of antiquity as a guide to aesthetics and civic virtue led to an explosion of images of Roman and Greek ruins, most masterfully rendered in the paintings of Giovanni Paolo Pannini and the prints of Giovanni Battista Piranesi in mid-century and towards the end of the century in those of Hubert Robert. In the early 1800s, the fascination with ruins continued to find expression in the works of various Romantic poets and painters and was further sustained as imperialist encroachments into India and Southeast Asia revealed another rich vein of ancient cultural remains.[67] In the hands of many Romantics, the taste for ruins shifted from the classical to the medieval. Works of Caspar David Friedrich, the German painter active in Dresden during the early nineteenth century, such as *Abbey in the Oakwood* (1808–10) or *The Dreamer* (1840), perfectly evoke the gothic sensibility of the age in crepuscular visions of ruined tracery.

Ruins symbolized the vagaries of history and the inexorable changeableness of human society,[68] as well as the power of nature, which not only promoted many of the destructive forces but also accelerated the decay as vegetative growth picturesquely overran the fragile handiwork of man.[69] At the same time, paradoxically perhaps, these ruins pointed to the future. In his celebrated book *Les Ruines, ou méditations sur les révolutions des empires* (*The Ruins, or Meditations on the Revolutions of Empires*; 1791), composed during the height of the French Revolution, the Comte de Volney built a utopian vision of mankind's future on a contemplation of the ruins of the ancient city of Palmyra in Syria. Volney's first view of the site prompts a melancholic frame of mind: "And now behold what remains of this powerful city: a miserable skeleton! What of its vast domination: a doubtful and obscure remembrance! To the noisy concourse which thronged under these porticoes, succeeds the solitude of death." But all at once an apparition appears, the Genius of tombs and ruins, and teaches Volney not to fall into despair but to learn from man's history on earth:

> [W]hat profound truths are written on the surface of your soil! remembrances of times past, return into my mind! places, witnesses of the life of man in so many different ages, retrace for me the revolutions of his fortune! . . . unveil to himself the causes of his evils! correct him by the spectacle of his errors! teach him the wisdom which belongeth to him, and let the experience of past ages become a means of instruction, and a germ of happiness to present and future generations.[70]

Ruins not only evoke sadness at the caprice of time but also carry valuable lessons for the future. Building on Volney's conceit, Hegel also recognized the spiritual burden of ruins: "What traveler, admidst the ruins of Carthage, Palmyra, Persepolis, or Rome, has not been led to contemplate the transiency of empires and of men, and to sorrow at a once vigorous and rich life that is now gone?" But like Volney he transformed this melancholic frame of mind to one of expectation. "This decline is at the same time the emergence of a new life – for although life leads to death, death also leads to life."[71] Hegel's critical insight, as indeed that of Volney, was that such transitoriness – the very mechanism of change – created at the same time the opportunity for learning and progress.

Hegel's unflinching vision of the mechanisms of history gave the lie to any notions of complacency about current accomplishments. Man was ever vulnerable to change, and even his own securely held beliefs would one day prove to be shibboleths. This philosophical insight was driven home in wry variations on the painterly ruin tradition. In 1796, Robert imagined the great gallery of the Louvre in the form of an ancient Roman wreck. In 1830, Sir John Soane exhibited two paintings by his assistant Joseph Gandy, depicting his celebrated Bank of England building, largely completed in the 1790s, in a future state of ruin. In 1840 the historian Thomas Macaulay imagined a time in the future when "some traveler from New Zealand shall, in the midst of a vast solitude, take his stand on a broken arch of London Bridge to sketch the ruins of St. Paul's." Macaulay's apocalyptic image of a future London in a dramatic state of decay was captured years later by Gustave Doré in a print from his book *London, A Pilgrimage* (1872) showing the New Zealander gazing across the Thames to the jagged edges of the broken masonry walls of the city. These ironic visions of anticipatory ruin served as warnings, but also palpable visual lessons in the inexorable process of historical change.

In his writings of the early 1850s – prior to his encounter with Schopenhauer – Wagner invoked the concept of destruction and annihilation in the same way, not as a celebration of renunciation but rather as a Hegelian step towards the emergence of a new and more evolved stage of culture. In discussions with Edward Devrient before the Dresden revolt, Wagner asserted that "before the world could be rebuilt . . . the old order first had to be destroyed"[72] and made this point crystal clear in his essay "The Revolution" printed in Röckel's *Volksblätter* on April 8, 1849: "Ay, we behold it, the old world is crumbling, a *new* will rise therefrom."[73] To Uhlig in December 1849 he continued the theme: "works of art cannot be created at present, they can only be prepared for my means of revolutionary activity, by destroying and crushing everything that is worth crushing and destroying. That is our task, and only people totally different from us will be the true creative artists. . . . Destruction alone is what is now needed." Wagner returned to the concept ten months later in October 1850 when he wrote to Uhlig again that "just as we need a water-cure to heal our bodies, so we need a fire-cure in order to remedy (i.e. destroy) the cause of our illness."[74] In *The Artwork of the Future*, Wagner looked for the "great stroke of fate which will *annihilate* [*vernichtenden Schiksalsschlage*] the whole immoderate mushrooming of this musical muck, *in order to clear the stage* for the artwork of the future . . . to which air and breath are absolutely denied on the current scene" (AF 46, emphases added). In employing the word "annihilate" in this context, Wagner was not advocating the rejection or renunciation of music as such, but merely seeking the extinction of one stage of cultural development to make way for a fresh new paradigm.[75] In similar vein, when Wagner called for the "Going-under of the State" in *Opera and Drama* he saw it as a necessary step towards a new stage of history which would accomplish "*the self-realisement of Society's religious conviction of its purely-human essence*" (OD 201). By the same token, in calling for "our own annihilation" in his 1854 letter to Röckel, Wagner was simply expressing impatience with the pace of historical progress and explaining that the prevailing conditions that had shaped modern civilized man had to give way – become eradicated – before liberated man with a higher consciousness could emerge.

This notion of dynamic historical change, constantly shifting from death to life to death again, continued to shape Wagner's conception of the *Ring*. I have already noted how in 1852 Wagner contemplated introducing a phrase for Wotan that united the concept of annihilation with germination: "O could I compress all godhead into a seed out of which a free man would sprout! In this way I could annihilate godhead." And in January 1854, while composing the music for the Erda scene in *Rheingold*, Wagner decided to alter the text, changing Erda's haunting message from one warning solely of the ring's curse to one that more clearly articulated the philosophical truth of nature and time: "All things that are – end."[76] In this way he returned to a fundamental principle of his revolutionary thought of 1849,[77] seeking to capture in Erda's wisdom what he originally had conceived almost five years earlier as the prophetic insight of his goddess "Revolution" – namely nature's state of constant flux and mutability. As the goddess had declared: "I am the e'er-rejuvenating, ever-fashioning life"; "Whatever stands, must fall: such is the everlasting law of Nature, such the condition of Life."[78] The 1854 letter to Röckel, written at the same time as this amendment to Erda's speech, demonstrates Wagner's intellectual commitment to the theme of unrelenting change, destruction, and renewal: "[T]he remainder of the poem is concerned to show how necessary it is to acknowledge change, variety, multiplicity and the eternal newness of reality and of life."[79] In the *Beethoven* essay of 1870, Wagner's reference to the ruined landmarks of ancient Greece evinces his continuing historicist and future-facing mindset as he was embarking on the composition of the music for *Götterdämmerung*: "A mere glance at a single fragment of the ruins remaining to us makes us realise with awe that we here face a culture which we are not in the very least equipped to judge. That world had acquired the privilege even out of its ruins to teach us for evermore how the further course of life in this world could be shaped."[80]

Advocates of the Schopenhauerian interpretation of the *Ring* and Wagner's allegedly proto-Schopenhauerian frame of mind in the early 1850s also like to point to Wagner's letter of 1853 to Franz Liszt in which he exclaimed, "Mark well my new poem – it contains the world's beginning and its end!"[81] But this bit of hyperbole must be read in context of Wagner's thinking at the time before one jumps to the conclusion that Wagner had adopted Schopenhauer's fatalism even before he had ever read a word of the philosopher. Just two months later, in April 1853, he would write to Lizst perhaps his most effusive defense of progress conceived in terms of the species life: "I believe in the future of the human race." Later, when Wagner had finally read Schopenhauer, he was able to articulate to Röckel exactly what philosophical mindset had first animated his creative efforts.

> My Nibelung poem . . . had taken shape at a time when, relying upon my conceptions, I had constructed a Hellenistically optimistic world for myself which I held to be entirely realizable if only people wished it to exist. . . . I believed I could express this idea even more clearly by presenting the whole of the Nibelung myth, and by showing how a whole world of injustice . . . is destroyed in order – – – *to teach us* to recognize injustice, root it out and establish a just world in its place.[82]

As Wagner himself clarified, he had originally intended the destruction of Valhalla to mark the end of one phase of history and to usher in a new phase that would take the lessons of the past to improve the lot of man. In 1850 Wagner wrote *Art and Climate* to make this worldview crystal clear in response to a reader's letter to the *Deutsche Allgemeine Zeitung*. That reader had averred that art had no capability to flourish in northern climes as it had once done in southern Europe during Hellenic times, and that no renewal of the Greek artistic spirit could be expected in Germany without a "new cycle of the world." Summing up the challenge in this way – "To clear the ground for such a Work of the Future, must the Earth, then, take the human race once more into her womb, and bear herself and it anew?" – Wagner countered that such an event would be a "sorry trick!" "for then would Mother Earth destroy at one fell swoop all those conditions whose actual presence, just as they are, now shows us – rightly understood – the Necessity of such a framing of the human Future" (AC 265). Mankind could not advance without learning from the multiple missteps and errors of its forbears who had created the conditions of the present time. "Out of error knowledge is born," Wagner declared in the first pages of *The Artwork of the Future* (AF 13). The future originally envisioned in *Götterdämmerung*, then, is not the end of the world, nor a pure blank slate renewal of nature, but is human history which necessarily builds on the rubble of the past.[83]

In light of Wagner's contemporary theoretical prescriptions and the message of redress and purification in the final scene it becomes clear that Brünnhilde's sacrifice was designed not as a despairing suicide *à la* Werther, or a Schopenhauerian withdrawal from the world's pain, as Berry and others want to stress.[84] Instead, what Berry sees in the *Ring* as the tension between a Schopenhauerian view of the world ("Being") and a Hegelian ("Becoming") can be reconceived in terms of Wagner's own *Weltanschauung* of the early 1850s as the conflict between the individual and his egotistical passions which will forever mark man and define his vulnerable sensual being – Carlyle's "clay-given mandate" or the problem of jealousy – and the longing for transcendence and progress which can only be achieved and indeed perceived through the species and time – Carlyle's search for Promethean agency or Hegel's infinite end of freedom. This tension of Being and Becoming is simultaneously embodied in Brünnhilde. For Wagner, Brünnhilde's spiritual crisis was just as much about the irreducible quantum of human sorrow as it was about the hope for future progress. Brünnhilde initially is Othello/Werther/Don José/Elsa – a passionate human dragged down to her core human vulnerability – but she re-emerges as a world-historical hero who has the power and insight to see beyond her catastrophic moment of passion. Brünnhilde reconciles this conflict between the particular and the absolute – man's innate tendencies to destructive emotion and the eternal call of freedom and reason – by subsuming her personal ends to that of the human race.[85] In *Götterdämmerung*, then, the theme of Being which Berry and others associate with Schopenhauer is not presented through the denigration or denial of the will but rather through acceptance of the undeniable force of the will – the glorious but equally destructive urge to erotic love that will always accompany the sensual man in his Adamite state. These congenital and unremitting emotional forces are not to be written off, rejected or held in contempt, as Schopenhauer would have it, but instead recognized as fundamental, necessary, and ultimately in the service of a grander historical purpose. The historical optimists of the early nineteenth century were not blind to the painful experience of life – but for all of them, as for Wagner at this time, the means to transcend individual disappointment, pain, and tragedy is not a Schopenhauerian withdrawal, but a faith in history and human potential borne of faith in the species – the belief that the species will collectively learn over time what the individual may not be able to fathom in the moment.

Notes

1 Rotenstreich explains that "[t]he unity of mankind may . . . be regarded as still another assumption of the idea of progress. . . . [T]he life of the individual cannot be conceived

as the model of human history. Only by Man with a capital 'M,' i.e. by the human race, can the ideal of human perfection be realized. . . . [O]nly the human species can be expected to realize the destiny of man." Rotenstreich, "The Idea of Historical Progress and Its Assumptions," 206–7.

2 Kant, *Political Writings*, 42–3.
3 Feuerbach, *Principles of the Philosophy of the Future*, 189 (§12).
4 Bancroft, *Progress*, 10.
5 See Kelly, *Discovery of Chance*, 197: "All the divine attributes are latent human powers, limited in individuals but infinite in the human species-being, and manifested progressively throughout history." In his *Critique of Hegel's Philosophy* Feuerbach quoted Goethe's insight that "[o]nly all men taken together . . . cognize nature, and only all men taken together live human nature." Feuerbach, "Towards a Critique of Hegel's Philosophy," as excerpted in Stepelevich, ed. *The Young Hegelians*, 97.
6 For Strauss, "[t]he incarnation of the Logos, the *Geist*, was not restricted to the particularity of Jesus but was received into the total human race. . . . Given Strauss' theoretic perspective, avowedly Hegelian, there could be no other practical consequence but that the individual, to be saved, i.e., to overcome his alienation, should consciously enter into the secular equivalent of the Christ, the community. The individual was called upon to participate fully 'in the divine-human life of the race.'" Lawrence Stepelevich, "Introduction," to Stepelevich, ed. *The Young Hegelians*, 7.
7 See Rotenstreich, "The Idea of Historical Progress and Its Assumptions."
8 Feuerbach, *Principles of the Philosophy of the Future*, 189 (§12).
9 Carlyle, "Characteristics," 351–2.
10 Strauss, *The Life of Jesus*, as excerpted in Stepelevich, *The Young Hegelians*, 49.
11 *Id.*, 48.
12 Wernick, "The Religion of Humanity and Positive Morality," in *Love, Order and Progress*, 225–33, 241: "Comte's Religion of Humanity can be seen as a French variant of the same post theistic teleological humanism that, via Immanuel Kant and Georg Hegel, surfaced more radically in Germany with Ludwig Feuerbach and the young Marx."
13 Feuerbach, *Thoughts on Immortality*, 142.
14 *Id.*, 17.
15 Richard Wagner, "Man and Established Society," in *Jesus of Nazareth and Other Writings*, 229. "We know that it is not on his own that the individual can be happy, but only when the whole of mankind is happy." Letter to Röckel, 25/26 Jan. 1854, SL 305.
16 Letter to Liszt, 13 Apr. 1853, SL 285.
17 In addition to "self-annihilation" Carlyle also used the term "renunciation," but as his biographer John Morrow explains, Carlyle "promoted renunciation as a necessary feature of aspiration and action." Morrow, *Thomas Carlyle*, 48. "He extolled earnestness, self-abnegation and sincerity and set these virtues in a context framed by concerns for social morality and engagement." *Id.*, 48. As another Carlyle scholar has noted, "the ultimate aim of [*Sartor Resartus*] is not Denial but Affirmation." P.A. Dole, "Sartor Resartus and the Inverse Sublime: The Art of Humourous Deconstruction," in *Allegory, Myth and Symbol*, ed. M.W. Bloomfield (Harvard University Press 1981), 302. In Carlyle's own words, he explicitly rejected "gloomy, austere, ascetic people, who have gone about as if this world were all a dismal prison-house! It has indeed got all the ugly things in it which I have been alluding to; but there is an eternal sky over it; and the blessed sunshine, the green of prophetic spring, and rich harvests coming – all this is in it too." Carlyle, "Inaugural Address at Edinburgh," as quoted in Morrow, *Thomas Carlyle*, 48.
18 Letter to Röckel, 25/26 Jan. 1854, SL 305. Queen Victoria's consort, Prince Albert, touched on this theme in his speech at the Lord Mayor's banquet in London in 1850. Speaking of the Great Exhibition which was soon to open, he explained that "knowledge acquired becomes at once the property of the community at large." As quoted in Gay, *Schnitzler's Century*, 144.

19 Wernick, "The Religion of Humanity and Positive Morality," in *Love, Order and Progress*, 226–7: "In worshipping, loving, and serving Humanity . . . we each become more perfectly integrated into it and in so doing advance the order and progress of the Great Being itself. . . . Under the aegis of its humbling and inspiring spirit . . . the ideal set before the worshipper is to become, through an active life of useful service, Humanity's worthy servant."

20 Schopenhauer, *The World as Will*, i, 276.

21 Theodor Adorno, *In Search of Wagner*, trans. Rodney Livingstone (Verso 2005), 133–4.

22 See Spencer, "*Zieh hin!*," 114: noting "that sense of compassion which was as basic to Feuerbach's willful view of the world as it was to Schopenhauer's."

23 Wagner adopted this point in *Opera and Drama*: "All understanding comes to us through love alone, and man is urged the most instinctively towards the essence of his own species" (OD 154).

24 Letter to Mathilde Wesendonck, 1 Dec. 1858, SL 432.

25 Hegel, *History*, 33.

26 Wernick, "The Religion of Humanity," 228.

27 Letter to Röckel, 25/26 Jan. 1854, SL 307 (emphasis added).

28 "Hans Sachs, then, differs from Wotan and [King] Marke in that he can both relinquish the world and help the hero to achieve supremacy in the new world." David Marcus, "The Break in the Ring," in *Penetrating Wagner's Ring: An Anthology*, ed. John DiGaetani, 201. See also Alain Badiou, *Five Lessons on Wagner*, trans. Susan Spitzer (Verso 2010), 109: "The master of art is he who is able to sacrifice himself in a timely manner so that the new can be incorporated into the old, so that artistic innovation can be synthesized with tradition."

29 Letter to Röckel, 25/26 Jan. 1854, SL 307.

30 Dahlhaus makes this point in *Richard Wagner's Music Dramas*. "But the 'end' that he 'wills' is not the end of the world, but the downfall of the gods. . . . [H]is resignation is the gods' 'self-destruction', whereby the way is opened for mankind to attain to consciousness of its freedom." Dahlhaus, *Richard Wagner's Music Dramas*, 103.

31 Mircea Eliade, *The Myth of the Eternal Return, Cosmos and History*, trans. William R. Trask (Princeton University Press 2005), 156: "For the modern man can be creative only insofar as he is historical."

32 Darcy, "Everything that Is, Ends," 446. The original German reads "*O könnte ich alles götterthum in einen samentropfen drängen, aus dem in freier mensch entsprosse! So möchte ich das götterthum vernichten.*"

33 Porges, *Wagner Rehearsing the 'Ring,'* 104. Thomas Mann also recognized in Wotan's deference "the loving abdication of the old power in favour of the eternally youthful." Thomas Mann, "Richard Wagner and *Der Ring des Nibelungen*," in *Pro and Contra Wagner*, trans. Allan Blunden (University of Chicago Press 1985), 190.

34 Carlyle, *The French Revolution*, 190.

35 *Id.*, 193. John Rosenberg maintains that "let us do otherwise" is the "one-line moral of *The French Revolution*." Rosenberg, *Carlyle and the Burden of History*, 95. In contrast to Carlyle, Herzen praised the French aristocracy for appreciating when their time was up. For Herzen, the August 4, 1789, meeting in the Constituent Assembly was a critical moment of courage for the aristocracy when "perceiving that its end was inevitable" they elected to "perish in glory" by willingly declaring the end of feudal privileges. Kelly, *Discovery of Chance*, 269.

36 Rapport, *1848, Year of Revolution*, 51–7.

37 Smith, "Hegel and the French Revolution," 259–60:

> [T]he end is not brought about by a superintending providence operating outside of history but through conscious human will and activity working in and through history. Consequently, it is never enough to wait patiently for the end; it is necessary to force the end, to act as if the end were already immanent in our

deeds. . . . The Hegelian . . . construction of an end of history is not a *Heilsge-schichte*, which sees divinity breaking into history from the outside, but is the outcome of purely immanent developments which can be either hastened or retarded by human activity.

As Carlyle proclaimed in a passage from his *History of Frederick the Great*, quoted by Wagner in his introduction to volumes iii and iv of his *Gesammelte Schriften und Dichtungen*: "Say Two Centuries yet, – say even Ten of such a process: before the Old is completely burnt out, and the New in any state of sightlines? Millennium of Anarchies; *abridge it, spend your heart's blood upon abridging it, ye Heroic Wise that are to come!*" J.S. Mill in his series of essays, "The Spirit of the Age," noted that "and if the multitude of one age are nearer to the truth than the multitude of another, it is only insofar as they are guided and influenced by the authority of the wisest among them." Mill, "The Spirit of the Age," 57. Kant made a similar observation: "human nature is such that it cannot be indifferent even to the most remote epoch which may eventually affect our species, so long as this epoch can be expected with certainty. And in the present case, it is especially hard to be indifferent, for it appears that we might by our own rational projects accelerate the coming of this period which will be so welcome to our descendants." Kant, *Political Writings*, 50. Schiller, too, recognized the power of human action to speed up historical processes. In his *On the Aesthetic Education of Man*, he explained that there are "three separate moments or stages of development, which not only the individual man but also the whole race must pass through, and in a particular order, if they are to complete the whole circle of their determination. For accidental reasons, which lie either in the influence of external things *or in the free choice of Man*, the several periods can certainly be now lengthened and now shortened but none can be entirely passed over." Schiller, *On the Aesthetic Education of Man*, 89 (emphasis added).

38 Kitcher and Schacht, *Finding an Ending*, 180–4: Brünnhilde struggles "against the world's darkness and mindlessness" and yet "she *acts*" "in a manner denying victory to the looming darkness." Brünnhilde "sees that . . . there are or can be actions that are meaning-creating in ways that transcend their transcience; she both sees and does. She vindicates the world that makes possible her own final action, affirming love, valor and justice despite their instability and frequent corruption; and she therefore vindicates her own life – as well as Wotan's, and even Siegfried's – in ending it. Brünnhilde ends the world – but she does not negate it"; Scruton, *The Ring of Truth*, 303: "the life of the free and accountable person remains, for us, the focus of meaning, and its many aspects are symbolized by Wagner in the leading characters of *The Ring*"; 271: "The moment of free commitment, the moment when I am fully myself in an act of self-giving – this has no place in the temporal order as science conceives it. And yet it is the moment that justifies my life, the moment that shows the absolute value of my being the thing that I am." In contrast to Kitcher and Schacht, Scruton arrives at this interpretation by accepting Schopenhauer's impact on the *Ring*; yet his celebration of the individual and her acts of free self-definition through erotic love and self-sacrifice is markedly inconsistent with Schopenhauer's wholesale rejection of the myth of the *principium individuationis*. Slavoj Zizek agrees: "Brünnhilde's final act is precisely that: an act, a gesture of supreme freedom and autonomy, not just resigned acquiescence to some higher power. This fact in itself, this *form* of act, makes it totally foreign to Schopenhauer's thought." Zizek, "Afterword: Wagner, Anti-Semitism and 'German Ideology,'" in *Five Lessons on Wagner*, 196.

39 Scruton, *The Ring of Truth*, 302.

40 Letter to Röckel, 25/26 Jan. 1854, SL 306.

41 See, e.g., Berry's reference to Feuerbach's "embarrassing paens to love." Berry, *Treacherous Bonds*, 262; Kitcher and Schacht, *Finding an Ending*, 194: Feuerbach's idea of "love triumphant"; Scruton, *The Ring of Truth*, 46: noting "Feuerbach's naively

optimistic philosophy" and the Feuerbach ending in which Brünnhilde announces "that the rule of the Gods will give way to a human society of love"; Treadwell, *Interpreting Wagner*, 85: "the hoard she bequeaths to [the future] – in orthodox Feuerbachian manner – is simply 'die Liebe,' love." Emslie, *The Centrality of Love*, 80: "If the full Feuerbach ending had survived we might have inferred that *The Ring* boiled down to a pretty straightforward attack on the sin of possessiveness and property at the expense of real, idealized love."

42 Feuerbach, *Thoughts on Immortality*, 146.

43 Magee argues that the plot of *Götterdämmerung* represents an insight about the human condition that is at odds with Wagner's original utopian intentions for the *Ring*, Magee, *Tristan Chord*, 180–1, but this interpretation sets up a false dichotomy. Wagner was not nearly as utopian in his thinking as Magee suggests, and "all you need is love," Magee, *Tristan Chord*, 122, 186, is not the theme of the Feuerbach ending.

44 Hegel, *History*, 29.

45 *Id.*, 33.

46 "In no time was man's life what he calls a happy one; in no time can it be so. A perpetual dream there has been of Paradises, and some luxurious Lubberland . . . ; but it was a dream merely; an impossible dream. Suffering, contradiction, error, have their quite perennial, and even indispensable abode in this Earth." Carlyle, "Characteristics," 342–3.

47 Letter to Röckel, 25/26 Jan. 1854, SL 302–3.

48 Wagner also uses this phrase to refer to Siegfried's blood as he draws it into the cup for his oath with Gunther, and a variation of the wording is used by Siegmund in his celebration of the Wälsung blood line: "*so blühe denn Wälsungen-Blut!*" (RN 139).

49 See, e.g., Darcy, "Metaphysics," 6, 39; Kitcher and Schacht, *Finding an Ending*, 181, 184: "Brünnhilde ends the world – but she does not negate it."

50 Roger Hollinrake acknowledges this broader message of the Feuerbach ending in one sentence of his essay "Epiphany and Apocalypse in the 'Ring'" in Stewart Spencer, *Wagner's Ring of the Nibelung: A Companion*, 44: "This is the legacy that Brünnhilde, made wise by Siegfried's love, vouchsafes on Siegfried's behalf to a future humanity, a legacy that redresses the trend of the action which otherwise, bereft of any promise for the future, veers dangerously in the direction of a nihilistic void." Treadwell also acknowledges a hint of "foresight" in this speech, but concludes it is "more retrospective than progressive." Treadwell, *Interpreting Wagner*, 85. Treadwell bases his skeptical conclusion on the fact that Wagner defines the future only by negatives, but this method of describing utopian visions was a common trope based on a tried and true rhetorical device. See Sarah Blakewell, *How to Live, or a Life of Montaigne* (Other Press 2010), 186: "Negative enumeration was a well-established rhetorical device in classical literature." As Montaigne wrote in his essay *Of cannibals*, "This is a nation . . . in which there is no sort of traffic, no knowledge of letters, no science of numbers, no name for a magistrate or for political superiority, no custom of servitude, no riches or poverty, no contracts, no successions, no occupations but leisure ones." Michel de Montaigne, *The Complete Works: Essays, Travel Journals, Letters*, trans. Donald Frame (Alfred A Knopf 1943/2003), 186. Treadwell also finds a regressive tinge in Brünnhilde's wording: "this new world is left 'behind' (*zurück*)," but this formulation simply proves that in Wagner's view there was a continuity of humanity after Brünnhilde's passing, from the old world to the new, not a completely new beginning where all the insights need to be tragically learned anew.

51 As quoted in Kelly, *Discovery of Chance*, 296.

52 Proudhon, *What Is Property?*, 194.

53 Letter to Röckel, 25/26 Jan. 1854, SL 305.

54 Carlyle, "Characteristics," 355–6.

55 As quoted in Kelly, *Discovery of Chance*, 425.

56 See, e.g., the characterization of Wagner's letter to Röckel in January 1854 as the "famous proto-Schopenhauerian interpretation of the Ring." *Wagner's Ring of the Nibelung: A*

Companion, 368 n. 125; Berry, *Treacherous Bonds*, 242: "that form which 'our own annihilation' is to take already appears to assume a metaphysical, world-renouncing tinge"; Rather, *The Dream of Self-Destruction*, 63, 89: detecting "a Schopenhauerian note already audible in *Opera and Drama*"; Roger Hollinrake, *Nietzsche, Wagner and the Philosophy of Pessimism* (George Allen & Unwin 1982), 68: idea of Wotan's retreat as an ethical advance "almost unintelligible without help from Schopenhauer."

57 Berry, *Treacherous Bonds*, 256.

58 Berlin, *Political Ideas*, 302, 303: "Hegel conceives of the universe as a kind of performance in which individuals, classes, groups, nations are each called upon to play their part before being destroyed by the next necessary actor to be called in"; "At these moments leaps occurred from one level, that of thesis and antithesis, to the higher level of the synthesis – the phoenix which arose from the ashes of the previous contenders." In *What Is Property?*, Proudhon adopted the Hegelian dialectic to explain his vision for a future freed of individual property rights. "The power of accumulation and property" was the source of "the downfall and death of societies," such as "Carthage, a commercial and financial city, continually divided by internal competition; Tyre, Sidon, Jerusalem, Nineveh, Babylon, ruined in turn by commercial rivalry." Proudhon set out the stages of history "by a Hegelian formula . . . .: communism, first mode, first cause of sociability, is the first term of social development, the thesis; property, the reverse of communism, is the second term, the antithesis. When we have discovered the third term, the synthesis, we shall have the required solution." Proudhon, *What Is Property?*, 187, 195.

59 Hegel, *History*, 33 (emphasis added).

60 "[T]he passing of a political or a social order, which, being bound up with a certain stage in the realisation of the spirit, with a particular outlook expressed in the arts, the sciences, the moral, intellectual and personal habits and customs of a given stage of civilisation, could only go down in a violent explosion attending the final conflict of thesis and antithesis. . . . The dialectic necessarily contains 'negative movements' which embody the needful destructive forces which kill the old to make way for the new." Berlin, *Political Ideas*, 303.

61 Hegel, *History*, 76. As George Windell has noted, "Reality [in Hegel's philosophy] ceased to be something given and therefore unchanging, as in the Christian tradition; it became dynamic, always evolving." Windell, "Hegel, Feuerbach and Wagner's *Ring*," 41.

62 Arnold Ruge, "Hegel's 'Philosophy of Right' and the Politics of our Times," as excerpted in Stepelevich, *The Young Hegelians*, 213.

63 As quoted in Lawrence S. Stepelevich, "Introduction," to Stepelevich ed., *The Young Hegelians*, 13.

64 Carlyle, "Characteristics," 346.

65 Carlyle, *On Heroes*, 39.

66 The image of the snake shedding its skin is also found in Hegel's *Phenomenology*. Hegel, *Phenomenology*, 332 (§545).

67 Sarah Tiffin, *South-East Asia in Ruins: Art and Empire in the Early Nineteenth Century* (National University of Singapore Press 2016).

68 *Id.*, 49–51.

69 *Id.*, 51.

70 Constantin Francois de Volney, *The Ruins or Meditation on the Revolutions of Empires and the Law of Nature*, trans. Peter Eckler (The Echo Library 2007; repr. of 1890 American edn.) 26, 37–8.

71 Hegel, *History*, 76.

72 As paraphrased in Joachim Köhler, *Richard Wagner: The Last of the Titans*, trans. Steward Spencer (Yale University Press 2004), 221.

73 Wagner, "The Revolution," 232.

74 Letters to Uhlig, 27 Dec. 1849, 22 Oct. 1850, SL 184, 219.
75 See Foster, *Wagner's 'Ring,'* 165–6.
76 Darcy, "'Everything that Is, Ends!,'" 447.
77 Wagner, "The Revolution," 235.
78 *Id.*, 235.
79 Letter to Röckel, 25/26 Jan. 1854, SL 307.
80 Richard Wagner, *Richard Wagner's Beethoven (1870): A New Translation*, tr. Roger Allen (The Boydell Press 2014), 169–71.
81 Letter to Liszt, 11 Feb. 1853, SL 281; Darcy, "'The World Belongs to Alberich!,'" in *Wagner's Ring of the Nibelung*, 52.
82 Letter to Röckel, 23 Aug. 1856, SL 357 (emphasis added).
83 I therefore disagree with Michael Ewans's conclusion that "Wagner's ending turns to the past but it does not truly build upon it." Ewans, *Wagner and Aeschylus*, 251.
84 Berry characterizes Brünnhilde's Immolation Scene as her "renunciation of the Will" (*Treacherous Bonds*, 268–9). Likewise Scruton, *The Ring of Truth*, 294: "All the loose ends of life, all the damage suffered and inflicted, can be knitted into a consoling totality in retrospect, when seen in the light of renunciation"; 295: "her death, which is also a renunciation"; and Emslie, *The Centrality of Love*, 79, 89: noting the "high redemptive Schopenhauerian final scene." See also Darcy, "'The World Belongs to Alberich!,'" in *Wagner's Ring of the Nibelung: A Companion*, 52.
85 By presenting Brünnhilde's jealous outburst as part and parcel of a spiritual crisis, and providing for her education of the next generations of man, Wagner implicitly mitigates the impact of her jealous rage. By placing Othello's story in a historical moment of radical transition, Wagner hints that the very intensity of her jealousy need not reflect a timeless quality of this emotion, but rather a product of a time and era where man's inner resources are shaken.

4 Brünnhilde's mercy

In the majority of interpretations of the *Ring*, Brünnhilde's final scena is associated with themes of compassion. Brünnhilde's transgression against Wotan, and her evolution into a mortal woman do indeed derive from the first stirrings of her compassion for Siegmund. But there is very little compassion demonstrated by Brünnhilde or others in the final opera of the cycle. Brünnhilde refuses to help her sister Waltraute; she takes revenge on her husband and reveals to Hagen where his spear will strike true; she scolds Gutrune, chiding her for bemoaning the fate of Siegfried as a child cries over spilled milk; she seals the fate of her father and the rest of the gods for their "guilt" by burning down Valhalla.

What she does exhibit in the end, then, is not compassion, but a different virtue, forgiveness.[1] First, she forgives Siegfried for his betrayal, announcing that "never did any man love more loyally" (RN 348). Next, she forgives Wotan. Instead of harshly condemning the father who failed her, and indifferently consigning him to the dustbin of history, she provides him a respectable ending, softly lulling him to sleep to weakened but still ennobling snatches of the Valhalla theme: "*Ruhe! Ruhe, du Gott!*"[2] In recognizing these two acts of forgiveness we acknowledge the authority which Brünnhilde has achieved through her suffering. Rather than simply reflecting a sensibility of human fellow-suffering – as compassion does – forgiveness, on the other hand, issues from a position of power and freedom.[3] Brünnhilde exercises her power, but in a way that achieves reconciliation. In this way, she exhibits a regal magnanimity and mercy. But her forgiveness is not simply the well-bred clemency of a Titus, or the noble forbearance of the Pasha Selim, common tropes of good leadership in the eighteenth century brought to musical life by Mozart. Rather, Brünnhilde's act of forgiveness can appropriately be understood in nineteenth-century Hegelian terms.

In the *Phenomenology of Spirit*, Hegel introduced the concepts of the "judging consciousness" and the "acting consciousness" and explained how the former, priding itself on adherence to a pristine idealism, passes judgment on the "acting consciousness," holding it responsible for how action in the real world falls short of the ideal. But over time, in response to the acting consciousness' confession of inadequacy, the judging conscious, also known as the "beautiful soul" or the "universal consciousness," finally relents and offers forgiveness. In Hegel's words, "The forgiveness which [the beautiful soul] extends to the other is the renunciation of itself . . . and acknowledges that what thought characterized as bad, viz. action, is good. . . . The word of reconciliation is . . . a reciprocal recognition which is *absolute* Spirit."[4] There is renunciation at work here, but it is not the renunciation of the will that Schopenhauer preached. Rather, it is the renunciation of the beautiful soul's moral arrogance that paves the way for the act of forgiving, through which the judging consciousness reaches a new stage of understanding. Engaging at long last with the confession of the acting consciousness, the beautiful soul finally comes to the realization that action is necessary in the world and cannot be disdained as impure, and goes further in acknowledging the relativism of both the judging and the acting postures. In undergoing this intellectual maturation process, the beautiful soul brings Spirit closer to actualization. In Hegel's romantic evocation: "The reconciling *Yea*, in which to the two 'I's let go their antithetical *existence*, is the *existence* of the 'I' which has expanded into a duality."[5] Forgiving becomes an affirmative act of reconciliation that by acknowledging not only the necessity of action but the practical limits on man's ability to actualize the Ideal paradoxically brings the Ideal closer.[6] Wagner was undoubtedly familiar with these Hegelian principles of philosophical and historical perspectivism and empathy, if not through the *Phenomenology* itself,[7] then through Lamartine's eloquent peroration which concludes his *Histoire*: "Let us . . . pardon the sons of those who struggled or were victims. Let us become reconciled over their tombs, in order that we may renew the interrupted work! . . . Let us resign ourselves to the conditions of human affairs."[8] In similar vein, in *The French Revolution*, Carlyle found in his heart some room for leniency for Robespierre, in spite of his otherwise scathing and uncompromising indictment of the "sea-green Incorruptible": "One thing therefore History will do: pity them all; for it went hard with them all. Now even the sea-green Incorruptible but shall have some pity, some human love, though it takes an effort."[9]

Hegel's allegory of the evolution of consciousness provides a useful framework for interpreting the relationship between Wotan and Brünnhilde. Wotan conceives his "grandiose idea" for winning back the ring at the end of *Das Rheingold* as he prepares to cross the rainbow bridge into Valhalla. To Wotan's credit, this plan for solving his dilemma through the "fearsome sword" and the Wälsung free agents is creative and forward-looking. And he is justly proud of his vision for the future. As he explains to Fricka, in a phrase uttered in a traditional-style recitative capped by a leitmotif characteristic of the drama of the future: the clarion call of the Sword: "Age old custom is all you can grasp: but my thoughts seek to encompass what's never yet come to pass." Wagner had already expressed this sentiment to his own wife, Minna, in the bitter letter he wrote to her from Paris at the start of his exile in April 1850: "You think of the past only with longing and regret, – I abandon it and think only of the future. All your desires are directed at a reconciliation with what is old, at compromise and conformism, and at re-establishing old ties, – I have broken with all that is old, and fight against it with every ounce of my strength."[10] But Wotan's valiant efforts to bring the future closer reach their inevitable impediments. In his famous monologue in Act II of *Die Walküre*, he admits to Brünnhilde his inability to accomplish his plan, thereby enacting the key moment when the "acting consciousness" confesses the limits of idealism in a world of partial solutions. In his autobiography Wagner identified this theme as the initial spark of inspiration for his opera on Friedrich I and later for his adaptation of the Nibelung mythology: "[the hero's] dignified resignation at the impossibility of realizing his highest ideals was to lead, while arousing sympathy for the hero as well, to a true insight into the manifold complexity of all action in this world."[11] While originally conceived as the dramatic message of Barbarossa's historical struggles with the Lombard League, this philosophical insight ultimately became the theme of Wotan's mythic struggle.

In *Die Walküre*, Brünnhilde is initially unable to comprehend Wotan's dilemma and righteously attempts to fulfill the god's plan on her own by intervening to save Siegmund. This transgression, though strictly inconsistent with Hegel's model of the beautiful soul who shuns action altogether as impure, reflects all the same an idealistic refusal to credit the practical constraints on Wotan's actions. Wotan upbraids her for her moral arrogance: "craven and foolish you thought me" (RN 184). Even after her awakening as a human, Brünnhilde is content to remain on the mountaintop, comforted by her idealized vision of the hero and the god's plan.[12] She has sent Siegfried, Wotan's heir, into the world to accomplish deeds of heroism, while she remains inviolate on the rock of her faith. But as circumstances would have it, Brünnhilde herself is dragged into the world of action and compromises. There she is forced to learn Wotan's own bitter lesson, that ideals cannot readily be reconciled to the brutality of real facts. As Siegmund's death was the catalyst for Wotan's painful insight into the harsh narrative of Spirit, so Siegfried's death awakens Brünnhilde to the same realization. In confronting the fate of Siegmund, Wotan had first articulated the fundamental truth that Brünnhilde herself must come to learn through the deepest pain and sorrow, that man's noble aspirations are fragile constructs and that the demands of real life may cruelly force us to kill the thing we love: "what I love I must relinquish, murder him whom I cherish" (RN 153).[13] And in the process of mourning her own loss and the destructive force of her own resentment Brünnhilde learns a lesson of humility. As the vulnerable victim of jealous rage, and willing participant in Siegfried's murder, she ultimately recognizes that she does not have a monopoly on truth. She herself has been caught in the snares of moral inconsistency.[14] Wagner had developed the utmost forbearance for his "jovial god who stands in need of self-annihilation," and in her final goodbye Brünnhilde arrives at the same attitude.[15] Through the act of forgiving Wotan, Brünnhilde implicitly acknowledges her own limitations. And by sweetly rocking Wotan to eternal sleep, Brünnhilde demonstrates an openness to the process of historical succession: although her new secular humanism embodies the antithesis to the thesis of Wotan's theology, she does not reject Wotan as evil, but gently bids him farewell *"senza rancor."*[16]

Nietzsche read *Götterdämmerung* as enacting the very "reconciling *Yea*" that Hegel described. The ancient Greek tragedy of *Prometheus* – attributed to Aeschylus in the nineteenth century by its German translator, Johann Gustav Droysen, and read by Wagner, who was deeply influenced by the Greek playwright[17] – pitted the bold sacrilegious act of the Titan Prometheus in favor of humanity against the order of the gods. In his analysis, Nietzsche marveled at "the profoundly Aeschylean demand for *justice*" which balanced "the immeasurable suffering of the bold 'individual' on the one hand" – read Brünnhilde – and "the divine predicament and intimation of a twilight of the gods on the other" – read Wotan – and "the way the power of these two worlds of suffering compels a reconciliation, a metaphysical union."[18]

Many commentators identify Brünnhilde's quiet lullaby passage – *"Ruhe, du Gott"* – in the Immolation Scene as representative of a form of Schopenhauerian renunciation.[19] The first problem with this interpretation is that Wotan is meeting his end through Brünnhilde's historical agency, not entering into a higher state of self-denial. And far from defining the emotional scope of Brünnhilde's final scena, the lullaby marks only a short-lived moment of repose in her peroration. In the very next strophe when Brünnhilde takes up the ring and then the torch, her vocal line reaches new heights of intensity and urgency – rising to high B's and B-flats; not the kind of quietude expected of a true Schopenhauerian. In addition, as noted prior, Brünnhilde's attitude of forgiveness indicates acceptance rather than censure of Wotan's past struggles. The musical setting bears this out. (See Figure 4.1.)

Brünnhilde's benediction of *"Ruhe! Ruhe, du Gott!"* is ushered in with a refreshing return of the Rheingold theme sounding in A-flat Major, which then turns to a gentle reprise of the Valhalla motif in its original key of D-flat Major. Before the listener has a chance to find comfort in these consonances, however, the restless theme of Wotan's striving (also known as "the Need of the Gods" or "Agitation"; Figure 4.2.) intrudes on the basses and cellos in a disorienting shift to the subdominant minor of D-flat Major: g-flat minor. (See Figure 4.1.)

Wotan's motif creates a state of tension with Brünnhilde's long held A-flat, but her step down to the G-flat meets Wotan's disruptive harmonization on its own terms; her further descending vocal line ultimately unites with the rising bass line – which leaps an augmented fifth to do so – finding unison on E-flat and a joint resolution on the D-flat tonic. There is respite from striving, yes, but this respite is a gift from Brünnhilde. And as the music shows, Brünnhilde's blessing of rest does not censure that striving, but instead acknowledges it harmonically, approaches it melodically and gently leads it to tonic resolution. Immediately thereafter, another snippet of the Valhalla theme returns, bestowing dignity to Wotan's memory; his ambitions are given their due. Understood in Hegelian terms, then, Brünnhilde's generosity of spirit marks a frank reconciliation to the necessity – and limits – of the phenomenological world – the "manifold complexity of all action in this world" – not an escape from that world. Brünnhilde has come to terms with the sins of Wotan. And in doing so, she acknowledges the necessity of historical action and Wotan's necessary place in the historical progression.

Kitcher and Schacht view Wotan's struggle not simply as a failure of his vision, but more broadly as the failure of the human endeavor.[20] But Wagner did not intend for Wotan's project to be dismissed as futile, but instead to be understood as part and parcel of the process of historical progression and emergence of self-consciousness. In Hegel's philosophy, the bud, and the blossom that supplants

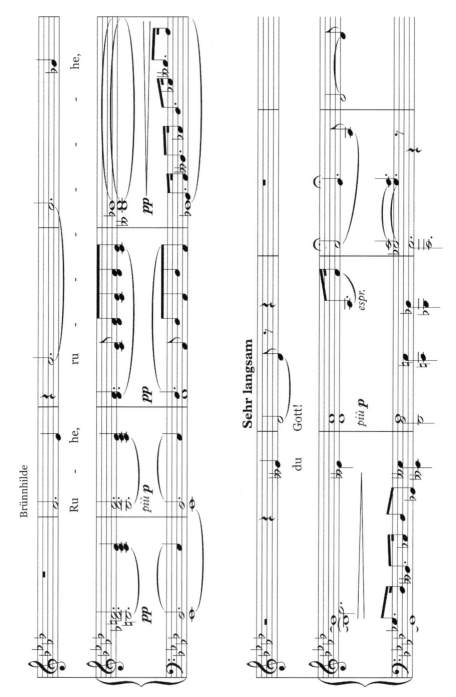

Figure 4.1 Brünnhilde's farewell to Wotan

Figure 4.2 Theme of Wotan's striving as it appears in *Siegfried*, Act III Prologue

it, are both "moments of an organic unity in which they not only do not conflict, but in which each is as necessary as the other; and this mutual necessity alone constitutes the life of the whole."[21] Wotan's struggle to implement his "grandiose idea" was a valid struggle of Spirit seeking to manifest itself in the world. His faulty steps were as necessary to the progress of consciousness as Brünnhilde's own struggle with passion. Intellectual historian Aileen Kelly has explained that Hegel's "dialectical vision of development through conflict and negation presented the dichotomies of the modern consciousness as a logical and necessary stage in the progressive deepening of humans' understanding of the self and the world."[22] Each generation must undergo the painful doubt and despair that accompany the self-questioning integral to the development of Spirit. *Weltschmerz*, then, is itself a sign of Spirit's struggle for renewal. Thus the disorientation of the nineteenth-century age of transition – the very disaffection that Wagner shared and that Wotan embodied "to a tee" – was evidence of history at work. As Carlyle captured the paradox: "Nay, is not even this unhealthy action of the world's Organisation, if the symptom of universal disease, yet also the symptom and sole means of restoration and cure?"[23] It is no surprise then that Hegel could describe the evolution of historical self-consciousness as at the same time "the inwardizing and the Calvary of absolute Spirit." Spiritual renewal emerges out of an emotionally and physically painful encounter with life.[24] Heine expressed this same idea through metaphors of birth and diurnal renewal. In highlighting Friedrich Schlegel's spiritual despair, he cautioned his readers against misinterpreting the often troubling signs of contemporary life:

> He recognized all the glories of the past and felt all the pains of the present. But he did not understand that these pains were sacred, and necessary for the future redemption of the world. He saw the sun going down, looked sadly towards the place it was setting, and mourned the nocturnal darkness he saw approaching. And he did not notice that there was already a new dawn coming up on the opposite side. . . . In the pains of our time he did not see the labor pains of a new birth, but rather the agony of death; and his death horror caused him to flee into the shaky ruins of the Catholic Church.[25]

Brünnhilde recognizes that Wotan's painful struggle does not mark the end of time, but helps clear the passageway to a new dawn.

This interpretation of Brünnhilde's act of forgiveness reveals another reason why the I-Thou relationship on the mountaintop cannot succeed. It represents pure idealism protected from the cruel facts of the phenomenal world. In the *Phenomenology*, Hegel had made clear that Spirit's progress could only arise out of the constant struggle between the ideal and the real. Only through thought's conflict with action, Spirit's "severe and unwilling working against itself," can Spirit learn to know itself.[26] While acknowledging that the French Revolution "received its first incitement from philosophy," Hegel warned in his lectures that "this philosophy is in the first instance only abstract thought, not the concrete comprehension of absolute truth, and this [is] an immeasurable distinction."[27] Wagner made this point clear to Lizst – that it was only through "active striving" that man could acquire knowledge and fulfill the "task of world history."[28] The glorious strains of exuberant joy that ring out from the mountaintop have not stood the test of hard facts. As Siegfried descends the mountain and travels up the river in jolly anticipation of noble deeds, the surging arpeggios of the Rhine motif turn sour as themes associated with the ring's sinister power, the renunciation of love, and the gold are recalled – echoes of the descent into Nibelheim – warning of the dangers and compromises of the world of action.[29] But Siegfried, as the man who sits outside history, who has no comprehension of what the next day will bring, cannot be the vehicle for insights that must be reaped from history itself. Whatever Siegfried accomplishes in awakening Brünnhilde to love, he can only advance Spirit so far. It is Brünnhilde, then, who fully puts her idealism to the test in the laboratory of the real world and, although bruised, betrayed, and despairing, comes to self-conscious realization that the wisdom she has won from her struggle reveals a new organizing framework that will guide mankind in the future. As Isaiah Berlin summarized Hegel's insight: "[C]itizens can be benefitted only by . . . having their faculties heightened – made 'more real' – by the conflict of war, participation in the historical process, identification with the great force which at once is and governs the world."[30]

Brünnhilde thus enacts two affirmative "yeas" in her final scene – the first, that of Carlyle, which recognizes that the ultimate source of meaning for humanity is the universal species consciousness – the second, that of Hegel, whereby the ideal of human values is reconciled to the historical process and each individual's struggle in the real world to realize that ideal. By contrast, Robespierre had utterly failed to master these hard lessons of history. His self-righteousness – the "ostentatious display of his tasteless 'vertu,'" as Wagner noted to Röckel – in other words, his inability to adapt or compromise his rigid idealism to the crooked timber of humanity – coupled with his lack of any consciousness of a "higher purpose" beyond his own egoistic need for power, led not to reconciliation and species progress, but to the guillotine.[31] The calm authority and generosity of spirit that mark Brünnhilde's end were therefore predictably absent from Robespierre's own departure from the world. As Carlyle narrated the well-known story, when it came time for Robespierre himself to face the machinery of death he had so ruthlessly employed against his enemies, "there burst forth from him a cry; – hideous to hear and see."[32] Death in Robespierre's world had come to mean nothing more than existential emptiness – the cutting off of heads of cabbages. Death, in Brünnhilde's hands, on the other hand, becomes a glorious passing of the torch from generation to generation reaching for the highest aspirations of the species' inherent potential.

Through Brünnhilde's own acknowledgement of the imperfection of historical solutions, the ultimate failure of pure idealism to hold sway in a complex human environment, Wagner modeled a new moral attitude that would define the new epoch. Feuerbach adopted as the motto of his philosophy of the future the famous line from a Terrence play, "*Homo sum, humani nihil a me alienum puto.*"[33] This thesis required the utmost clarity about the sensuous reality of man, but, taken seriously, also the utmost charity. The embrace of the whole man – base passions and all – necessitated a new form of judging his actions. Carlyle exclaimed, "Man, with his so mad Wants and so mean Endeavours, had become the dearer to me; and even for his sufferings and his sins, I now first named him Brother" (SR 144). Man's errors do not make him more objectionable, subjecting him to censure, but rather render him more worthy of respect for having to struggle mightily against such fundamentally contradictory forces. Thus, the nineteenth-century commentators on *Othello* for the most part did not damn him for his murderous excess of passion. To the contrary, they held the hero in great esteem. As A.C. Bradley explained, after the "Chaos has come and gone," there returns "a greater and nobler Othello still." Wagner viewed Brünnhilde in the same fashion and treated his character as she herself treats Wotan. Her own outbreak of jealousy and willing participation in Hagen's conspiracy do not condemn her to ignominy and shame, but in fact permit her to rise to a new plane of nobility and spiritual insight.[34] And her new consciousness implicates a new creed of compassionate forgiveness.

These themes play an important role in Goethe's *Werther*. In a discussion with his dear friend Albert, Werther makes the case for compassionate mercy.

> True, it is wrong to steal: but if a man goes thieving to save himself and his family from starvation, are we to pity him or punish him? Who will first cast a stone if a husband sacrifices his unfaithful wife and her worthless seducer in the heat of his righteous wrath? or if a girl abandons herself for one joyful hour to the irresistible pleasures of love? Even our laws, cold-blooded and pedantic as they are, are moved to relent and forgo punishment.[35]

Later, when Werther learns of the crime of passion committed by the faithful servant from Wahlheim, he rushes to the side of the murderer. Overcome with pity, Werther is "seized by an inexpressible longing to save the man. He felt him to be so unhappy, even as a criminal he considered him so blameless." Werther pleads the young man's cause before an officer of the peace. But the representative of the law is unmoved, explaining that "that was the way to render every law useless and destroy the security of the state. . . . [E]verything would have to take its usual orderly course, in the prescribed channels."[36] Man's rational law-bound order denies the subtleties of nature, and its inadequacies are continually exposed in the clumsy day-to-day application of rigid rules to the complexities and ambiguities of human experience. This theme of the conflict of law and equity would be developed throughout the nineteenth century, but nowhere more vividly than in the fiction of Victor Hugo: first in the titanic struggle between Jean Valjean and Inspector Javert in *Les Misérables* (1862) and later in his novelistic account of the

Terror, *Quatrevingt-treize* (*Ninety-Three*; 1874), in which Cimourdain, advocate of an inflexible legal system, condemns Gauvain (his beloved former student) to death for his humanitarian – but legally forbidden – release of a prisoner of war.

The unruly nature of human frailty thus challenged the very core of a rational man-made order. The rule of law, deemed so necessary to the true ordering of society, could not adequately rationalize the contradictions of the heart, or promote the truth of nature. Accordingly, Feuerbach taught that "[m]ercy is the *justice of sensuous life*" (EC 52). In other words, formal legalisms could no longer guide mankind's organic growth; he was now due on earth the same merciful outlook that man had once projected only as God's other-worldly justice. Building on Hegel's insights in the *Phenomenology*, Feuerbach developed the principle of mercy, explaining that "[t]he understanding judges only according to the stringency of the law; the heart accommodates itself, is considerate, lenient, relenting. . . . The law condemns; the heart has compassion even on the sinner . . . Since, then, God is regarded as a sin-pardoning being, he is posited, not indeed as an unmoral, but as more than a moral being – in a word, as a human being" (EC 50–2). In calling for reconciliation with the past, Lamartine urged his readers, "Let us leave human nature its heart, that is the surest and most infallible of its principles."[37]

Wagner too regretted the inevitable friction between "pure Human Nature" and "politic-juristic Formalism" (CF 355) and endorsed the "instinctive forbearance of Love" as the antidote to the "chilling edicts of moral compacts" (OD 204).[38] In words echoing Werther's forgiving romantic sensibilities, he explained that "[i]n this sense a criminal case had the same interest for me as a political action; I could only take the side of the suffering party, and indeed, in exact measure of vehemence as it was engaged in resisting any kind of oppression" (CF 355). Adopting Hegel's potent image for historical progress, Wagner longed to "strip off from the phenomena their formal shell, fashioned from the traditions of Juristic Rights," in order to "light upon their inward kernel of purely human essence" (CF 355). Wagner dramatized this tension between the juristic demands of human social order and the equitable needs for human forbearance in a number of ways in the *Ring*: First, in his portrait of Siegmund who comes to the aid of a "sorrowing child" who had been forced to marry without her consent. Like Werther, Siegmund sees the world differently from others: "Whatever I held to be right others thought was wrong; to whatever seemed to me bad others gave their approval" (RN 128–29). Then, in his portrayal of Wotan. In his first approach to the *Ring – Siegfried's Tod –* Wagner externalized the antipodes of nature and civilization in the representative figures of Siegfried and Hagen. As he worked his way back in the *Ring*, however, he developed the tragic conflict between these two forces into a psychological drama, internalizing the struggle in the character of Wotan. In the story of the tragic god, he captured how the civilized mind is relentlessly bedeviled by the contradictions implicit in the social order. Thus Wotan must attempt to reconcile his goals for the hero engaged in an incestuous liaison with his sister – the call of nature and freedom – and the laws of marriage that he is obligated to enforce – the constraining rules of civilization. Wotan is tormented by the fact that he must yield to Fricka's invocation of custom's inviolable dictates.[39] Like Siegmund and Werther, he longs to liberate the condemned individual from the fate that custom has decreed. But as the enforcer of the law, he has no such freedom. Instead, like Captain Vere in *Billy Budd*, he must reject his compassionate instincts and follow the law. "Starry Vere" had confronted the "clash of military duty with moral scruple – scruple vitalized by compassion." But he was forced to acknowledge, "do these buttons that we wear attest that our allegiance is to Nature? No, to the King."[40] In a deeply moving soliloquy Wotan concedes his failure to lay the groundwork for his continued rule. Trapped in his own contradictions he is overcome with a destructive fury: "Within my breast I harbour the rage that can plunge into dread and confusion a world which once smiled upon me in joy" (RN 155). Tellingly, at this moment of deepest *Weltschmerz* – clear parallels with Werther – when Wotan realizes that he must stand by the law and let his beloved son be killed, Wagner puts into Wotan's mouth words that echo those of Othello at the height of his despair: "Farewell, then, imperious pomp! Godly show's resplendent shame! Let all I raised now fall in ruins!"[41]

But as noted, Wagner was not content to rest on Shakespearean laurels. His reflective Othellos – Wotan and Brünnhilde – would find a means to transcend their despair. Wotan thus learns a lesson of charity from this pain, and when it comes time to punish Brünnhilde he relaxes the strictness of his sentence upon her plea for mercy. The covenant which he makes with her, and which Brünnhilde tragically must see broken, represents an act of compassion for her fate – mercy as a new justice. Wotan's world is dominated by a master/slave dynamic. Wotan as ruler knows only masters and obedient subjects. But when confronted with his daughter Brünnhilde's transgression he is moved to see the other as a person worthy of respect and indulgence. In Terry Pinkard's terminology, through his act of compassionate mercy, his worldview shifts from a monadic – rule driven – to a dyadic – personhood driven – framework that is more receptive to notions of freedom and justice.[42] Wotan thus reenacts Creon's final insight at the end of Sophocles's *Antigone* – that at the sight of his dead son, he learned to be a father again; and his renewal of love's instinct signaled the death knell of the State: "The sword of his son's love drove a deadly gash into his heart: wounded deep within, *the State* fell crashing to the ground, to become in death a *Human Being*" (OD 190).

Wotan's feeling of the first stirrings of compassion for his daughter, as Brünnhilde once did for Siegmund, marks the first crack in the noble edifice of his theocratic regime. This dialectical fault line opens a passageway to a new paradigm of human freedom and equity which Brünnhilde then follows through. In lulling Wotan to sleep, Brünnhilde does not impose a harsh legal censure on past missteps; she implements instead a reign of loving forgiveness. Like Heine's wise old lizard, she understands that the "poor old gods" do not deserve to be humiliated as they are evicted from their palace, but should "be placed into retirement in some honourable way."[43] The chiastic structure of these two dramatic moments reinforces their connection. With her reciprocal act of forgiveness, Brünnhilde mirrors Wotan's enlightened gesture and demonstrates her understanding that she cannot rule like Wotan attempted to do with the unyielding rigor of the Spear and its dictates. What is required is a more fluid process of accommodation and understanding and a recognition that humanity is constantly engaged in a delicate balancing act. As Aileen Kelly summarizes Friedrich Schiller's insights in *On the Aesthetic Education of Man*, "personal wholeness" requires "a continuing effort at modulation of our drives in response to the situations we encounter, neither blindly following instinct nor holding rigidly to rules and principles."[44] Proudhon, likewise careful to resist the temptations to utopian casts of thought, summed up this perspective of humility with respect to human advancement when he recognized that egoism and communism were simply "two facets of our nature, ever adverse, ever in the process of reconciliation, but never wholly reconciled."[45] In the truest sense of Hegelian *Aufhebung* (sublation), Brünnhilde's new worldview is at once both a cancellation and a preservation of what has preceded it.[46]

By reading Brünnhilde's lullaby as forgiveness, her noble gesture of reconciliation can also be understood as a resolution of the central problem of the *Ring's* drama – Alberich's curse. Alberich's resentment and the curse that encapsulates that sentiment define the tragedy of the *Ring*, animating the evil will to power in the Nibelung dwarfs and the Gibichungs. And Wagner gives Alberich's resentment musical depth in an insistent phrase, charged with syncopated rhythms, that repeatedly snaps like a tightly wound coil throughout the drama. The curse, which is a direct manifestation of this resentment, is also given musical expression in a motif that is a recurrent burden on the score, regularly bringing the action back to the first cause. As Treadwell has noted, the curse is "a musical sign of . . . fatefulness," "bringing a kind of death . . . to the fabric of time itself."[47] Wotan, for all his noble intentions, is also caught in the same psychological trap, accepting Alberich's definition of the rules of the game and valuing the battle for control over the ring over all other aims. Wotan's rage and despair at his inability to secure the ring's power are but emotional variations on Alberich's hate. As Wotan himself summarizes his struggle, "I bequeathed the world to the Nibelung's spite" (RN 258). This resentment feeds the second generation as well. Alberich poisons Hagen's psyche by bringing him up to feel "stubborn hatred." Brünnhilde herself is for a time poisoned by resentment, which Wagner highlights by calling on Alberich's motif just as Brünnhilde reveals to Hagen the secret to killing Siegfried: "But – if you struck him in the back" (RN 327).

In the end, however, by ultimately engaging in forgiveness, Brünnhilde directly confronts the dangerous sentiment that animates the curse, and refuses to let the rancor that has infected Wotan's reign further define her actions. In Comte-Sponville's insightful commentary on ethical principles, we learn that mercy, "the virtue of forgiveness," is the "virtue that triumphs over rancor, over justified hatred . . . over resentment, over the desire for revenge or punishment."[48] By engaging in forgiveness, a person refuses to perpetuate the sentiments of anger and revenge or to partake in the hatred that has led to prior error. Wagner highlights the impact of this enlightened outlook by introducing the Curse motif just prior to the *"Ruhe, du Gott"* passage, thus positing the act of benediction as a clear alternative to Alberich's corrupting worldview. Brünnhilde's forgiveness not only breaks the spell of the curse but also interrupts the infinite regress that the curse had imposed on the world of the *Ring*. *Ressentiment* faces backwards, always focused on a sense of past wrong that cannot be allayed. By freeing herself from this sentiment and annulling the evil effects of the retrogressive rancor, Brünnhilde allows mankind to restore the fabric of time and step forward.

In the end, then, it is not Siegfried and his sword – in which both Wotan and Brünnhilde initially put their faith – who can redeem Wotan's end – the collapse of the inflexible structure of the State – and point the way out of Wotan/Othello's despair, but Brünnhilde who clears the way for a new generation to reap the collective benefits of knowledge and understanding, and through her forgiveness transforms the tragedy of broken promises and lost loves into a parable of latter-day justice.

Notes

1 See André Comte-Sponville, *A Small Treatise on the Great Virtues: The Uses of Philosophy in Everyday Life*, trans. Catherine Temerson (Metropolitan Books 2001), 119–20: "Mercy is not the same as clemency . . . or compassion. . . . Compassion . . . is concerned with suffering. . . . Mercy, on the other hand, is concerned with wrongdoing. . . . Mercy is the rarer virtue and more difficult." Scruton and Tanner are among the few commentators to acknowledge the presence of "forgiveness" in Brünnhilde's final gesture towards Wotan. As Scruton explains, "through a new kind of wisdom – the wisdom of forgiveness – she can learn to die as she should." Scruton, *The Ring of Truth*, 287; Tanner, *Wagner*, 178: noting that Brünnhilde forgives "Wotan for causing all the trouble in the first place." At one point in his analysis of the *Ruhe du Gott* passage, Berry hints at "mercy." Berry, *Treacherous Bonds*, 265.

2 Likewise, Wagner noted that there should be no "bitterness in her speech to Gutrune" when Brünnhilde reappears on stage at the end of the *Ring*. Porges, *Wagner Rehearsing the Ring*, 143.

3 See Comte-Sponville, *A Small Treatise*, 123; and Zizek, "Afterword: Wagner, Anti-Semitism and 'German Ideology,'" 184: "the notion of Mercy is strictly correlative to that of Sovereignty: only the bearer of sovereign power can dispense mercy."

4 Hegel, *Phenomenology*, 407 (§670).

5 *Id.*, 409 (§671).

6 "Through mutual respect each side recognizes itself in and through the other; the self sees itself in the other as the other sees itself in the self. . . . The act of mutual reconciliation and recognition among moral judges *is*, Hegel claims, the advent of absolute spirit." Frederick C. Beiser, "'Morality' in Hegel's *Phenomenology of Spirit*," in *The Blackwell Guide to Hegel's 'Phenomenology of Spirit,'* 223–4.

7 We know that Wagner read at least some of the *Phenomenology* while in Dresden, and there is some evidence that he grasped the concept of the beautiful soul directly from that source. In a vivid passage of the *Phenomenology*, Hegel described how the "hard-hearted" beautiful soul, by virtue of the contradiction in its "unreconciled immediacy," becomes "disordered to the point of madness, wastes itself in yearning and pines away in consumption." Hegel, *Phenomenology*, 407 (§668). Inevitably, as we have explained, the hard heart softens, and the beautiful soul offers forgiveness. *Id.*, 407 (§670). Wagner adopted a similar personification in *The Artwork of the Future* where he described "speculative thought and system-building in the fields of theology and philosophy" as "that intelligence which so arrogantly set itself apart from life" and which "finally has no choice, in order to avoid genuine madness, but to accept unconditionally the singular force of [the life-drive]" (AF 15).

8 Lamartine, *History of the Girondists*, 546.

9 Carlyle, *French Revolution*, 606. Wagner, himself, also expressed some compassion for Robespierre in his 1854 letter to Röckel. Though labeling him "deeply unsympathetic," Wagner was willing at the same time to acknowledge that he was a "deeply pitiful man." SL 305–6.

10   Letter to Minna Wagner, 16 Apr. 1850, SL 196.

11   *My Life*, 376.

12   I do not share Corse's view that Brünnhilde's remaining behind on the mountaintop represents a patriarchal view of marriage. Corse, *Wagner and the New Consciousness*, 168. Rather, it is consistent with her role as the trusting believer. And ultimately she has her defining moment at the end of the drama when she emerges as the true world-historical hero. Windell makes this point explicit when he observes how, in his portrait of Brünnhilde, "Wagner abandoned the romantic stereotype of the passive woman who redeems sinful man by her constancy alone." Windell, "Hegel, Feuerbach and Wagner's *Ring*, 47–8.

13   Herzen recognized this painful insight as integral to the historical process. In an essay of July 1848 he argued, "It is time for man to put the republic on trial, along with its legislation . . . all our notions about the citizen and his relations to other citizens and the State. There will be many executions: things nearest and dearest will have to be sacrificed – merely to sacrifice the detestable is not the problem. This is the whole point: to surrender what we love if we are convinced that it is not true." As quoted in Kelly, *Discovery of Chance*, 347. Later in the century Oscar Wilde would famously declare in the *Ballad of Reading Gaol*, "some love too little, some too long/Some sell, and others buy;/Some do the deed with many tears,/And some without a sigh:/For each man kills the thing he loves,/Yet each man does not die." Wilde saw a tragic kernel at the heart of human love which rendered all men guilty – although social custom only singled out some for punishment.

14   "The word of reconciliation is the *objectively* existent Spirit, which beholds the pure knowledge of itself *qua universal* essence, in its opposite, in the pure knowledge of itself *qua* absolutely self-contained and exclusive *individuality* – a reciprocal recognition which is *absolute* Spirit." Hegel, *Phenomenology*, 408 (§670). See also my discussion of the confrontation between Henry and Margaret Wilcox in E.M. Forster's *Howard's End*. Alexander H. Shapiro, "McEwan and Forster: The Perfect Wagnerites," *The Wagner Journal*, Vol. 5, No. 2 (2011), 35–6.

15   As Kelly astutely notes of Hegel's approach to philosophy, "empathy is an essential quality of the true philosopher." Kelly, *Discovery of Chance*, 193.

16

> What Hegel's idea of reconciliation means is that the in modern world, we are able to recognize the failures of our ultimate ethical, spiritual, and rational demands as the natural result of the collision between thought and the world. And having understood the source of these failures, we need no longer conclude that the world cannot reflect the reality of thought. Instead we can see the history of culture, the passage from the ancient to the modern world, as itself the work of thought's demands.
>
> (Krasnoff, *Hegel's Phenomenology*, 145)

17   Mark Owen Lee, *Athena Sings: Wagner and the Greeks* (University of Toronto Press 2003), 66–8; Barry Millington, *The New Grove Guide to Wagner and His Operas* (Oxford University Press 2006), 96.

18   Nietzsche, *The Birth of Tragedy*, 70. Other, more recent commentators, have noted striking parallels between the Droysen version of *Prometheus* and the *Ring*. Hugh Lloyd-Jones, "Wagner and the Greeks," in *The Wagner Compendium*, ed. Barry Millington (Thames and Hudson 1992), 158–61.

19   See, e.g., Scruton, *The Ring of Truth*, 142, 265: Wotan and Brünnhilde "united in an act of renunciation that will give meaning to their suffering"; Berry, *Treacherous Bonds*, 258: noting the "Schopenhauerian repose of feeling as one with all mankind and its suffering"; Hollinrake associates the musical setting of the passage with Wagner's Schopenhauerian outburst to Mathilde Wesendonck in 1858, "I can conceive of only

one salvation. It is rest! Rest from longing! The stilling of every desire." Hollinrake, "Epiphany and Apocalypse in the 'Ring,'" 46.

20 Kitcher and Schacht, *Finding an Ending*, 134, 178–9, 183–4: Brünnhilde and Wotan's "experiences are indicative of the hard truth that there simply is no viable solution to the problem of stable order that Wotan set for himself. . . . Neither [Brünnhilde] nor *Götterdämmerung* offers us a way to resolve this predicament in general; indeed, both she and the drama itself suggest that that the general problem is insoluble"; "All that remains for [Wotan] is to arrange the conditions for the consummation of the gods, leaving the world to its own sad devices and sorry fate, and to await those ends, without hope, in infinite sadness."

21 Hegel, *Phenomenology*, 2 (§2).

22 Kelly, *Discovery of Chance*, 151.

23 Carlyle, "Characteristics," 361.

24 Terry Pinkard, *Does History Make Sense?*, 123–33.

25 Heinrich Heine, *The Romantic School* (1835), as excerpted in Heine, *On the History of Religion*, 166.

26 Hegel, *History*, 59; Bykova, "Spirit," *Blackwell Guide*, 274:

> Self-consciousness is necessarily mediated through the actual forms of life of individual thinking subjects, because without this 'real-life' mediation there is no self-consciousness.

Krasnoff, *Hegel*, 111–12:

> Hegel's hope is that the narrative of history will provide us with a kind of reconciliation to the particularity of our agency. To see this particularity as not in fatal conflict with our infinite freedom, to see our agency as not threatened by our entanglement in culture and history, we need to see that culture and that history as teaching us that we have overcome our earlier, futile efforts to insist on an unrestrained conception of freedom. To reconcile freedom with culture requires a kind of maturity, and only a historical narrative can show us that we have achieved it.

Once again, George Bancroft, in his Oration of 1854, hit all the relevant points of the Hegelian agenda, including the need to reconcile fact and idealism:

> [T]heoretic principles . . . struggle unrelentingly to conform society to the absolute law of Truth and Justice; and this, though it kindle the purest enthusiasm, can likewise never perfectly succeed, because the materials of which society is composed partake of imperfection, and to extirpate all that is imperfect would lead to the destruction of society itself. And there may be a third [strand], which seeks to reconcile the two [fact and idealism], but which yet can never thrive by itself, since it depends for its activity on the clashing between the fact the and higher law.
> (Bancroft, *Progress*, 11–12)

27 Georg Wilhelm Friedrich Hegel, *Lectures on the Philosophy of History*, trans. Ruben Alvarado (Wordbridge Publishing 2011), 400.

28 Letter to Liszt, 13 Apr. 1853, SL 284.

29 Curiously, Deathridge views Siegfried's journey as the "exact opposite" of Wotan's descent into Nibelheim since he travels "up the Rhine," Deathridge, *Wagner*, 52, but in point of fact he is really descending "down" from Brünnhilde's rock – and thematically, the movement from the rock to the river mirrors the descent from the bliss of true love to the hell of Hagen's world. The concept was captured in Wagner's account of his reaction to a letter from Herwegh while he was traveling in the Alps in July 1852, which had the effect of "dragging me down from my lofty Alpine impressions into the unpleasant everyday world." Wagner, *My Life*, 483.

30 Berlin, *Political Ideas*, 316. Terry Pinkard has explained that for Hegel idealistic phi-losophy and the concrete facts of lived history are two sides of the same coin. Terry Pinkard, *Does History Make Sense?*, 167. Likewise Carlyle, acknowledging that "[o]ur Life is compassed round with Necessity," understood that the task of man was to balance the competing demands of life. "[M]ust there not be a confusion, a contest, before the better Influence can become the upper?" SR 140.
31 Letter to Röckel, 25/26 Jan. 1854, SL 306.
32 Carlyle, *French Revolution*, 744; Lamartine's book, which we know Wagner lingered over in Paris in 1849, describes Robespierre giving out a *"rugissement de douleur physique qui fut entendu jusqu'aux éxtremités de la Place de la Révolution"* ("a cry of anguish that was heard to the opposite side of the Place de la Révolution"). Lamartine, *Histoire des Girondins*, 926.
33 Feuerbach, *Principles of the Philosophy of the Future*, 243 (§55).
34 Berry notes that Brünnhilde "makes no apology – neither for herself nor for Siegfried." Berry, *Treacherous Bonds*, 265.
35 Goethe, *Werther*, 61.
36 *Id.*, 109.
37 Lamartine, *History of the Girondists*, 546.
38 See Cohen, "To the Dresden Barricades," 49–51.
39 Wagner noted "the restless inner discord of [modern man], who between 'will' and 'can' had created for himself a chaos of tormenting notions, driving him to war against himself, to self-laceration and bodiless abandonment to the Christian death" (OD 169).
40 Melville, *Budd*, 361.
41 "O now, forever/Farewell the tranquil mind! Farewell content!/Farewell the plumed troops, and the big wars/. . . . Farewell . . . /Pride, pomp, and circumstances of glorious war!/ . . . Farewell! Othello's occupation's gone!" *Othello*, Act III, sc. iii., 70.
42 Pinkard, *Does History Make Sense?*, 25–9.
43 Heinrich Heine, "Lucca, the City," in *Travel Pictures*, Part IV (1831), as excerpted in Heine, *On the History of Religion*, 127.
44 Kelly, *Discovery of Chance*, 223.
45 Kelly, *Discovery of Chance*, 146. Kelly notes of Proudhon, his "model of socialism" was "as an unstable equilibrium reconciling individual ambition and initiative with col-lective goals through the cultivation of *humanitas* – 'the distributive justice of social empathy.'" Kelly, *Discovery of Chance*, 320.
46 Pinkard, *Does History Make Sense?*, 30–1.
47 Treadwell, *Interpreting Wagner*, 91, 93; Foster, *Wagner's 'Ring,'* 255–6: noting "linear circularity" of the theft of the gold theme in the *Ring*.
48 Comte-Sponville, *A Small Treatise*, 118–19.

5   Renunciation on the Rhine?

There is little question that Wagner's introduction to the works of Schopenhauer in September or October of 1854 was a key turning point in his intellectual development.[1] The final significance to the *Ring* of Schopenhauer's philosophy as set forth in *Die Welt als Wille und Vorstellung* (*The World as Will and Representation*; 1819/1844) is a much more difficult issue to resolve. The historical record discloses Wagner's path of ambivalence on this very issue. At the height of his preoccupation with Schopenhauer, in May 1856, Wagner began sketching new verses as a substitute for the Feuerbach ending, introducing the jarringly extrinsic notion of a Buddhistic nirvana "*redeemed from incarnation*."[2] In a letter to Röckel some three months later, Wagner disclaimed the Feuerbach lines as "tendentious" and attempted to convince Röckel that despite his best intentions for the *Ring*, he had been "unconsciously following a quite different, and much more profound intuition, and that, instead of a single phase in the world's evolution, what I had glimpsed was the essence of the world itself in all its conceivable phases, and that I had therefore recognized its nothingness."[3] But when it came time to make a public printing of the libretto in 1863, Wagner retained the original Feuerbach ending.[4] Equally important, while composing the music for the Immolation Scene in 1872 Wagner was still juggling both texts. Stewart Spencer asserts that during composition, "it was Schopenhauer's lines which he considered rather than Feuerbach's."[5] But Cosima's diary reveals otherwise: up until April 1872 Wagner was still considering the original Feuerbach text. On April 4, 1872, Cosima quoted her husband: "I have cut several things, for example, '*Glücklich in Leid und Lust*,' etc. [sic] I shall retain it in the reading text, but what is this maxim doing in the drama? One knows it anyway, having just gone through it all. It would seem almost childish if she were yet again to turn to the people to proclaim her wisdom."[6] The key phrase here is "one knows it anyway," suggesting that its themes were already expressed in the course of the drama. In the end, Wagner scrapped *both* conclusions to Brünnhilde's speech, choosing instead to include them *together* as dueling addenda in his published libretto of 1872 (volumes v and vi of the *Gesammelte Schriften und Dichtungen*). In introducing the second (1856) alternative ending, he did tip the scales in its favor: "Finally it could not escape the composer that, since the meaning of these lines was already expressed with the greatest definition in the tenor of the musical drama, their actual delivery

had to be eliminated from the performance."[7] But this is virtually the same sentiment that Wagner expressed privately to Cosima about the Feuerbach ending! For
the scholarly commentator, these two separate and conflicting references to the
implicit dramatic message virtually cancel each other out, leaving no clear extrinsic guidance for the hermeneutic inquiry into the opera's final message.[8] In the
end, Wagner refused to signpost his philosophical intent and left it to the spectators themselves to evaluate what the "tenor of the musical drama" communicates
in light of the finished product he presented to the public at Bayreuth in 1876, the
printed score of *Götterdämmerung* published that same year, and the full historical and intellectual context of the work's gestation.[9]

In spite of Wagner's post-hoc attempt to discover an "unconscious" intuition
at work in his poem, the entire plot design and language of the *Ring*, as I have
endeavored to show, expressly follow the logic of the original Feuerbachian and
Hegelian agenda that consciously informed and shaped the project in the late 1840s
and early 1850s.[10] And given that the Feuerbach ending was written contempora-
neously with the rest of the text means that it is highly probative of the import of
the work as a whole. But even without the Feuerbach verses to point the way, the
final product is consistent with its meaning. As noted, the opera does not end with
the death of Siegfried and a blank message of untempered mourning and despair.
Rather, there is an elaborate coda in which Brünnhilde returns to make historical
and philosophical sense of the events that have taken place. And as Brünnhilde
comes through the test of time and struggle of love and passion, she does not arrive
at a moment of rejection and renunciation. She does not exhibit the "willlessness"
or the "greatest indifference to all things" which are the hallmarks of renunciation.[11] She does not abdicate any further responsibility for the world. Instead, she
engages in deeds, deeds that do not deny or relinquish the will to power but utilize
it in creative new directions and in the service of a higher species consciousness.
Brünnhilde exerts her authority throughout the last scene, directing the Gibichung
personnel to "Do as Brünnhilde bids," dispatching the two ravens home to Valhalla, repossessing the ring as her "inheritance," first grasping the gold, then giving
it away. Wagner directed Amalie Materna, his first Brünnhilde, to turn "one way
and then the other with sweeping arm movements" as "she delivers her words of
command."[12] In preparing the funeral rites for Siegfried, Brünnhilde engages in a
ritual act that honors the dead man and his role in the world – an act that affirms
human meaning rather than denies it. But most important, she conclusively brings
the compromised world of the gods to an end and accomplishes this task by taking from Wotan control over the power of fire. It is no longer Wotan who summons
Loge – "tamed," as the Third Norn says, "by the spell of his spear" – but Brünnhilde
who wields the torch.[13] And although Brünnhilde carries no spear, Wagner makes
it clear that it is Wotan's power she exercises; as Brünnhilde ignites the flames, the
Spear motif forcefully sounds in the brass. Brünnhilde's Promethean act of defi-
ance of the gods thus becomes full-blown revolution and usurpation – at the same
time destructive and creative. Through Isaiah Berlin's insight, we can understand
this dramatic moment in its proper philosophical framework. "Hegelianism has a
revolutionary element . . . and revolutionary action was justified if it fought on the

side of dynamic reason against static actuality, if it embodied that criticism of the past, and destruction of it, without which the future could not be born."[14]

And Brünnhilde does not hold the ring high as a symbol of the world's unalterable corruption and tragic stasis – the curse that life is. Instead, she delivers it, and herself, to the funeral pyre in the expectation of cleansing absolution and renewal. "Let the fire that consumes me cleanse the ring of its curse; in the floodwaters let it dissolve" (RN 350). Equally important, the release of the ring does not signal an end to her love or a rejection of it as an illusion. She does not conclude that her passion was misguided (as indeed Othello does – "one that loved not wisely, but too well"). Continuing to extol Siegfried as a hero and a husband, she longs for union with him. Indeed, her final apostrophe to Siegfried – as Nietzsche noted, perhaps the most anti-Schopenhauerian of Wagner's creations[15] – is full of sensual expressiveness undiminished by her encounter with the disappointments of the phenomenal world: "Feel how the flames burn in my breast, effulgent fires seize hold of my heart: to clasp him to me . . . and in mightiest love to be wedded to him!" (RN 350). Finally, Brünnhilde's affirmative act of suicide is completely antithetical to Schopenhauer's teachings on renunciation. "Far from being denial of the will, suicide is a phenomenon of the will's strong affirmation," Schopenhauer maintained. "For denial has its essential nature in the fact that the pleasures of life, not its sorrows, are shunned."[16] Brünnhilde's immolation is not a passive death reflecting a will that has weakened to a dying ember, but one that is determined "from the full force of [her] being" (AF 79).

Thus, although Brünnhilde has passed beyond her tragic moment of passion and reached a moment of reflection, there is nothing that suggests cosmic stasis or indifference in the Immolation Scene. In light of Brünnhilde's concrete acts of honoring Siegfried's memory with a funeral pyre, seizing the torch, extinguishing the reign of the gods, and returning the ring to the Rhine, it is simply a non sequitur to argue that the Immolation Scene communicates a "sense of repose" that signals that "the will-to-power stands upon the verge of abdication" or that "Renunciation of the Will remains the ideal," as Berry does.[17]

As for Wotan – the traditional model of renunciation – he does not pass away in Buddhistic peace either, but is driven by will to the very end: first, in summoning Erda in Act III of *Siegfried* to find a way out of his predicament: "I'd thank the store of your wisdom to be told how to hold back a rolling wheel" (RN 255); next, in confronting Siegfried on the mountain; and finally, consumed with anxiety in Valhalla, tightly grasping the broken symbol of his former power, the splinters of his spear, and still searching for a last-minute reprieve in the ring's release.[18] Take for example the meeting of Wotan and Siegfried at the mountain pass. When he sees Siegfried approaching, Wotan cannot help but confront the young man. Insulted by Siegfried's indifference to the wisdom of old age, Wotan becomes enraged and stands in Siegfried's way. (In this way, incidentally, he unilaterally changes the conditions of his promise to Brünnhilde – for while he promised her the bravest of men who could fearlessly breach the wall of flames, he did not require that the hero would also have to break past the ruler of the gods to reach her.) Wagner was particularly proud of this scene, explaining to Röckel how it brought out the essence of Wotan's character: "Faced with the prospect of his own annihilation, he finally becomes so instinctively human that – *in spite of his supreme resolve* – his ancient pride is once more stirred, provoked moreover (mark this well!) by – his jealousy of Brünnhilde. . . . He refuses, so to speak, to be thrust aside, but prefers to fall – to be conquered."[19] Wagner thus admired Wotan not simply for his resolve to pass on, but equally for the passionate way he struggled against "the prospect of his own annihilation" with a show of "ancient pride," feelings of "jealousy," and a drive to fight bravely until the end.

An even more compelling textual refutation of the Schopenhauerian reading is that Wotan's resolution to step aside is not made in a vacuum but with full knowledge of Siegfried's heroic exploits; it is therefore predicated on the expectation of a succession plan: "I now perform freely in gladness and joy: though once, in furious loathing, I bequeathed the world to the Nibelung's spite, to the lordliest Wälsung I leave my heritage now" (RN 258). Wotan takes the decision to relinquish his power only once he knows that there is someone to take over from him, to inherit the world. He does not speak of forfeiting his estate and the world altogether, but bequeathing it to Siegfried as his heir and the anticipated agent of his original plan. The very act of bequeathing an inheritance is antithetical to and inconsistent with a belief in the meaninglessness of life, or, as Berry states, "the futility of *all* power relations."[20] Berry has no means to justify Wotan's future-facing perspective in Schopenhauerian terms except to characterize Wotan's notion of an inheritance as "utter delusion."[21] But evidence of such delusion is not to be found in this scene. To the contrary, Wagner reinforces the authenticity of Wotan's decision with a new "triumphant sounding"[22] musical motif known as the World's Inheritance.[23] Wotan's movement from a state of despair and bitter surrender of the world to Alberich, to a sense of purpose and hope about the future when he recognizes he can pass his baton on to Siegfried, can only signal an emerging optimism about the future prospects for his world, not a deepening conviction of life's emptiness.[24]

Finally, we cannot discount the imagery that Wagner specified to accompany the last measures of the score: "A red glow breaks out with increasing brightness from the cloudbank that had settled on the horizon. By its light, the three Rhinedaughters can be seen swimming in circles and merrily playing with the ring on the calmer waters of the Rhine, which has little by little returned to its bed." Then "the hall of Valhalla comes into view. . . . Bright flames seem to flare up in the hall of the gods, finally hiding them from sight completely." This vision is accessible not only to the audience but also to those who have survived the catastrophe. As the stage directions make clear, "From the ruins of the fallen hall, the men and women watch moved to the very depths of their being, as the glow from the fire grows in the sky" (RN 351).[25] Humanity has not been effaced, but survives to observe the historic moment – the return of the ring and the passing of the gods. This is manifestly not the end of the world, then, but simply the end of *a stage* of world history. Human beings pick their way among the ruins, transformed "to the very depths of their being" by the apocalyptic vision. Wagner thus concludes with a *tableau vivant* that silently evokes the principle image and key concept of his Feuerbach ending – that a world dramatically altered by Brünnhilde is to be inherited by those who remain behind.[26] It is also a visual trope that would have been all too familiar to his audience – the visitor in a state of awe before the sublime ruins.[27] Civilizations come and go, but the human species endures to learn the lessons of the past.

If there is a Schopenhauerian cast to the *Ring*, it cannot readily be found in the final version of the text. The focus of any such analysis must therefore be on the music Wagner wrote for *Götterdämmerung*, in particular, Brünnhilde's Immolation Scene. But before we explore the musical ending, it is important to pause for a moment on some of the philosophical and historical details that complicate the perhaps too facile story of Wagner's complete and irreversible conversion to Schopenhauer.

First, it bears noting that on reading Schopenhauer Wagner did not immediately dismantle the *Ring* libretto in disgust; to the contrary, he proudly sent the 1853 printed version – complete with the final Feuerbach ending – to Schopenhauer himself.[28] Clearly Wagner was not unduly embarrassed to share his forward-looking theme of "blossoming life" with the philosopher of pessimism.

Second, whatever one thinks of Schopenhauer's metaphysics, one need not accept his own prescription for redemption, namely that denial of the will is the only way to true enlightenment. Thomas Mann observed that "the denial of the will is the moral-intellectual component of Schopenhauer's philosophy, which is of little essential significance. It is merely secondary."[29] Wagner himself was deeply ambivalent about Schopenhauer's message of renunciation and never completely gave up his earlier faith in the key tenets of Young German sensualism. For the Young Germans, sexual freedom had been a rallying point, and throughout his writings of the 1840s and early 1850s Wagner had sought to restore sensuality to a place of importance in man's life and not discredit it in deference to Christian piety. Schopenhauer's theory of the will, on the other hand, resonated strongly with the Christian belief in man's inherent sinfulness,[30] and renunciation in his philosophical program required sexual abstinence.[31] Instead of embracing this ascetic demand, Wagner did intellectual backflips – expressed most notably in his famous letter from Venice to Mathilde Wesendonk in December 1858 – to try to show how "sexual love" really achieved the prescribed quelling of the will rather than the proscribed kindling of it.[32]

Third, the Schopenhauerian interpretation of the *Ring* also fails to account for the significant passage of time between Wagner's first encounter with the Sage of Frankfurt and the composition of his finale. Wagner started composing the score for *Götterdämmerung* in October 1869, finishing the complete draft of the first act in July 1870. The second act was written after about a year-long hiatus, from June 24 to November 19, 1871. Wagner commenced the third act on January 3, 1872,[33] finishing the complete draft of the score about seven months later on July 22/23, 1872. Thus, by the time that Wagner came to compose the music for *Götterdämmerung*'s ending, about 18 years had passed since his first introduction to the philosopher, and in that time his own personal outlook on life had changed dramatically. No longer a lonely exile in an unhappy marriage with no prospects of returning to his homeland or having his works produced, he was now a German citizen again; graced with the patronage of Ludwig II, King of Bavaria, and recognition at the court of Wilhelm I (the new Reich was declared on January 18, 1871, and Wagner was received in Berlin in April 1871); married (as of August 25, 1870) to a woman he adored; and proud father of several children, including a son (Siegfried Helferich Richard, born on June 6, 1869). Wagner's letters at this time exude a new optimism and faith in the future, emerging from the confidence that he had achieved his life's goal. In January of 1870, Wagner mused to Anton Pusinelli, the family friend and doctor, "if my life thus far has been aimless and storm tossed, my ship of life has had to suffer the most unprecedented hardships before reaching port. But I have now reached port. And now I must live gladfully and joyfully. A handsome sturdy son, high of forehead and bright of eye, Siegfried Richard, will inherit his father's name and preserve his works for the world."[34] Wagner's sense of confidence resided, like that of Wotan, in the security of knowing that he had an heir who could carry on his life's work. The next year he gushed to Alwine Frommann, a friend and acolyte in Berlin, that "everything is prospering" and "my confidence in the future has been revived."[35] By 1872, he was writing to Nietzsche that his son "is now teaching me what it is to feel hope again."[36] Wagner returned to composing the *Ring* during this period of renewed professional and personal gratification and indeed attributed his newfound enthusiasm for the work to his son: "[O]verjoyed as I was [by the birth of 'a handsome son'], I finished composing 'Siegfried,' which had been interrupted for 11 years. An unheard-of case! No one thought I would ever return to it."[37] On January 3, 1872, the day he turned to composing Act III of *Götterdämmerung*, Wagner told his wife with tears in his eyes, "a person who is happy as I am dares to face life and he accepts the world's challenge."[38]

By 1872, moreover, Wagner had been introduced to Carlyle's own unique brand of transcendentalism and faith in historical evolution. (Cosima's diary reveals that they were reading *Frederick the Great* together in early 1871, although as previously noted there is good reason to believe Wagner had encountered the thought and writings of Carlyle well before.)[39] But even more telling is the fact that by the time he returned to complete the *Ring*, Wagner had met the remarkable professor of philology Friedrich Nietzsche, who had become a friend and frequent visitor to his home in Tribschen. In a letter to the classicist Erwin Rhode, Wagner shared his amazement at this new evolved form of man: "[H]ere is a genus, perhaps even a whole generation, for the sake of which it has been worth my while to have spent half a century shut up in prison!"[40] Wagner read Nietzsche's lecture for the Frei Akademische Gesellshaft in Basel on *Socrates and Tragedy* in February of 1870 and urged his friend to write a longer and more comprehensive work on the subject.[41] The gestation of *Die Geburt der Tragödie aus dem Geiste der Musik* (*The Birth of Tragedy out of the Spirit of Music*; 1872), conceived in part under Wagner's own tutelage,[42] thus took place while Wagner was composing the music for *Götterdämmerung*. The book in its final form had an enormous impact on Wagner.[43] He received the completed proofs on January 3, 1872, the same day that he embarked on the composition of Act III.[44] He devoured it right away and was soon joking with Cosima that "my love for you is both Dionysian and Apollonian."[45] He confessed to his wife that "[t]his is the book I have been longing for,"[46] and in his thank-you letter to Nietzsche, he exclaimed, "Never have I read anything more beautiful than your book! How splendid it all is!.... reading it has left me so inordinately excited that I must first await the return of reason before reading it *properly*."[47] By January 10, 1872, just a week later, Wagner had read the book twice,[48] and he "carefully" read it over again in the summer of that year.[49]

In *The Birth of Tragedy*, Nietzsche had begun his philosophical campaign to light a path out of the dark tunnel of Schopenhauerian pessimism.[50] In a preface to a later edition, Nietzsche expressed regret that his work had placed such reliance on that philosopher's structures of thought: "in those days I still lacked the courage . . . to permit myself in every way an individual language of my own . . . and that instead I tried laboriously to express by means of Schopenhauerian and Kantian formulas strange and new valuations which were basically at odds with Kant's and Schopenhauer's spirit and taste!"[51] Irrespective of how he framed his thoughts, Nietzsche expressly praised the "profound Hellene" for resisting the temptations of "a Buddhistic negation of the will."[52] While acknowledging a deep well of sorrow in the world, he sought all the same to celebrate "the eternal joy of existence."[53] Nietzsche, the *wunderkind* academic, gave renewed intellectual credence to many of the ideas that Wagner had originally developed in the *Ring* but which had seemed to lose their vitality in the face of Schopenhauer's compelling prose. Like Wagner, Nietzsche did not sugarcoat the harsh truths of human existence. Reiterating Erda's fundamental insight – and Wagner's revolutionary tenet – that "all that comes into being must be ready for a sorrowful end," Nietzsche called on man not to "become rigid with fear" (as Wotan had), but rather to take "metaphysical comfort" in the contemplation of the wonder and glory of the life force of nature, the "eternally creative primordial mother, eternally impelling to existence."[54] Suffering would no longer serve as the excuse for shunning life but rather as the spur to higher engagement, striving, and wisdom: "the struggle, the pain, the destruction of phenomena, now appear necessary to us, in view of the excess of countless forms of existence which force and push one another into life, in view of the exuberant fertility of the universal will."[55] For those who witness these "tremendous struggles and transitions," the response is not to renounce the world, but to "take part and fight."[56] Nietzsche thus recast Schopenhauer's dark vision of the mindless will back into a Young Hegelian wonder at the plenitude of human species life and strivings.

I do not mean to suggest that there is a perfect correlation between Nietzsche's thought and Wagner's Hegelian thesis for the *Ring*. Nietzsche, it needs be said, hesitated to recognize the accretion of learning from generation to generation – "the amazingly high pyramid of knowledge in our own time" – as the saving grace for mankind. But for all his critique of science and Socratic optimism, he was not above endorsing a faith in spiritual regeneration, the ability of a culture to "endure" the pain of existence more effectively even if that existential pain at its core could never fully be mitigated. Nietzsche hailed the developments in German music, from Beethoven to Wagner, as the road to a rebirth of tragedy and hence a return to the Hellenic magic mountain: "Let no one try to blight our faith in a yet-impending rebirth of Hellenic antiquity; for this alone gives us hope for a renovation and purification of the German spirit through the fire magic of music."[57] As Nietzsche not so subtly implied, by tapping into fundamental mythic themes of the Germanic tradition and pushing the emotional and formalistic boundaries of music to new frontiers, Wagner was sowing the seeds if not actually cultivating the flower of a rebirth of tragedy – within the German cultural tradition. Wagner's revolutionary aesthetic dreams of 1849–51 were coming true. Nietzsche had stepped forward as Wagner's Evangelist, giving the composer new cause to believe that his unfinished masterwork would still have *historical* significance.

Given that Nietzsche's book emerged out of an intense period of intellectual exchange between Wagner and his disciple, it is not hard to see in *The Birth of Tragedy* reflections of Wagner's own mindset – call it post-Schopenhauerian – at the time he embarked on the final act of the *Ring*.[58] Indeed, already in his *Beethoven* essay of 1870, drafted between the composition of the first and second acts of *Götterdämmerung*, Wagner had begun to renew some of the revolutionary faith and Rousseauvian idealism that had guided him in the early 1850s. In that encomium to the composer, he gave full throated endorsement of art, and German music in particular, as the key to a new social order:

> It may certainly seem that our civilisation, to the extent that it fashions the artist in particular, can be given soul anew only out of the spirit of our music, the music which Beethoven freed from the bonds of fashion. In this sense the task of bringing the religion permeating this civilisation to the new, more spiritual civilisation which is perhaps [*vielleicht*] being shaped by this means can evidently be granted only to the German spirit . . .[59]

Although Wagner hedged just a tad by slipping in the qualifier "perhaps," he appears to have found a way back to his historical optimism in a "more spiritual civilisation" even after having grappled with the harsh truths of Schopenhauer. Nietzsche would remark years later in 1885 – perhaps with no small tinge of competitive self-congratulation – that *The Birth of Tragedy* had been "for Wagner the happiness that had the greatest resonance in his life; he was ecstatic, and in *Götterdämmerung* there are magnificent things that he brought forth in his condition of an unexpected, extreme hope."[60] And there is good reason to believe that Wagner's composition of the last act of *Götterdämmerung* was influenced by the themes in the book.[61] Wagner wrote to Nietzsche on January 10, 1872, that "I must have it [*The Birth of Tragedy*] in order to get myself in the proper mood for working after breakfast, as I am again hard at work on the last act [of *Götterdämmerung*] *since* reading your book."[62] Wagner's sense of hope continued to mature, and by 1880, Wagner asserted in *Religion and Art* and its supplements that Schopenhauer's ethics could serve as a basis for the historic regeneration of man. In doing so, he sought to excuse Schopenhauer's pessimism as consistent with the corrupt state of affairs he saw all around him: "these paths, which well may lead to hope, are clearly and distinctly pointed out by our philosopher, and it is not his fault if he was so fully occupied with the correct portrayal of the only world that lay before him, that he was compelled to leave their actual exploration to our own selves."[63] In other words, Schopenhauer's philosophical pessimism was simply a product of his historical time and place!

The musical phrase that ends *Götterdämmerung* has been interpreted in a variety of ways, whether as the celebration of love, the triumph of compassion, the glorification of Brünnhilde, or the call to renunciation and the end of the world.[64] I argue that none of these conceptual correspondences accurately captures the dramatic import of the final motif. Bryan Magee asserts categorically that Wagner's music embodies his new Schopenhauerian frame of mind: "*The Ring* as we have it now does in fact have a Schopenhauerian ending, but one that is articulated solely in terms of music."[65] Scruton does the same: "One thing is certain . . . which is that, musically speaking, the cycle ends in a spirit of resigned acceptance rather than visionary hope, and that the renunciatory outlook of the completed cycle is one to which Wagner was brought by his own artistic intuition, and not by philosophy."[66] Warren Darcy is the only one to attempt to justify this reading in musical terms.[67] His analysis of the Immolation Scene fails to convince, however, because it assumes what it needs to prove. According to Darcy, the "imperious melodic descent of the Twilight motive" symbolizes not only the demise of the gods, which the logic of the text and musical structure supports, but also the entire "dissolution of the phenomenal world." In similar vein, Hagen's final cry of "*Zürück vom Ring*" reflects not just his own selfish ambition but "a thoroughly unrepentant humanity"; repetition of a theme in stepwise ascent represents not just transcendence, but "Schopenhauerian" transcendence. Darcy finally concludes that as the final statement of the Glorification theme yields to "harmonic security" it suggests "the wheel of eternal becoming is stilled at last."[68] Darcy does not adequately explain how the broad interpretive freedom he takes in construing these passages as expressions of Schopenhauerian pessimism is supported by the text or musical "con-text" of the *Ring*.

Darcy's analysis fails to account for the unique significance of the Glorification theme within the semantic framework of the score. It has frequently been argued that Schopenhauer's privileging of music as the royal road to the blind will had an impact on Wagner's compositional mindset when he returned to complete the score of the *Ring*, thereby upsetting the delicate balance of the branches of art that had originally defined the *Gesamtkunstwerk*.[69] Ironically, however, the leitmotif system, as original conceived, and as methodically pursued through to the last measures of the score, was as programmatic as music could be. Music as a complex pattern of symbolic units is designed to communicate not through the dumb intuition of the will, but through extra-musical association with ideas and phenomena.[70] As Dahlhaus explains, "[i]t is only when a musical motive has been explicitly associated with something on the stage, with the gold, the ring, Valhalla or the restraints placed on Wotan's actions by his contracts and obligations (music cannot, of itself, express objects of concepts), that it can become a motive of reminiscence or a leitmotiv."[71] Thus, "the linking of the 'melodic elements' [i.e., the leitmotifs] . . . is founded on the 'poetic intention' and not in abstract principles of musical form."[72] Wagner made the point clear in *Opera and Drama* when he maintained that the purpose of the leitmotiv system was to achieve the "highest unity of musical Form, – a Form which the musician has hitherto put together at his own caprice, but through the poet's aim can for the first time shape itself into a necessary, a truly unitarian, i.e. an *understandable* one" (OD 347). Maynard Solomon has eloquently expressed the tension inherent in such a program: "The programmatic in music can have multiple purposes. . . . But not least among its purposes is to place limits on music itself, to pretend that music is something other than what it is, that it is merely another language, that is reducible to the rational and verbal, to an expressible idea, image, or scenario."[73] In completing the final bars of *Götterdämmerung*, Wagner hewed close to his original design and did not reject the elaborate musical syntax he had adopted throughout the tetralogy.[74] In doing so, he chose a form of meaning that is directly susceptible to rational and associative analysis and whose very premise necessarily *invites* such analysis. Thus, insofar as *Götterdämmerung*'s musical ending continues to embrace the original Apollonian design for the *Ring*, it contradicts at its structural core any notion of a truly Schopenhauerian musical finale.

Among all the leitmotifs that have sounded over again throughout the cycle and which carry the weight of so much history with them, the Glorification theme has been heard only once before in *Die Walküre* – when Sieglinde learns that she is carrying a child in her womb. The theme is introduced at a dramatically critical and emotionally charged moment in the drama which Porges called "a scene of turmoil quite unprecedented in the theater."[75] Brünnhilde has violated Wotan's command by trying to save Siegmund, and as Act II of *Die Walküre* ends, Wotan exits in a fit of rage to track her down and punish her for her insubordination. The third act, set according to Wagner's meticulous instructions, "[o]n the summit of a rocky mountain" where "rocks of varying height form the parapet of the precipice," opens with a vivid orchestral prelude marked by sonorous brass fanfares, antiphonal exchanges of the jagged dotted-rhythm Valkyrie motif, and swooping cries of victory from the Valkyries flying in from the battlefield, all against an unrelenting backdrop of rising and falling string flourishes. This harsh mountain setting and vertiginous musical accompaniment combine to evoke the terror and astonishment of Edmund Burke's sublime as captured in a painting by Caspar David Friedrich.[76] Brünnhilde bursts onto the scene fleeing her father's wrath but still focused on her rash plan to secure Sieglinde's safety. *"Breathlessly"* she calls on her sisters to "[s]hield me, and help me in direst need!" (RN 172). Wotan fast approaches in a thunderous storm cloud. When "Wotan's terrifying voice is heard," Porges noted, "the excitement reaches its highest pitch."[77] In the little time left to her before Wotan arrives, she must find a way to save Sieglinde, a harried anxious fugitive consumed with despair and resolved to die. Wagner instructed that Sieglinde must initially sing "in deathly tones, as from the grave."[78] But into this frightful hurried moment of deep anxiety and foreboding Brünnhilde is able to introduce a ray of hope, a revelation that lifts Sieglinde out of despair and arms her with renewed inner strength. Sieglinde is to bear a child; not simply any child, but "the world's noblest hero." In a highly uncharacteristic moment of exuberance Sieglinde cries out in utter amazement and joy, *"O hehrstes Wunder! Herrliche Maid!"* to the tones of a new musical phrase. (See Figure 5.1.) Porges captured Wagner's intention when he noted the "terror and delight . . . expressed by Sieglinde after her initial violent shock."[79]

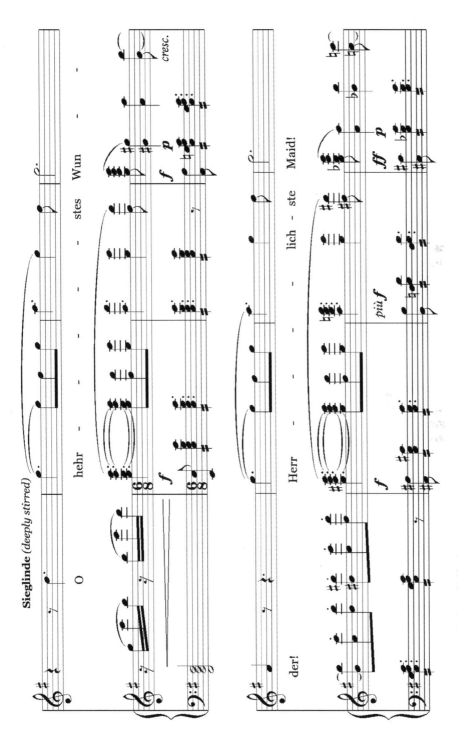

Figure 5.1 Annunciation of Life theme

This melodic effusion has been called the Glorification theme based on Wagner's comment to Cosima that it served as a "glorification of Brünnhilde" [*die Verherrlichung Brünnhildens*] when re-introduced at the end of the drama.[80] But Sieglinde does not simply extol Brünnhilde – "*herrliche Maid*" – but also exults in the glorious prospect – "*hehrstes Wunder*" – of her son's birth. Notably, the falling minor seventh that so defines the musical phrase falls on the word "*Wunder*" and not "*herrliche Maid.*" Wagner wanted Josephine Scheffzsky, the soprano singing Sieglinde at the first Bayreuth performance, to "put all the intensity of which she is capable" into this moment; "she must release a great flood of emotion, enraptured and enrapturing."[81]

The word "*Wunder*" had great significance for Wagner. A word that had traditionally been understood to mean "miracle" in the Christian sense – a false view of the world associated with the unnatural tarnhelm – was recast by Wagner in *Opera and Drama* to signify the dramatist's ability to forcefully communicate "life-energy" to the spectator – in a word, the sublime. According to Wagner, "this strengthening of a moment of action could only be achieved by lifting it above the ordinary human measure, through the poetic figment of the Wonder – in strict correspondence with human nature, albeit exalting and enhancing its faculties to a potency unreachable in ordinary life; – of the Wonder, which was not to stand beyond the bounds of Life, but to loom so large from out its very midst . . . ."[82] Wonder served as an essential technique of the artist to heighten the emotional impact of the music drama, not only by magnifying its features in sublime imagery and nobility of character and action but also by communicating the fundamental message of the myth, namely that nature existed "not as an aimfully constructed Mechanism" but rather "as a living Organism" that "was not a thing *created*, but herself the *forever becom-ing*" (OD 217). The experience of the sublime thus drove home the fundamental philosophical tenet that the world was not a static clockwork universe, as the Enlightenment philosophers had posited, but an organic force that was continually in a process of change and renewal – the very characteristic of nature that Kant and Leibniz had identified as the engine of progress. The wonder that nature evoked in man also recaptured a measure of the spiritual void that had been lost with the death of the gods. Carlyle had characterized the utilitarian clockwork vision of man as a mere dictionary definition: "To the eye of vulgar Logic . . . what is man? An omnivorous Biped that wears Breeches." But there were greater depths to man's experience. "Stands he not thereby in the centre of Immensities, in the conflux of Eternities?" (SR 51).[83] "Wonder," in Carlyle's Romantic worldview, was "the only reasonable temper for the denizen of so singular a Planet as ours. 'Wonder . . . is the basis of Worship'" (SR 53). Brünnhilde's revelation to Sieglinde is thus a key moment of "Wonder" in the *Ring*, whereby, in a moment of highest dramatic tension in the plot, Wagner delivers a musical, scenic, and spiritual vision of the sublime force of nature – its awesome, awe-inspiring, "forever-becoming" power to bring forth a new hero and drive the species to new heights of development.

This emotionally charged scene on the rocky precipice also marks a significant transformation in Brünnhilde's philosophical mindset. Whereas in Act II of

Die Walküre Brünnhilde was called upon to deliver an Annunciation of Death (*Todesverkündikung*) to Siegmund, in Act III she now brings an Annunciation of Life to Sieglinde. When confronting Siegmund, Brünnhilde had acted as agent of Wotan and the enforcer of a religion that ultimately favored the hero's magical immorality in Valhalla over life itself; she asked him in disbelief: "You're so little heedful of bliss everlasting?" (RN 162).[84] But later, when she embraces Sieg-mund's wife, in continued open rebellion and in contravention of Wotan's resolve to abandon the Wälsungs, she acts in a completely different guise as the prophet of a new living savior. As Porges noted, Brünnhilde's announcement evinces a "prophetic fervour."[85] This new Annunciation supersedes the prior ritual that cel-ebrated life after death in Valhalla. In *Opera and Drama*, Wagner heartily rejected the Christian mythos "that utters itself as dread and loathing of actual life, as flight before it, – as longing for death" (OD 159). In the same vein, Brünnhilde, hav-ing responded with compassion to Siegmund's love for Sieglinde, learns to move beyond the ritual of death associated with Wotan's rule and celebrates instead the glory of a new human life – a prophecy that anticipates her own future as well.

Wagner's handling of the musical motifs associated with these two incidents articulates just this intellectual trajectory. During the Annunciation of Death scene, Wagner intones the haunting Fate motif – three notes that cover a half-tone and minor third interval. (See Figure 5.2.) This motif immediately gives way to the Annunciation of Death theme which employs the same three notes in a mourn-ful rising phrase that is weighted down by falling half-steps and a descending bass line. (See Figure 5.3.)

In fashioning the musical phrase for the contrasting Annunciation of Life, Wag-ner started with the same three-note framework of the Fate motif. But for this new variation, Wagner took the minor triad of the Fate motif and reoriented it as the leading note and supertonic of a major scale. He then opened up the static three-note motivic cell by transforming it into a flowing forward-moving sentence with

Figure 5.2 Fate motif

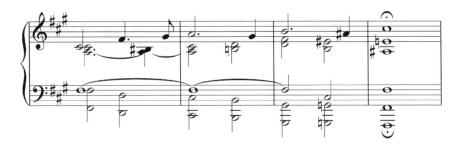

Figure 5.3 Annunciation of Death theme

a bright rising fourth to begin and a sweeping falling minor seventh to end.[86] (See Figure 5.1.) Through symphonic manipulation of the thematic material, Wagner signaled in the Annunciation of Life theme that the binding strictures of fate – Wotan's law – have been loosened, and human life and agency can now – in leaps of fourths and sevenths – move freely in time.[87] Taken together, then, these two themes, each derived from the Fate motif, map the historical and theological paradigm shift that Wagner was dramatizing – from the cramped Christian mindset obsessed with death and the myth of immortality of the soul to the new religion of man focused on the species life; from a theological world governed by an overarching providential determinism (fate) – or at the opposing end of the philosophical pendulum swing by an Enlightenment utilitarianism that reduced man to a mere machine – to an ever fluid and developing world of nature charged with potential and the promise of progress. (See Figure 5.4.)

Certain commentators have held that when the Annunciation of Life theme returns at the end of the music drama its meaning is necessarily ambiguous because it has not been utilized in multiple contexts.[88] To the contrary, the very fact that it has only been heard once in the entire *Ring* cycle means that its signification is not clouded or complicated by successive and overlapping associations.[89] And far from incidental, the Annunciation of Life theme arises as we have seen out of a dramatic and spiritual turning point laden with tension and expectation. Understood as a theme associated with the regenerative power of nature and a liberated spiritual mindset focused on life, not death, its reemergence in the last pages of the score takes on a new significance.

In the Immolation Scene, Wagner fully exploits the dichotomy between these two themes. As Brünnhilde turns her attention from Siegfried to the gods, the somber tones of the Annunciation of Death theme sound in the bass trumpet and trombones, and her ensuing address to Wotan is shaped throughout by the mournful contours of the Fate motif, punctuated with the menacing drumbeats of the *Todesverkündikung*. But when it comes time to contemplate her own immolation,

FATE MOTIF

ANNUNCIATION OF DEATH THEME

ANNUNCIATION OF LIFE THEME

Figure 5.4 Derivation of Annunciation of Life and Annunciation of Death themes from Fate motif

Brünnhilde adopts an entirely different *Affekt*. As she prepares to meet Siegfried in death, it is not fate which continues to toll the inexorable, but instead the agile Annunciation of Life motif which springs back into action. The theme reappears for the first time since *Die Walküre*, gushing forth in Brünnhilde's vocal line as the Violins I and II pass the phrase back and forth with ecstatic intensification. Then, after the destruction of Valhalla is complete, the curse is broken, and Hagen is consigned to the depths of the Rhine, the theme once again returns to crown the drama, now in a more serene guise, the note values lengthened, sounding high in the registers of the flutes and violins. A final peaceful reprise of the theme in D-flat Major brings the massive four-night music drama to a close. The contrast could not be more pointed. The gods are consigned to oblivion in the grim and antiquated ritual of death that had marked their reign. Brünnhilde, on the other hand, exalts in her own demise with a joyful new song that celebrates the miraculous cycle of life. Just as the theme first communicated the end of Sieglinde's despair, so at the end of the drama it marks Brünnhilde's own transition from grief to hope, from egocentric pain and resentment to an enlightened universalist historicist perspective – an evocation of her "Everlasting Yea." Brünnhilde is not crushed by a fate greater than she; she has become master of her own destiny and history's guide, willingly choosing the time and place of her death armed with the freedom of consciousness and the consciousness of freedom that emerge with the evolution of Spirit. The extended treatment of the Annunciation of Life theme in the final orchestral coda only serves to reinforce the import of the revolutionary message initially voiced by Brünnhilde.

Porges's notes of the first Bayreuth rehearsals lend further credence to this interpretation. There he recorded that it was "well known" that the Annunciation of Life theme, "banishing the terror of death, is employed at the close of *Götterdämmerung* as the song of redemption that overcomes the power of fate."[90] Feuerbach had taught that the means to banish the "terror of death" was to reject the Christian myth of the immortality of the soul – which merely addressed the fear with a false palliative – and instead draw comfort from the future of the species life. And Teufelsdröckh's spiritual renewal arises out of just such a confrontation with the fear of death. Reduced to utter misery, Teufelsdröckh wanders onto the Rue Saint Thomas de l'Enfer, a "dirty little" street somewhere in Paris, where he angrily confronts his despair: "Despicable biped! what is the sum-total of the worst that lies before thee? Death? Well, Death; . . . Let it come then, then; I will meet it and defy it!" Having thus rejected the "Everlasting No," Teufelsdröckh finds his way to the "Everlasting Yea" by embracing the new faith of the nineteenth century: the "Godlike that is in Man" (SR 128–9, 146). Wagner had taken these lessons to heart when he explained to Liszt his new secular theory of the "hereafter" as quoted in Chapter 3 and when he preached to Röckel in 1854 that "without the necessity of death, there is no possibility of life" and that one must "abandon oneself as a sentient human being to total reality . . . and to choose to live – and die – a life of happiness and suffering."[91] Wotan – so dependent as he is on Freia's apples – has not fully grasped this truth about death, and to the end remains gripped by anxiety and fear about his passing. As Deathridge and

Holloway note, the final reprise of the Valhalla motif in the orchestral coda tracks the form of Waltraute's earlier narrative, evoking the image of Wotan as "silent, disconsolate, and still clutching the shattered fragments of his spear, not unlike the melancholic rulers of the German baroque dramas."[92] Fate in Wotan's world had meant strict conformity with the god's rule of law and immortal life after death chosen by Wotan's Valkyries for those heroes worthy of the honor. But with the death of the god so goes the fallacy of "bliss everlasting" as well as the unbending dictates of Wotan's spear. The consolatory music that accompanies Brünnhilde's *"Ruhe, du Gott"* perfectly evokes Feuerbach's new enlightened perspective on death and life: "The sweet life of a new consolation . . . consoles you . . . With the angelic spirits of precious children,/The future masters of the present masters:/These call you away from life/And whisper you into a peaceful grave." As Wotan's daughter and heir to his world, "the future master of the present master," Brünnhilde "whispers" Wotan into a "peaceful grave." Moments later, inspired with Erda's wisdom about the inevitability of change and the truth of the species life, Brünnhilde chooses the time and place of her own death with composure and strength, invoking a theme that anticipates the human lives that will succeed her own and itself supersedes the Fate motif by redefining the modal significance of its static three-note phrase.[93] In Feuerbach's words, "the individual dies within history because he is only one member of the historical totality."[94]

The other motivic connection noted between the Faith in Siegfried theme and the Annunciation of Life theme (see Figure 2.2.) illuminates yet another dimension of Brünnhilde's spiritual evolution. Brünnhilde had embraced Siegfried on the rock with trust in his noble deeds. In the Immolation, she no longer addresses him with those tones – that theme's momentum and integrity were broken on Siegfried's betrayal. Instead, she now appropriates as her own Sieglinde's ecstatic effusion over the wonder of a new human life. As prescribed by Wagner in his theoretical treatise on the artwork of the future, Brünnhilde has moved from the love of the individual other – Siegfried – to the highest level – the love of all humanity. Although Brünnhilde's words are addressed to the memory of Siegfried, the Annunciation of Life music with its falling seventh continues to signal a prophetic vision – looking not back to Siegfried's exploits and love but forward to the next heroes who are to come. The anticipatory joy in Siegfried's individual potential has evolved into an all-encompassing faith in ever-renewing human life and humanity's time-enabled power to progress over successive generations.

Berry characterizes the final refrain as "enigmatic" and as "intrinsic, as insoluble, as that of the 'Tristan chord.'"[95] But harmonically there is nothing mysterious or unresolved about the phrase. The theme is bright, diatonic, and clear. After the dark tonalities and chromaticisms of the final act, and the obsessive recycling of the various leitmotifs that form the core of the score and continue to carry the heavy burden of the past, the listener is refreshed and relieved by a clarion theme that is virtually new to the ear and unencumbered by harmonic complexities. As Grey notes, it appears as a "beautiful surprise" that connotes "happiness."[96] Emerging from the dark foreboding of the world of Hagen and Alberich, the disarming simplicity of the Annunciation of Life theme recalls Beethoven's finale to the Ninth Symphony, as if to say: *"O Freunde, nicht diese Töne!"* Wagner's delight in the Ode to Joy provides yet another key to understanding how he intended his similarly fresh and simple melody to conclude his own monumental exploration of despair and consolation. For Wagner, the Ninth Symphony was "the human gospel of the art of the future" and a work closely associated in his mind with the revolution. His performance of the symphony at the Palm Sunday concert a week prior to the Dresden revolt was viewed by contemporaries as an "overture to the uprising."[97] Bakunin told Wagner on that same occasion that "we should risk our own lives to preserve" the symphony, even "if all music were to be lost in the coming world conflagration."[98] Beethoven's Ninth was also the work Wagner chose for the cornerstone-laying ceremony for the new Bayreuth opera house, which took place on May 22, 1872, while Wagner was completing the *Götterdämmerung* score.[99] In *Opera and Drama*, Wagner characterized "true Melody" as "the utterance of an inner organism" and found in Beethoven's symphonic work the genius to "restore this organism from its mechanical state, to vindicate its inner life, and to show it at its livingest in the very act of Bearing" (OD 108, 110). Beethoven's final theme, then, symbolized for Wagner the culmination of a philosophical journey, recapturing the truth about nature's regenerative power and restoring the sublime wonder to the universe that had been lost in the excessively rational and utilitarian ("mechanical") theories of the last century – just the philosophic vision associated with the concept of "Wonder" and precisely the message that Sieglinde's theme represents.[100]

The upheavals in European history during the period in time that Wagner was composing *Götterdämmerung*, and the nineteenth-century framework for understanding such events, provide further context for understanding the meaning of the final musical passage of the *Ring*. The year before Wagner turned to the musical finale of *Götterdämmerung*, his youthful dream of Paris in flames had actually come to pass. The German siege of Paris in the winter of 1870–71 had given way by Spring 1871 to the Commune. In the bloody civil war that ensued – driven by Adolphe Thiers, head of the provisional government, whose strategy had been rebuffed by Louis Philippe some 23 years earlier[101] – Paris was on fire, and by the end of May 1871 many of the city's great monuments, the Tuileries Palace, the venerable Hôtel de Ville, the Ministry of Finance on the Rue de Rivoli, the Palais de Justice, had been reduced to rubble. Photographic images of the torched city circulated quickly throughout Europe, and tourists flocked to Paris to experience the charred remains firsthand.[102] The French were at once horrified and fascinated to see their beloved city in the guise of picturesque ancient ruins. But consistent with the Hegelian structured mindset of the day, many saw this destruction as just deserts for the corrupt reign of Napoleon III, and the start of a new beginning. Georges Sand wrote to Gustave Flaubert on April 28, 1871:

> For me, the ignoble experiment that Paris is trying out or undergoing proves nothing against the laws of the eternal progression of men and things, and if I have a few mental principles, good or bad, that I've acquired, they have not been shaken or changed. Long ago I accepted patience the way one accepts the weather, the length of winter, old age, lack of success of all kinds. But I think that (sincere) partisans should change their formulas and come to see the emptiness of any *a priori* formula.[103]

This faith in the future – albeit in the face of the necessarily painful accommodation of principles to the harsh realities of life – would remain alive for the rest of the century. In 1892, Émile Zola published his fictional account of the Commune, *La Débâcle* (*The Debacle*). As the protagonist, Maurice, lies dying, he reflects on the carnage: "But this bloodbath was necessary, and it had to be of French blood, the abominable holocaust, the living sacrifice, in the midst of purifying fire. Henceforth, Calvary had been ascended to the most terrifying of agonies, the crucified nation was expiating its faults and was going to be reborn."[104] Hegel's Calvary of the Spirit continued to serve late into the century as the appropriate metaphor for the trials of historical progress.

Wagner was acutely aware of the political upheavals in France during this time period[105] and made reference to them in his preface to volumes iii and iv (1872) of his *Gesammelte Schriften und Dichtungen*, in which *Art and Revolution* appears. Quick to align the Commune with the anarchic disruptions unleashed by the French Revolution, Wagner quoted at length a passage from Carlyle's *Frederick the Great*, in which the Sage of Chelsea employed the imagery of fire and destruction to communicate the mechanism of historical regeneration. Describing the French Revolution as "that universal burning-up, as in hell-fire, of Human Shams," Carlyle had predicted that centuries would undoubtedly pass before the "Old is completely burnt out, and the New in any state of sightliness?" He therefore called upon the "Heroic Wise that are to come" to shorten the time of anarchy. Wagner noted that when he wrote *Art and Revolution* in 1849 he had been "in complete accord with the last words of this summons of the grey-headed historian," and by the end of the preface was not disavowing this summons in any way, but rather proposing that the German race was the best suited to supply those heroes (AR 23–9).[106]

A "whole political world in the throes of 'Spontaneous Combustion'" (AR 29) and Carlyle's Hegelian vision of history were thus clearly on Wagner's mind as he approached the final passage of the *Ring*. Taken together, the Immolation Scene and final musical coda dramatize in sound the nineteenth-century conceptual framework for understanding history. In *Sartor* Carlyle eloquently declared his faith in the forward march of history through a moving poetic evocation of the historical dialectic: "a process of devastation and waste . . . will effectually enough annihilate the past Forms of Society," but in the ruins and ashes of a defunct world, there is reason for hope: "in that Firewhirlwind, Creation and Destruction proceed together; ever as the ashes of the Old are blown out, do organic filaments of the New mysteriously spin themselves; and amid the rushing and the waving of the Whirlwind-Element, come tones of a melodious Deathsong, which end not but in tones of a more melodious Birthsong" (SR 178, 185).[107] It is certainly curious that in striving for an apt metaphor of transcendence in human spiritual evolution, Carlyle moved imperceptibly from his well-worn sartorial images of filaments and spinning to musical metaphors. In this way, he appears to have intuited Nietzsche's bold insight in *The Birth of Tragedy* that "it is only through the spirit of music that we can understand the joy involved in the annihilation of the individual."[108]

No other passage of nineteenth-century philosophy or literature, in my view, more effectively captures what I believe Wagner meant to convey in the musical coda to his epic music drama. In the final scene, motifs of "Creation and Destruction proceed together" as Erda's theme – the mirror-image rising and falling dotted-rhythm sequences alternatively evoking the power and the twilight of the gods – returns. When Brünnhilde seizes the torch, Loge's erratic flickering flame music ushers in the catastrophic "Firewhirlwind" that will consume Siegfried, Brünnhilde, the palace, and Valhalla. The flooding waters of the Rhine then complete the erasure of the Gibichung culture accompanied by a "rushing and waving" "Deathsong" – the Rhinemaiden's chant – that melodiously engulfs Hagen. But out of these catastrophic images and sounds of destruction, Wagner weaves a new melodic filament – "more melodious" still – that offers consolation and calm – a "Birthsong" – that signals ever-renewing life – in short, the Annunciation of Life theme.[109] The return of Sieglinde's and now Brünnhilde's theme announces the wonder of the Hegelian historical dialectic. Out of death and destruction inevitably comes a new life, and with that new life hope for the progress of the species.[110]

Let us not forget, moreover, that Wagner intended this final theme to sound alongside the visual icon – so immediately evocative of the recent political upheavals and at the same time a powerful symbol of nineteenth-century historicism – of the ruins of the Gibichung palace and the survivors standing in a mute state of awe. In this regard, just before the final iteration of the Annunciation of Life theme reaches its cadence in D-flat Major, Wagner employs the winds, brass, and violas to touch on the eerie subdominant minor (g-flat minor) that had earlier introduced Wotan's striving into Brünnhilde's farewell. Wagner reminds us that there will be more compromises and Calvaries along the road of human history. But this momentary *chiaroscuro* only throws into starker relief the harmonious resolution.[111] The Annunciation of Life theme unabashedly offers a frank and cheering turn to the score, hard won from the crucible of pain, sorrow, and destruction.[112] The consoling quality of the Annunciation of Life's final ethereal iterations high in the orchestral firmament aptly captures the ennobling truth of the historical process as proclaimed by Hegel – and acknowledged by Brünnhilde in her generous farewell to Wotan – that despite the travails of history "the wounds of the Spirit heal, and leave no scars behind."[113] The pain and violence of each historical epoch can be overcome and superseded. The Terror has been domesticated.

Other philosophers of the 1860s and 1870s had not let the disappointments of 1848 and the pessimist teachings of Schopenhauer stand in the way of a hope for the future. Alexander Herzen, for one, understood the core arbitrariness of life, but saw the very contingency of human existence as an opportunity to be exploited, privileging the role of reason in helping shape the future of man.[114] Like Herzen, Wagner appears to have found a way – through a historicist view of mankind – to thread the needle of despair; forced to acknowledge the naivete of the radical optimism of pre-revolutionary utopians he was at the same time ultimately able to hold at bay the rank pessimism of Schopenhauer. But even were we to concede no further evolution in Wagner's worldview once he had come to grips with the bracing tonic of Schopenhauer's philosophy, Wagner's own understanding of *music*'s role in culture had changed by the time he had come to compose the final bars of *Götterdämmerung*. In the *Beethoven* essay of 1870, completed just before he embarked on the music for the second act of *Götterdämmerung*, Wagner came to the conclusion that it was music's purpose to encompass the "world itself in which pain and joy, good and bad, alternate." Most significant, the artist's own *personal* "view of the world" had no place there.[115] Moreover, what Wagner also would have understood from Nietzsche was that tragic art drew its cathartic power from the tension between the Dionysian id and the Apollonian ego.[116] Thus, whatever personal Schopenhauerian doubts he may have continued to harbor about man's Sisyphean predicament, he need no longer shudder at the thought of completing his Grecian style masterwork with the optimism inherent in his original vision for the cycle. By celebrating the dream of historical renovation in the final bars of the opera while at the same time acknowledging the destructiveness of love and Brünnhilde's all too human grief, Wagner was engaging in the great Attic tradition and aspiring to the highest achievements of Aeschylus. In his *Beethoven* essay, Wagner praised the composer for accomplishing a similar vision of sublime transcendence in his Ninth Symphony, the final theme of which speaks to "someone waking with a shout of anguish from a terrible dream and near to madness after every quieting of his repeated despair," with the consoling words "*yet* man is good!"[117] The Ode to Joy's "childlike innocence" evoked the "inexpressible joy of Paradise regained."[118] Music drama thus could reach for the stars while at the same time acknowledging the abyss. And on the aesthetic plane, at the very least, Siegfried could return unblemished by man's encounter with history. Viewed from this somewhat more cynical critical perspective, the final theme of the *Ring* constitutes, to employ Schiller's terminology, a *sentimentalisch* attempt at the *naiv*.

Let us return to Shaw. As I have attempted to show, Wagner's vision of love was not saccharine at all but deeply conscious of the destructive forces inherent in erotic passion, and to the extent that he entertained any view of love as panacea it was to demonstrate its ultimate inadequacy – in Siegfried – as a philosophy of life and history. Rather than erotic love or compassion for fellow suffering, therefore, the final message in *Götterdämmerung* is about process, not substance – the regenerative force of nature as the mechanism of human development and transcendence. Thus while Shaw misread *Götterdämmerung* as melodrama, he accurately identified the main theme of the *Ring*. And Dahlhaus is correct that Wagner's first conception was his last –not because he returned to a love theme, but because he revived the Feuerbach ending's celebration of "*blühenden Lebens*" with a musical symbol heralding that promise of the future life of the species.

Notes

1 Magee, *Tristan Chord*, 128.
2 The versified Schopenhauer ending reads:

> Were I no more to fare to Valhalla's fortress, do you know whither I fare? I depart from the home of desire, I flee forever the home of delusion; the open gates of eternal becoming I close behind me now: to the holiest chosen land, free from desire and delusion, the goal of the world's migration, redeemed from reincarnation, the enlightened woman now goes. The blessed end of all things eternal, do you know how I

attained it? Grieving love's profoundest suffering opened my eyes for me: I saw the world end. --

(RN 363)

3 Letter to Röckel, 23 Aug. 1856, SL 357–8.
4 Hollinrake, *Nietzsche*, 65, 76. It was this version that introduced the titles "*Siegfried*" and "*Götterdämmerung*" in place of "*Der junge Siegfried*" and "*Siegfried's Tod.*"
5 Spencer, "*Zieh hin!,*" 111.
6 CT, i, 473 (4 Apr. 1872) (emphasis added).
7 Richard Wagner, *Gesammelte Schriften und Dichtungen*, vi, 256, as translated in Dahlhaus, *Richard Wagner's Music Dramas*, 140. Wagner introduced the Feuerbach verses in this way: "Although the poet had sententiously attempted in these lines to anticipate the drama's musical effect, it became clear to him in the course of the long interruptions which prevented him from setting the poem to music that that effect would be better realized by a different version of the last parting strophe, which he here similarly appends." As translated by Spencer in "*Zieh hin!,*" 119.
8 The story is further complicated by the subsequent publication history of the libretto. In 1873, Johann Jakob Weber, Wagner's publisher in Leipzig, who had produced the first public printing of the text of the *Ring* in 1863, came out with a second edition of the 1863 version which included the Feuerbach ending. Richard Wagner, *Der Ring des Nibelungen. Ein Bühnenfestspiel für drei Tage und einem Vorabend*, 2nd edn. (J.J. Weber 1873), 440–2. When Cosima received the book on May 26, 1873, she noted to her chagrin that it contained "all the old printing mistakes!!" CT, i, 640 (26 May 1873). It is not at all clear that she was referring to the Feuerbach lines, however. But when in 1876, B. Schott and Sons, publishers of the full score of the *Ring*, printed yet another edition of the libretto, they continued to retain the Feuerbach lines intact. Richard Wagner, *Der Ring des Nibelungen. Ein Bühnenfestspiel für drei Tage und einem Vorabend* (B. Schott's Söhne 1876), 84–6. Another printing in 1876 by Schott of just the *Götterdämmerung* text repeated the Feuerbach lines, but this time with a bracket indicating that "*diese Stelle ist nicht componirt*" ("this passage is not composed"). No mention, however, of the alternative Schopenhauer verses. Richard Wagner, *Götterdämmerung: Dritter Tag aus der Trilogie: Der Ring des Nibelungen* (Schott's Söhne 1876).
9 In this regard, Shaw's interpretive principle bears repeating: "These works must speak for themselves: if *The Ring* says one thing, and a letter written afterwards says that it said something else, *The Ring* must be taken to confute the letter just as conclusively as if the two had been written by different hands." Shaw, *The Perfect Wagnerite*, 101.
10 "Wagner's attitude to Schopenhauer . . . was one of imaginative, retrospective identification rather than of literal dependence." Roger Hollinrake, "Philosophical Outlook," in *The Wagner Compendium*, 145.
11 Schopenhauer, *The World as Will*, i, 379–80.
12 Porges, *Wagner Rehearsing the 'Ring,'* 144.
13 While Wagner was drafting the final musical passages of the *Ring* in April 1872, he commented to Cosima about "this great discovery" of fire "which at once places human beings on the level of the gods, which banishes the night; and how rightly and beautifully the Greeks had distilled it all in the legend of Prometheus." CT, i, 478 (19 Apr. 1872).
14 Berlin, *Political Ideas*, 320.
15 Roger Hollinrake, "Philosophical Outlook," in *The Wagner Compendium*, 145: "Nietzsche remarked of Siegfried that 'nothing could be more contrary to the spirit of Schopenhauer.'"
16 Schopenhauer, *The World as Will*, i, 398.
17 Berry, *Treacherous Bonds*, 259, 265, 268–9. Kitcher and Schacht recognize that Brünnhilde's actions contradict the notion of a Schopenhauerian abnegation and yet,

at the same time, advance a message of Schopenauerian futility in describing the opera as heralding the end of the world. Kitcher and Schacht, *Finding an Ending*, 180–4.

18 These facts undermine Berry's conclusion that Wotan "will truly *conquer* fear." Berry, *Treacherous Bonds*, 253. Spencer agrees that "the Wanderer of *Der junge Siegfried* is not a passive figure calmly awaiting his own annihilation, but a power-seeker anxious to avert that end." Spencer, *"Zieh hin!*," 102. Williams likewise notes that Wotan "has not accepted his decline philosophically. On the contrary, he is filled with terror of the end. He returned home from his defeat by Siegfried cowed and depressed, not serene and accepting his fate." Williams, *Wagner and the Romantic Hero*, 99.

19 Letter to Röckel, 25/26 Jan. 1854, SL 308 (emphasis added).

20 Berry, *Treacherous Bonds*, 246. As Scruton eloquently states it: "Wotan's bequest to Siegfried, therefore, is conceived and executed in such a way as to affirm Wotan's sovereignty in the very moment of renouncing it." Scruton, *The Ring of Truth*, 291.

21 Berry, *Treacherous Bonds*, 245.

22 *Id.*, 245

23 Scruton recognizes the spiritual importance of this moment when he writes, "And, from the mingled anxiety and weariness, he extracts the great affirmative theme, with which he bequeaths the world again – not to the son of Alberich this time, but to Siegfried, the free being who will act for himself alone." Scruton, *The Ring of Truth*, 208. Spencer suggests that Wotan's invocation of the World Inheritance theme is rendered ironic and delusional by the fact that the theme is "followed in the orchestra by the descending interval of Hagen's motif recalling the evil which is immanent in the world and which is independent of the fate of the gods." Spencer, *"Zieh hin!,"* 114. However, the appearance of this descending half-tone motif is merely a passing discordant grace note keyed to the textual reference to the "Nibelung's spite," in an extended passage, the entire tenor of which is one of great majesty and hope. Moreover, even if read as pointing to Hagen, the reference anticipates for the audience the future challenges to Wotan's vision, challenges that he personally cannot be aware of, since Hagen has not implemented his plot as yet. To the extent that there is any degree of delusion implied by Wagner's musical treatment, it is not about Wotan's belief in the future as such, but rather his misplaced reliance on Siegfried as the architect of that future. (By contrast, Berry hints that Wotan intuits Siegfried's inadequacy. Berry, *Treacherous Bonds*, 245–6.)

24 In October 1873, while speaking with Cosima about the "old Nordic sagas," Wagner remarked that "that insoluble riddle; resignation, the breaking of the will" represented the wisdom of the Norse god Odin – the mythic prototype for Wotan's character – as well as the "ethical theme of *Der Ring des Nibelungen*." CT, i, 682 (4 Oct. 1873). But when rehearsing the orchestra for the premiere of *Siegfried* in 1876 he told the players that the World Inheritance theme "must sound like the proclamation of a new religion" and that "the whole scene must be imbued by this revelation of spiritual renewal." According to Porges, the scene was designed to reflect a "sense of a boundless flow of feeling . . . the fusion of a movingly tragic act of heroic resignation with an exalted sense of the joy of life." Porges, *Wagner Rehearsing the 'Ring,'* 103–4. This paradoxical "fusion" linking Wotan's "resignation" to the "joy of life" can be read in two ways: (a) on the one hand as reflecting Wagner's own quixotic need to reconcile his Feuerbachian aims with his Schopenhauerian instincts, itself a Hegelian approach which renders a Hegelian sublation or synthesis; (b) on the other hand as a statement simply consistent with the concept of generational deference so fundamental to species consciousness and historical progress. Either way, this statement alongside the reference to "spiritual renewal" make clear that by the time he came to perform his *Ring* cycle, Wagner was not interpreting his work in terms of Schopenhauerian futility.

25 Darcy tries to explain away this key theatrical detail as an illusion: "these human figures no longer represent the Gibichung men and women, who have been swept away

with everything else; rather, they are now *a projection of the audience*, which has been, so to speak, sucked into the vortex of the drama to preside over the concluding scene of cosmic destruction." Darcy, "Metaphysics," 39 n. 59. This would make an interesting directorial choice, but is not convincing as textual interpretation.

26 The first stanza of the Feuerbach ending contains Brünnhilde's instruction to the survivors: "heed well what I tell you now!. . . . For when you've seen the Rhine's daughters return the ring to its depths,to the north then look through the night: when a sacred glow starts to gleam in the sky, then shall you know that you've witnessed Valhalla's end!" (RN 362).

27 Sarah Tiffin notes how for late eighteenth- and nineteenth-century viewers, ruins conjured the "awful astonishment" of the sublime. Tiffin, *South-East Asia in Ruins*, 46.

28 Hollinrake, *Nietzsche*, 58.

29 Thomas Mann, "The Sorrows and Grandeur of Richard Wagner," in *Pro and Contra Wagner*, 126. Treadwell warns that "Wagnerian notions of renunciation need to be treated with a lot of suspicion." Treadwell, *Interpreting Wagner*, 175. And yet, for all his stated skepticism, Treadwell persists in reading the *Ring* as a work that reinforces the circularity of mythic time rather than historical progress. Treadwell, *Interpreting Wagner*, 89.

30 *See* Margaret Nussbaum, "The Transfigurations of Intoxication: Nietzsche, Schopenhauer and Dionysus," *Arion*, Third Series, Vol. 1, No. 2 (Spring 1991), 91: noting "Christian and even Catholic origins of Schopenhauer's loathing for the will. . . . The body and its urges are bad, are both guilty and delusive; and nature as a whole, becoming as a whole, is infected with that guilt and those delusions."

31 Schopenhauer, *The World as Will*, i, 378–82.

32 Dahlhaus goes so far as to argue that with this theory, Wagner "eventually revoked the Schopenhauerian interpretation." Dahlhaus, *Richard Wagner's Music Dramas*, 104; see also Spencer, "*Zieh hin!*," 113: Wagner struggled "to achieve a compromise by positing the idea of love's being the means towards self-denial of the will." Adorno concludes that the *Ring* is full of ambivalence on this point: "the ascetic ideal is itself confused with sexual desire. The gratification of instinct and the negation of the Will-to-Life are jumbled together in a moment of rapture, in that 'laughing death' of Siegfried and Brünnhilde." Adorno, *In Search of Wagner*, 135.

33 The *Wagner-Werk-Verzeichnis* puts the date at January 4, 1872, but I have chosen to follow the date Cosima notes in her diary, as does Hollinrake. Hollinrake, *Nietzsche*, 64.

34 Letter to Anton Pusinelli, [13] Jan. 1870, SL 764.

35 Letter to Alwine Frommann, 1 Feb. 1871, SL 779–80.

36 Letter to Nietzsche, 23 Oct. 1872, SL 81.

37 Letter to Anton Pusinelli, [13] Jan. 1870, SL 765.

38 CT, i, 445 (3 Jan. 1872).

39 CT, i, 299, 320, 339 (24 Nov. 1870; 10 Jan. 1871; 20 Feb. 1871). In 1879, Wagner referred to Carlyle and Schopenhauer in the same breath as two individuals he would have like to have known had he been born ten years earlier. CT, ii, 291 (12 Apr. 1879).

40 Letter to Erwin Rhode, 28 Oct. 1872, SL 815.

41 Letter to Nietzsche, 4 Feb. 1870, SL 770–1.

42 See Magee, *Tristan Chord*, 296–301; Berry, "Politics of Music Drama," 670: noting the "largely unacknowledged debt Nietzsche owed to Wagner"; Berry, "Nietzsche," 27: Wagner is a "figure of crucial, positive importance in the development and formulation of Nietzsche's mature philosophy"; Georges Liebert, *Nietzsche and Music* (University of Chicago Press 2004) 40–4: It was in Tribschen, "through animated conversations with the composer, that *The Birth of Tragedy* took shape."

43 Kimberly Fairbrother Canton, "Redeeming the Rhinemaidens: A Reconsideration of their Dionysian and Apollonian Attributes," *The Wagner Journal*, Vol. 2, No. 2 (2008).

44 CT, i, 445 (3 Jan. 1872).

45 CT, i, 446 (4 Jan. 1872).

46 CT, i, 447 (6 Jan. 1872).

47 Letter to Nietzsche, Jan. 1872, SL 787–8.

48 *The Nietzsche-Wagner Correspondence*, ed. Elizabeth Foerster-Nietzsche, trans. Caroline V. Kerr (Liveright 1949), 99.

49 Letter to Nietzsche, 15 June 1872, SL 810: "carefully rereading"; Letter to Nietzsche, 23 Oct. 1872, SL 814: "I reread your book last summer: my wife devoured it again more recently."

50 See Nussbaum, 98, noting Nietzsche's "most fundamental break with Schopenhauer: Nietzsche's complete rejection of the normative ethics of pessimism, in favor of a view that urges us to take joy in life, in the body, in becoming"; Walter Kaufmann, "Translator's Introduction," to Nietzsche, *The Birth of Tragedy*, 11: "Nietzsche's very first book, *The Birth*, constitutes a declaration of independence from Schopenhauer. . . . From tragedy Nietzsche learns that one can affirm life as sublime, beautiful, and joyous in spite of all suffering and cruelty." Magee notes among the "leading ideas of Nietzsche's philosophy" "the elevation of life itself as the supreme value, and therefore of the will to power, the saying of Yes to life as the supreme principle of action . . . ; the achievement thereby of a higher stage in human development, that of the superman." Magee, *Tristan Chord*, 318.

51 Friedrich Nietzsche, "Attempt at a Self-Criticism," in *The Birth of Tragedy or: Hellenism and Pessimism*, trans. Walter Kaufmann (Vintage Books 1967), 24.

52 Nietzsche, *The Birth of Tragedy*, 59.

53 *Id.*, 104. Compare Carlyle's inaugural address at Edinburgh University in which he explicitly rejected "gloomy, austere, ascetic people, who have gone about as if this world were all a dismal prison-house! It has indeed got all the ugly things in it which I have been alluding to; but there is an eternal sky over it; and the blessed sunshine, the green of prophetic spring, and rich harvests coming – all this is in it too." Carlyle, "Inaugural Address at Edinburgh," as quoted in Morrow, *Thomas Carlyle*, 48.

54 Nietzsche, *The Birth of Tragedy*, 104.

55 *Id.*, 104.

56 *Id.*, 98. Compare with Hegel's injunction to his readers that when confronted with the "tediousness that this reflection of sadness [about world history] could produce in us," they should not "return to the selfishness of standing on a quiet shore where we can be secure in enjoying the distant sight of confusion and wreckage." Hegel, *History*, 24.

57 Nietzsche, *The Birth of Tragedy*, 123.

58 Roger Allen, "Introduction" to *Richard Wagner's Beethoven (1870): A New Translation* (Boydell 2014), 23–4: "ferment of ideas" generated by Nietzsche and Wagner.

59 Wagner, *Beethoven* (Allen, trans.), 185–7.

60 Liebert, *Nietzsche*, 48; Hollinrake, *Nietzsche*, 64.

61 Magee entirely discounts any Nietzschian influence on the *Ring*. Magee, *Tristan Chord*, 288, 290: "[C]hronology rules out the possibility of his having had any influence on the operas," but the historical chronology suggests otherwise. See, by contrast, Canton, "Redeeming the Rhinemaidens," 41–3; Liebert, *Nietzsche*, 48; Hollinrake, *Nietzsche*, 64.

62 *Nietzsche-Wagner Correspondence*, 99 (emphasis added).

63 Wagner, "What Boots this Knowledge," in *Religion and Art*, trans. W. Ashton Ellis, 257–63.

64 See, e.g., Dahlhaus, *Richard Wagner's Music Dramas*, 140–1: "rapturous love"; "Brünnhilde's love for Siegfried features as the alternative to Wotan's resignation and renunciation of the world and looks forward in hope to reconciliation in the future"; Geck, *Richard Wagner*, 308–9: motif described by Wagner as "glorification of Brünnhilde" reflecting her compassion and "self-sacrificial love"; Scruton, *The*

Ring of Truth, 294–5: "moments of love and gift," "deeds of sympathy and gratitude"; Windell, "Hegel, Feuerbach and Wagner's *Ring*," 57: "final serene measures" achieve "what Feuerbach had sought to convey in mere words: 'What faith, creed, folly separates, love unites'"; Corse, *Wagner and the New Consciousness*, 38: "The ending of the *Ring* means that Brünnhilde has made a mark for self-determination for herself and for Siegfried and has brought to the consciousness of society the need for love"; Williams, *Wagner and the Romantic Hero*, 101: Brünnhilde represents "compassion as a force that changes people and brings about a less destructive world" and "a utopia has come into view in our imagination if not in actuality"; Spencer, "*Zieh hin!*," 114: noting theme's reference to "Brünnhilde's act of self-sacrifice . . . an example of that sense of compassion which was as basic to Feuerbach's willful view of the world as it was to Schopenhauer's"; Berry, *Treacherous Bonds*, 262–4: rejecting both Adorno's and Dahlhaus's readings and identifying the final theme as representative of a Schopenhauerian *caritas*; Darcy, "Metaphysics," 34, 39–40: transcendence of the phenomenal world; Kitcher and Schacht, *Finding an Ending*, 180–3: Brünnhilde provides a "kind of resolution to Wotan's problem after all" through a new form of "*ecstatic loving*" – "the *Ring*'s version of the humanly divine, with its hallowing power"; "This theme certainly has to do with love; but what it evokes is the possibility that despite all, love can achieve a form of triumph, giving meaning and value to what would otherwise be blank and bitter defeat." Treadwell, for his part, pointedly refuses to assign a meaning to the final theme, asserting that "the appearance of the motif known optimistically as 'redemption' works more like a question than a statement, because we don't know what it is about." In the end he concludes that there is no future for the world of the *Ring*. Treadwell, *Interpreting Wagner*, 86–94. See also Tanner, *Wagner*, 179: theme is "consolatory and suggests a promise, though we can have no clear idea what it is a promise of." Shaw more bluntly concludes that "there is no dramatic logic whatever in the recurrence of this theme to express the transport in which Brynhild immolates herself." Shaw, *The Perfect Wagnerite*, 84.

65 Magee, *Tristan Chord*, 181.
66 Scruton, *Ring of Truth*, 47.
67 Darcy, "Metaphysics."
68 *Id.*, 25, 30, 39.
69 Magee, *Tristan Chord*, 181, 200–1, 262–3.
70 As Grey notes, the *leitmotifs* are a "means of making music speak or signify" creating a "compelling musical rhetoric to supplant the conventional designs of 'absolute' operatic melody Wagner had chosen to dismiss." Grey, "Leitmotif, Temporality, and Musical Design in the *Ring*," 88.
71 Dahlhaus, *Richard Wagner's Music Dramas*, 86.
72 Dahlhaus, *Richard Wagner's Music Dramas*, 108. Emslie defines the *leitmotifs* as "musical signatures" that "signal non-musical things." Emslie, *The Centrality of Love*, 59.
73 Maynard Solomon, "Beethoven's Ninth Symphony: The Sense of an Ending," *Critical Inquiry*, Vol. 17, No. 2 (1991), 298. Michael Steinberg reinforces the point in this way: "Music drama rationalizes and systematizes the transgressive energy of opera and the voice. Leitmotivic writing becomes composition by total administration." Steinberg, "Music Drama," 179.
74 Deathridge eloquently describes the "increasingly petrified landscape of Wagner's allegorical motifs." Deathridge, *Wagner*, 95.
75 Porges, *Wagner Rehearsing the 'Ring,'* 66.
76 In this way, by situating the Ride of the Valkyries as of a piece with the entire scene, an attempt by Wagner to capture the sense of the sublime scenically, musically, and dramatically, I endeavor to rescue this famous musical passage from the familiar view of it as "a gratingly raucous but shallow introduction to a splendidly dramatic act." Kitcher and Schacht, *Finding an Ending*, 192. While versifying *Die Walküre* in June

of 1852, Wagner told Liszt that he was longing to "go up into the Alps." The next month he did travel in the Bernese Alps where he "had an awesomely sublime view of the mountain ice, the snow and the glacier world." Letter to Liszt, 16 June 1852; Letter to Uhlig, 15 July 1852, SL 262–3.

77 Porges, *Wagner Rehearsing the 'Ring,'* 69. Porges further highlighted the dramatic tenor of the scene: "From this point the tension increases from moment to moment: In fear and trembling we anticipate what is going to happen." Porges, *Wagner Rehearsing the 'Ring,'* 67. The amount of time that Wagner spent in explaining this scene in his rehearsal for the Bayreuth festival attests to the importance he attributed to this dramatic encounter. Porges, *Wagner Rehearsing the 'Ring,'* 66–9.

78 Porges, *Wagner Rehearsing the 'Ring,'* 67.

79 Porges, *Wagner Rehearsing the 'Ring,'* 68.

80 Darcy, "Metaphysics," 8.

81 Porges, *Wagner Rehearsing the 'Ring,'* 68.

82 Wagner, *Opera and Drama*, 221.

83 See Gay, *Schnitzler's Century*, 170: noting the Romantic "crusade to re-enchant the world."

84 Wagner explained that "for a Valkyrie it was undreamed of that a man should reject the honour of being taken as a hero to Valhalla." Porges, *Wagner Rehearsing the 'Ring,'* 62.

85 Porges, *Wagner Rehearsing the 'Ring,'* 68.

86 Darcy, "Metaphysics," 25: "the Glorification theme may be heard as a transmutation of the Fate motive."

87 Robert Donington reads the connection between these two themes differently, noting in the Annunciation of Life theme the "strong reminiscence of the melodic outline of [the Fate motif] as if to recall that the transformation here suggested comes only when destiny has somehow not only been accepted, but accepted as part of the character concerned." Donington, *The Ring and Its Symbols*, 293. Thus Donington interprets the Annunciation of Life theme as an affirmation of fate's power rather than its antithesis. This interpretation depends on the listener perceiving the Fate motif as embedded as a kernel of reminiscence in the Annunciation of Life theme, which is difficult if not impossible to hear. Donington's interpretation thus discounts the radically different aural and emotional effect of these two musical phrases. I view the Fate motif, rather, as the motivic outline for a wholly new melodic and harmonic treatment – a symphonic evolution rather than a pure preservation.

88 Grey, "Leitmotif, Temporality, and Musical Design in the *Ring*," 114; Treadwell, *Interpreting Wagner*, 87: "the fact that it only appears twice means that it cannot have a strong semiotic value."

89 I agree therefore with Borchmeyer, who avers that the two iterations of the theme reflect "an economy designed to ensure that there is no doubt as to its meaning." Borchmeyer, *Drama and the World of Richard Wagner*, 236.

90 Porges, *Wagner Rehearsing the 'Ring,'* 69n.

91 Letter to Röckel, 25/26 Jan. 1854, SL 302–3.

92 Deathridge, *Wagner*, 96; Robin Holloway, "Motif, Memory and Meaning in *Twilight of the Gods*," in *On Music: Essays and Diversions* (Claridge 2003), 39.

93

> This *dying*, with the yearning after it, is the sole true content of the Art which issued from the Christian myth; it utters itself as dread and loathing of actual life, as flight before it, – as longing for death. For the Greek, Death counted not merely as a natural, but also as an ethical necessity; *yet only as the counterpart of Life*, which *in itself* was the real object of all his viewings, including those of Art. The very actuality and instinctive necessity of Life, determined of themselves the

tragic death; which in itself was nothing else but the rounding of a life fulfilled by evolution of the fullest individuality. To the Christian, however, Death was *in itself* the object.

(OD 159–60)

94 Feuerbach, *Thoughts on Immortality*, 129.
95 Berry, *Treacherous Bonds*, 271.
96 Grey, "Leitmotif, Temporality, and Musical Design in the *Ring*," 114.
97 Köhler, *Wagner*, 219–20, 233.
98 Wagner, *My Life*, 384.
99 Preparations for the performance took place all throughout the period that Wagner was composing the third act of *Götterdämmerung*. CT, i, 448–88. In January of 1872, Cosima wrote to Nietzsche that "in the evening we read Schopenhauer aloud, in the afternoon we read the 'Birth of Tragedy' separately, and during dinner discuss the performance of the Ninth Symphony which is to be given on the evening of the cornerstone laying." *Nietzsche-Wagner Correspondence*, 97. Wagner was very particular about how he wanted the baritone to phrase his entry in the Fourth Movement, Cosima noting in her diary, "Betz [the baritone] has not yet quite achieved the accents R. wants for '*Freunde, nicht diese Töne.*'" CT, i, 487 (21 May 1872).
100 Later, in the *Beethoven* essay of 1870, Wagner would be even more explicit about the virtues of the *Ode to Joy*: "If we survey the historical progress which music made through Beethoven, we can define it succinctly as the acquisition of a capacity which, it was previously thought, had to be denied to music: it has transcended the aesthetically beautiful and entered the sphere of the sublime." *Beethoven* (Allen, trans.), 135.
101 Rapport, *1848, Year of Revolution*, 54.
102 Peter Brooks, *Flaubert in the Ruins of Paris: The Story of a Friendship, a Novel, and a Terrible Year* (Basic Books 2017), 71–82.
103 As quoted in *Id.*, 44.
104 As quoted in Brooks, *Flaubert in the Ruins of Paris*, 50.
105 Spencer and Millington, "Introductory Essay 1864–1872," SL 598.
106 Geck notes a sense of "triumph and frenzied ecstasy" in the finale of the *Ring* as an "echo of the mood of euphoria" accompanying the establishment of the new German Reich. Geck, *Richard Wagner*, 310–12. But see Deathridge, *Wagner*, 71: *Götterdämmerung* is "not the work of someone whose head had been turned by the outcome of the Franco-Prussian war."
107 Carlyle captured the same image in *The French Revolution*: "Behold the World-Phoenix, in fire-consummation and fire-creation: wide are her fanning wings; loud is her death-melody, of battle-thunders and falling towns; skyward lashes the funeral flame, enveloping all things: it is the Death-Birth of a World!" Carlyle, *French Revolution*, 179. Herzen, as we have already noted, characterized the revolution as "birth pangs" by which "history, in its prodigal way, will begin a new pregnancy." Kelly, *Discovery of Chance*, 363.
108 Nietzsche, *The Birth of Tragedy*, 104.
109 The very term "leitmotif" derives from Wolzogen's *Leitfaden* ("guiding *threads*"), commentaries he prepared on the *Ring* themes for the original Bayreuth production. Grey, "Leitmotif, Temporality, and Musical Design in the *Ring*," 87.
110 Scruton comes closest to identifying the theme's meaning when he notes on the last page of his book, almost as an afterthought: "But yet more important, the concluding music of the cycle seems to say, is the love for the unborn, for what is yet to be." Scruton, *The Ring of Truth*, 308. Borchmeyer also remarks briefly on the theme's association with birth, but gives it a mythic spin as a theme of cyclical "birth and rebirth." Borchmeyer, *Drama and the World of Richard Wagner*, 236. In similar vein, Donington notes how the *Ring* ends with the "archetypal imagery of the purifying

fire," but regards this imagery as a "basic theme of mythology," not of progressive historical evolution. Donington, *The Ring and Its Symbols*, 254.

111 See Badiou, *Wagner*, 59: closure "all the more conclusive" when delayed.

112 As Maynard Solomon writes of Beethoven's Ninth, "Elysium is gained only by over-coming terrifying obstacles." In late Beethoven generally, he explains, "happy end-ings are not abandoned but made more valuable, because they emerge from labyrinths, crucibles and battlefields." Solomon, "Beethoven's Ninth Symphony," 295–6. Porges recalled Wagner's "unforgettable rendering of the Ninth Symphony" at the cornerstone-laying ceremony and the "the way he conducted the shattering trumpet fanfare of the introduction to the finale." Porges, *Wagner Rehearsing the 'Ring,'* 85.

113 Hegel, *Phenomenology*, 407 (§669).

114 Kelly, *Discovery of Chance*, 447–8; Isaiah Berlin, "Alexander Herzen," in *Russian Thinkers*, eds. Henry Hardy and Aileen Kelly (Penguin Books 2013), 230: noting the "curious combination of idealism and scepticism" in Herzen's thought.

115 Wagner, *Beethoven* (Allen, trans.), 131.

116 "Now it is as if the Olympian magic mountain had opened before us and revealed its roots to us. The Greek knew and felt the terror and horror of existence. That he might endure this terror at all, he had to interpose between himself and life the radiant dream-birth of the Olympians. . . . Here, when the danger to his will is greatest, *art* approaches as a saving sorceress, expert at healing." Nietzsche, *The Birth of Tragedy*, 42, 60.

117 Wagner, *Beethoven* (Allen, trans.), 133.

118 *Id.*, 135.

6   Myth versus history

It would not do justice to the complexity of the *Ring* not to acknowledge that this theme of historical evolution, Brünnhilde's faith in the "roaring billows of Time," raises some challenging questions about Siegfried. As observed earlier, Brünnhilde is the true change agent of the *Ring*. It is her knowledge, insight, and sacrifice which seal the fate of the gods and hold the promise for future generations. She is the revolution, while Siegfried is only a possible future that the revolution is intended to bring about. But in working his way back into *Der junge Siegfried* Wagner deeply complicated this message of *Götterdämmerung*. For there is a striking disjunction between the character of Siegfried in the eponymous opera and in *Götterdämmerung* that cannot be explained – as others have done – as a revelation of a fault of character or failure of the revolution. In *Götterdämmerung*, as this book has argued, Siegfried plays the role of the naive child of nature. In *Siegfried*, Wagner develops this character, but then introduces elements of a mythic heroism that equip Siegfried with the strength to defy the forces of evil. Wagner even grants his hero some of the powers necessary to defeat the corruptions of Hagen's world. In a telling moment, touched by the blood of the dragon Fafner, Siegfried suddenly has the capacity to understand the underlying meaning and intent of Mime's lying double-speak. Siegfried thus gains the consciousness to pierce the veil of civilization's hypocrisy and safely rejects the potion proffered by the dwarf. It is this and other elements of epic heroism – not least his shattering of Wotan's spear – that make Siegfried such an appealing candidate for the role of the revolutionary. But his gifts of action and insight are short-lived; once he enters the world of the Gibichungs his mythical strengths are largely rendered powerless, and he accepts without a second thought the poisoned draught offered by Gutrune.[1] In *Götterdämmerung*, Nothung, once a radical tool of power, now serves impotently as a barrier enforcing customary morality and etiquette. However glorious in the world of pre-historic myth the hero does not have the tools to survive in the cruel reality of civilization.

Approaching the question from a dramatic perspective, Geck tries to smooth over the transition by arguing that the "youthful and carefree fairy-tale hero . . . is progressively turned into a tragic hero driven to his death in the tradition of classical tragedy."[2] The fundamental assumption here is that there is a consistent relationship between the Siegfried who discovers Brünnhilde in *Siegfried* and the

Siegfried who leaves her in the prologue of *Götterdämmerung*. But Wagner provides little basis to align the two Siegfrieds, and Geck's assertion that the carefree hero is "progressively" turned into a tragic figure assumes a continuity that simply is not there. In fact, there is no progression at all. Siegfried accepts Hagen's potion, and the poison acts immediately and conclusively. There is no gradual mental decline as we witness in Othello, or in Wotan for that matter, a soul fighting against itself. The transformation is immediate and absolute.[3]

Alternatively, commentators have tried to explain this change by presuming an evolution in Wagner's perception of his hero over the long span of years that separated the creation and completion of the *Ring*.[4] But this argument also fails to convince: Wagner's own marginal edits to *Siegfried's Tod* indicate that within weeks of completing the first draft in November 1848, he was already rethinking the fate of the gods and Siegfried's role as the god's redeemer.[5] By the time he completed *Der junge Siegfried* in June of 1851, his theory of his character as a man of nature who would ultimately be crushed by civilization had taken shape – as *A Communication to My Friends* written immediately thereafter attests. And finally, in the verse draft of the tetralogy as completed in December 1852 Wotan's reign is conclusively eradicated and Siegfried's death passes without any redemption specifically attached to it. Thus, well before Wagner's encounter with Schopenhauer and his composition of the score, Siegfried's role in *Götterdämmerung* as natural naif and victim of history had been fixed.

We must be careful, therefore, to distinguish between the two modalities of Siegfried's persona, natural man and epic hero, and in the end may have to accept the fact that they live uncomfortably side by side, to borrow a phrase from Berry, "in unresolved friction."[6] But the dichotomy can perhaps be explained in terms of the conflict between myth and history.

In dramatizing the heroic tale of Siegfried in *Der junge Siegfried*, Wagner was tapping into a contemporary need for myth and hero worship. At the dawn of the nineteenth century Friedrich Schlegel in his *Gespräch über die Poesie* (*Dialogue on Poetry*; 1800) had called for a new mythology. Decades later, in *The Birth of Tragedy*, Nietzsche made a similar diagnosis of the emptiness of contemporary life. "And now the mythless man stands eternally hungry, surrounded by all past ages, and digs and grubs for roots, even if he has to dig for them among the remotest antiquities. The tremendous historical need of our unsatisfied modern culture, the assembling around one of countless other cultures, the consuming desire for knowledge – what does all this point to, if not to the loss of myth, the loss of the mythical home, the mythical maternal womb?"[7] In the 1830s Carlyle had recognized that while the philosopher could readily debunk and dismantle the belief frameworks of the past, it was not so easy to find new principles to live by. Apostrophizing Voltaire he observed, "Sufficiently hast thou demonstrated this proposition, considerable or otherwise: That the Mythus of the Christian Religion looks not in the eighteenth century as it did in the eighth. . . . Wilt thou help us to embody the divine Spirit of that Religion in a new Mythus, in a new vehicle and vesture, that our Souls, otherwise too like perishing, may live?" But Voltaire was apparently silent on the subject. "What!

Thou has no faculty in that kind? Only a torch for burning, no hammer for build-ing?" (SR 147). In the aftermath of the death of God, man needed a new set of myths to guide him and comfort him.

In place of God, many in the nineteenth century found the hero as an object of reverence.[8] The quintessential articulation of this new faith is to be found in Thomas Carlyle's lectures *On Heroes, Hero-Worship, and the Heroic in History* in which he extolled the qualities of a hero: "a flowing light-fountain . . . of native original insight, of manhood and heroic nobleness."[9] By celebrating the best qualities of humanity in extraordinary prototypes, mankind as a whole could find some clear footing and direction in a world become devoid of certainties.[10] As Carlyle opined in his opening lecture: "One comfort is, that Great Men, taken up in any way, are profitable company. We cannot look, however imperfectly, upon a great man, without gaining something by him."[11] While Shakespeare and Cromwell may have sufficed as models for an English audience, in Germany it was the *Nibelungenlied* that took hold of the Teutonic imagination, and Siegfried became a new nineteenth-century model of German heroism.[12]

After *Lohengrin*, the *Nibelungenlied* became the inspiration for Wagner's new operatic endeavor. At the same time, however, he was also contemplating dramas on other heroic figures, Achilles, Jesus, and then Friedrich Barbarossa.[13] While a true historical figure, Barbarossa had also acquired mythic stature in German folklore as the savior who would return one day in the future to restore greatness to Germany.[14] In short, like Jesus, he was promised a second coming. As Barry Millington has noted, "Fundamental to all these abandoned projects is the notion of a solar hero, a sun god who will bring redemption to the world."[15] Siegfried ultimately fit the requirements for Wagner's new drama of heroic redemption, and consistent with his other contemplated projects Wagner originally conceived of Siegfried as a kind of Christ figure, dying to purge the sins of the world and return the gods to an unblemished state of rule. Wagner's mytho-historical essay on *Die Wibelungen: Weltgeschichte aus der Saga* (*The Wibelungen: World-History as told in Saga*; 1848–49) makes this clear: "In the German Folk survives the oldest lawful race of Kings in all the world: it issues from a son of God, called by his nearest kinsmen *Siegfried*, but *Christ* by the remaining nations of the earth; for the welfare of his race, and the peoples of the earth derived therefrom, he wrought a deed most glorious, and for that deed's sake suffered death."[16]

Such traditional forms of mythic heroism with their promise of eternal return, however, were at odds with the whole notion of historical progress and the nature-driven mechanics of eternal change which commanded the European worldview of the time. As Mircea Eliade has explained, the tropes of myth and history are in conflict with each other. "Insofar as an act . . . acquires a certain reality through the repetition of certain paradigmatic gestures, and acquires it through that alone, there is an implicit abolition of profane time, of duration, of 'history.'"[17] Myth reinforces repetitive patterns and archetypes.[18] History, on the other hand, feeds on time and creative change. The Young Hegelians understood this. Feuerbach, for one, had made clear that the myth of Christ signaled the death knell of history itself: "The incarnation of the species with all its plenitude into *one* individuality would be an absolute miracle, a violent suspension of all the laws and principles of reality; it would, indeed, be the *end of the world. . . . Incarnation* and *history* are absolutely incompatible."[19]

In the end, as the Feuerbach ending reveals, Wagner chose to redeem the world of the *Ring*, not by inviting divine intervention, but by embracing the march of history. Through Wagner's rejection of his projects on Jesus, Barbarossa, and Siegfried as redeemers, we can infer that he came to realize that these myths of eternal return were not the metaphysical answer to life and did not satisfy the need of the revolution – in fact, to the contrary, they were stale constructs of a discredited mythic program. Historical evolution was what the nineteenth century demanded, not comforting cyclicality and absolution. And so Siegfried quickly evolved from a quasi-Christ figure saving man (and God) from sin in a symbolic sacrificial death into the noble man of nature who, too impractical for the contemporary culture of *macht politik*, must die and cede place to the true modern hero of the nineteenth century – the world-historical individual who achieves the power through both the joy and the sorrow of love to direct the course of history, not remain its object. Brünnhilde's form of world-historical activism by its very nature calls into question the power of myth. Thus, even though Wagner rejected historical subject matter as an inappropriate starting point for the drama of the future, and instead embraced ancient Nordic mythology as his thematic blueprint, he proceeded not to restore a historical myth but to create a new myth about history.[20]

Siegfried's fairytale heroism conforms to the mythic framework, not the historical. Thus, as Wagner moved away from divine redemption as the core of his music drama of the future, he evidently thought it important to show how that model must be superseded, and subtly undermined the paradigm of the epic hero.[21] But this more jaundiced view of Siegfried's role, if you will, emerged not late in the *Ring*'s evolution but quite early in its formulation. This critical stance towards Siegfried as epic hero is integral to the original formulation of the tetralogy, and not a later gloss colored by Schopenhauerian pessimism and political capitulation.

If we take seriously Wagner's key dramatic point that it is Brünnhilde, not Siegfried, who grapples with the loss of faith and is the one left "god-forsaken," then Siegfried's accomplishments take on a very different hue. If Brünnhilde is the first to consciously recognize the impotence of the gods and break free from their rule, then everything that has come before – including Siegfried's great deeds – must be read as part and parcel of a moribund theology. And, indeed, throughout *Siegfried* there is an aspect of Siegfried's role that belies his freedom. As Simon Williams has pointed out, in reforging Nothung, Siegfried is still bound by history. But his smithy work is more than that: Siegfried is actively fulfilling the great plan of Wotan and proceeding only within the framework that Wotan has created. In other words, he is not thinking outside the box the god has constructed. Indeed, his deeds are fully anticipated by Brünnhilde even before he is born.[22] As Wotan tells her before putting her to sleep, "one man alone shall woo the bride, one freer than I, the god!" (RN 190). Geck recognizes that the "hero who forces his way through the fire to Brünnhilde's rock seems to be drawn by unseen strings or at the very least to be driven by a higher calling."[23] Siegfried finds his heroic achievements only by direction from others.[24] Mime leads him to Fafner's cave and prompts him to kill the beast; the song bird directs Siegfried to Brünnhilde's rock. As Siegfried frankly admits to Wotan: "a forest songbird directed me: it gave me good advice" (RN 259). Siegfried is acting along a prescribed plan – an unwitting subject of fate (but not history). Curiously, Wagner did not originally contemplate a confrontation between Siegfried and Wotan, and it was only at the very end of the drafting process in late 1852 that he added the encounter between grandson and grandfather and the consequent shattering of the spear.[25] But even this added scene, Siegfried's "defeat" of Wotan, does not amount to much; it is good theater, but in the final analysis a shadow play directed by Wotan. Wotan has already resolved to defer to Siegfried and actively chooses the engagement with the hero – which, as noted, is not necessary to the covenant Wotan made with Brünnhilde. The shattering of Wotan's spear thus does not advance the drama in any significant way but simply serves as a self-fulfilling prophecy to the god of his pre-determined withdrawal. In contrast to many other moments in the drama, including the immediately preceding encounter between Wotan and Erda, Wagner wanted this scene to be performed "without any passion."[26] Moreover, Siegfried's iconoclastic act does not conclusively do away with Wotan or his will. The god still continues to imagine a way out of his predicament by contemplating a return of the ring to the Rhinemaidens; Waltraute, secretly acting on his wish – as Brünnhilde had once done – pleads with Brünnhilde for compassion. In the end, therefore, Siegfried, like his father before him, continues throughout the third opera to function as an instrument of Wotan's divine plan, and his heroism, for what it is worth, appears to derive its relevance and power from a theologically structured world. Consistent with this interpretation, when Siegfried enters the cynical real world of *Götterdämmerung* he is truly off script and completely exposed. Without the divine infrastructure to guide him, he emphatically fails.

This perspective on Siegfried's heroism makes absolute sense when read in light of the common nineteenth-century understanding of Germany's unique cultural and historical destiny. Heine boldly took on advocates of revolutionary disruption in defending the more intellectual qualities of the German spirit: "Take note of this, you proud men of deeds. You are nothing but the unconscious servants of those men of thought, who, often in modest silence, have plotted out all of your doings in advance. Maximilien Robespierre was nothing but the hand of Jean-Jacques Rousseau."[27] In these words we hear a curious pre-echo of Wagner's plan for the *Ring*. Siegfried, the "proud man of deeds," is nothing but the instrument of Wotan's plan. The revolution belongs to Brünnhilde – Wagner's new Athena – who true to the unique German historical destiny directs the future of mankind through thought and wisdom. Wagner hinted at this when he closed his encomium to Beethoven with the brave assertion – notable in light of the patriotic militarism current among Germans of the time – that "the world's benefactor outranks the world's conqueror!"[28]

It is therefore left to Brünnhilde to enact the death of the gods. But by actively destroying the gods, Brünnhilde also destroys the mythological framework that imbues them with meaning – and that includes Siegfried's form of epic heroism. She engages in a creative act of history that breaks the mold that had defined human existence until then. Carlyle recognized that great men – and in Wagner's case great women – serve not only as noble paradigms, but also as catalysts for change: "I liken common languid Times, with their unbelief, distress, perplexity, with their languid doubting characters and embarrassed circumstances, impotently crumbling down into ever worse distress towards final ruin; – all this I liken to dry dead fuel, waiting for the lightning out of Heaven that shall kindle it. The great man . . . is the lightning."[29] The Siegfried who so appeals to us, wielding the sword, killing the dragon, and saving the maiden, is ultimately a fantasy, an older mythical formulation, that must fade away along with the gods.[30]

When Siegfried dies in the third act of *Götterdämmerung*, he has progressed no farther than he did at the end of the previous opera. After the hunt, Siegfried replays the events of his life. Wagner wanted one passage of his tale to "sound 'as though from another world.'"[31] Then Hagen administers the antidote, and Siegfried remembers his encounter with Brünnhilde on the rock. Siegfried's last breaths are drawn to the music of Brünnhilde's awakening as he recalls his first kiss ("to die upon a kiss"; "*un bacio*"!). Thus, even after being liberated from the potion's effect, Siegfried is stuck in the cycle of the eternal return, constantly replaying his glorious life story which culminates in the perfect love but never moves forward.[32] Some read the reprise of the Awakening theme as a sign of a new consciousness emerging in Siegfried.[33] And indeed as Simon Williams perceptively observes, his newfound capacity for storytelling hints at an emergent form of historical consciousness.[34] But in the end, Siegfried's story remains the fairytale; he still has no understanding of what has taken place in the course of *Götterdämmerung*, and his ecstatic vision simply transforms an all-too-brief erotic moment of fulfillment into an archetype of everlasting bliss; the epic hero has become the classic romantic tenor invoking love as panacea.[35] Moreover, the musical motif that accompanies his final vision recalls Brünnhilde's first awakening as a human being, not the older and wiser Brünnhilde who has by that time moved well beyond her first state of mind. To the extent that the return of the Awakening theme can be interpreted not simply as a reminiscence but reflecting the emergence of some deeper insight, it is not Siegfried's, but more logically Brünnhilde's second awakening, her transcendental "aha" moment taking place simultaneously on the moonlit banks of the Rhine. Indeed, Siegfried's final words are directed to a newly enlightened Brünnhilde: "Ah! Those eyes – now open for ever!" When Brünnhilde herself returns to the stage she will not sing "as from another world," but bring tidings of a new world.

James Treadwell, among others, insists that the *Ring* reinforces a mythic view of the world as cyclical and non-progressive. "The cyclical motion governing the *Ring* does indeed turn away from the promises of futurity which are so regularly raised in the course of the tetralogy."[36] For Treadwell, the curse motif is "a musical sign of . . . fatefulness," "bringing a kind of death . . . to the fabric of time itself."[37] The dramatic structure of the *Ring* certainly highlights this thesis, as the characters are condemned to repeat the errors of the past, in archetypal reenactments of their mythic fates. Thus, Siegfried violently wrests the ring from Brünnhilde, as Wotan had done from Alberich, and Hagen kills his brother Gunther for exclusive possession of the ring, just as Fafner had done. But the critical dramatic fact must be acknowledged that the curse is broken at the end of the opera, ending these perpetual cycles of mythological time and ushering in a new era of history. Treadwell reads the descent of Erda into eternal sleep and the breaking of the Norns' rope as symbolizing the end of the world. The breaking of the rope is not representative of the "downfall of the existing order of things," but rather, "the rupture of the line leading from present to future, the disappearance of futurity that is so powerful a theme in Wagner's 'revolutionary writings.'"[38] At the same time, however, Treadwell views the Norns as themselves defining the circularity of the *Ring*: "the Norns' scene makes redundant the whole of the action of *Götterdämmerung*, since the ultimate end happens at the opera's beginning." If the Norns and their power of prophecy represent the dominance of mythic fate and the futility of human existence, then how can the breaking of their rope mean the same thing? What could it mean if not the freeing of man from the constraints of myth and fate?[39] Contrary to Treadwell's view, Wagner did not consider the ancient runic wisdom of the gods as the last word on the meaning of the world. Instead, humans remain to write the history of the future. The Norns' rule passes away with the gods – time now belongs in the hands of passionate world-historical heroes who will shape history to fulfill the species' need. And we have already explored how Wagner brings this transition to life through the transformation of the Fate motif into the Annunciation of Life theme. By reconstituting the Fate motif, Wagner musically articulates the substitution of human history for the confining, deterministic strictures of mythic time. And far from predicting the future and thus rendering the drama redundant, as Treadwell asserts, the Third Norn actually gets the facts wrong. As she sings, "[t]he shattered spear's sharp-pointed splinters Wotan will one day bury deep in the fire-god's breast: a ravening fire will then flame forth, which the god will hurl on the world- ash's heaped-up logs" (RN 283). But Wotan does not have the courage, in the end, to bring about his own end. It is left to Brünnhilde to enact his demise by summoning the "ravening fire." Thus the Norns continue to preserve a worldview that is still dominated by the god and his aims and fail to account for the intervening agency of human consciousness and will – symbolized by the broken rope of fate.[40]

Borchmeyer's, and others', reading of the ending of the *Ring* as symbolizing a mythological cycle of perpetual birth and rebirth likewise misses the import of Wagner's historicist mindset and intentions.[41] For Wagner, as seen in his writings and his published texts of the *Ring* in 1853 and 1863, the progress of knowledge was key to the historical development of the species. Wagner intended for Brünnhilde's hoard of wisdom to be bequeathed to the next generations. Wiping the slate clean, as Wagner himself noted, would be a "sorry trick." The claim that the world is restored at the end of the *Ring* to its "first, paradisiacal state" or "a primordial state of natural and human simplicity"[42] is also belied by the music. The tetralogy does not end as it began with the perpetual arpeggios of E-flat major. And, when the Rhinemaidens' chant returns in the musical coda to the *Ring* it merely plays backup to bolder themes created out of the dramatic stuff of the narrative. The "reestablishment of a natural order" that Borchmeyer identifies relies on the iteration of a musical phrase that is charged with themes of *human* engagement, the expression of *human* love and gratitude, and the promise of future *human* species life – not the indifferent primordial world of the Rhinemaidens.

But, for all his embrace of change as the rule of nature, Wagner, like many of his contemporaries, remained anxious about the forces of history and sought to ground himself against the vertigo of endless time. As seen in his famous letter to Röckel, Wagner briefly entertained the fantasy that Siegfried could be restored – notably, not by divine grace and mythic cycles, but by historical progress.[43] But the return of the original man of nature simply did not fit the dialectic of progress. Hegel – and Brünnhilde – proved the fallacy of a return to the state of nature. Time does not go backwards. "[T]he march of evolution of all things human is no returning to the old, but a constant stepping forward," Wagner bravely asserted. "[E]ach turning back, whatever, shews itself no natural, but an artificial movement" (OD 290).[44]

In the absence of mythic cycles, existential comfort would have to be achieved by the logic of history. For Wagner, as for Kant, nature was not random; nature ensured that the positive potential in all things would come to fruition over time through the "ordered movement of a mighty stream" (AR 56).[45] But even more significant, the means to accomplish (or at least accelerate) the infinite ends of history was ultimately under man's control. It is this theory of man's integral role in purposeful change that gave Wagner the courage to hail the revolution; for the purpose of revolution was to correct the aimlessness of contemporary civilization and to shape the future. The dysfunction of European culture was not simply its rigid Christian morality, rampant egoism, and denial of species values, but its very indifference to the principle of change and, hence, coherent progress. As Carlyle so aptly noted about the *ancien régime*: "The Government by Blindman's-buff, stumbling along, has reached the precipice inevitable for it."[46] Taking this lesson of history to heart, Wagner excoriated the complacency of German society and government:

> To *Chance* she leaves the intellectual perfecting of certain of her members, while *forcibly* debarring the majority from any higher evolution; to **Chance** she leaves it, whether the few shall morally improve themselves, whereas she everywhere engenders and protects both vice and crime. To Chance she commits the training and growth of our bodily forces. . . . To *Chance*, our standing Society abandons *all*, our spiritual, our moral and corporeal progress; 'tis *Chance* decides if we shall near our destiny, attain our right, be happy.[47]

It was the task of the revolution, therefore, to drive "the war of *consciousness* with *chance*, of *mind* with *mindlessness*, *morality* with *evil*."[48] By reflecting on her sorrow and adding to the store of human knowledge, Brünnhilde asserts control over the destiny of man and defeats the tragic cycles of fate. But equally important, by her creative and thought-driven act of will, she at the same time defeats the vagaries of Chance, thus exorcising the terrifying specter of a random universe.

* * *

In the dialectic of Spirit, the apostolic succession of world-historical heroes passes from Wotan to Brünnhilde. Both are outsize actors on the stage of history searching for ways to understand and structure the world. Wotan fails in his endeavor, and has the good sense to yield, but he mistakes Siegfried as his rightful heir. Both Brünnhilde and the audience are misled, until it becomes clear in the end that it is Brünnhilde herself to whom the torch must pass. In his lectures on history, Hegel summarized this evolution. When Cronos first ruled it was "Time" itself. "What was produced, the children of Time, were devoured by time." Then came Zeus who "conquered Time" and "set a limit to [its] devouring activity." But then "Zeus and his race were themselves devoured by that productive principle itself: the principle of thought and of cognition, the principle of knowledge, of reasoning, of insight based on reasons and on the demand for reasons."[49] For Hegel, the era of divine order is superseded by the human world of consciousness and curiosity, those generative agents who, devoted to the "productive principle," create the potential for change. It is no longer the immortal gods – and their heroes – who rule the world by consuming Freia's apples and stopping time, but rather a new generation of world-historical heroes with creative instincts and questioning insights who, not afraid of death, move time forward and advance mankind along the trajectory of progress.[50] In the final musical passage of the *Ring*, Wagner summarized the thesis of his work, setting the symbols of these episodes or stages of history side by side, in sequence, in order to demonstrate this process of history. (See Figure 6.1.)

First, the Valhalla theme boldly recalls the glory of Wotan's aspirations. Next comes the Siegfried motif which is quickly cut short in the prime of its melodic ascent by Erda's descending theme signaling not only Siegfried's untimely death but the brevity of all living things and the ever-changing fluid nature of reality. Erda's theme then sets the harmonic stage for a return of the Annunciation of Life theme which transmutes the sorrowful truth of the individual's painful and painfully short existence into a transcendent vision of a generative and ever-progressing species life and a new world of human agency. Over four nights, the audience has witnessed these phases in the history of the world. They have seen Valhalla built, but also Wotan's despair; they have watched Siegfried's sorrowful journey from bold youth to lost soul; they have witnessed Brünnhilde's destructive act of jealousy, but also her act of mercy borne of suffering and knowledge. "The realm of Spirits which is formed in this way; in the outer world constitutes a succession in Time in which one Spirit relieved another of its charge and each took over the empire of the world from its predecessor."[51] Now all that remains of these vital dramatic passion-driven moments of the tetralogy are the timeless

Figure 6.1 The final pageant of motifs

talismanic leitmotifs that carry the memory of these events – each a "recollection" or "*inwardizing*" of that experience. Hegel made clear that true history did not consist simply of events, but critically also the narration of those events. Only through narration could human life emerge into consciousness and evolve.[52] In this way, we can resolve the regressive tendencies of Wagner's leitmotiv system which, like "boats against the current," seems to pull the *Ring* "ceaselessly into the past."[53] Only by confronting the past and making sense of it, through the singularly human act of inwardizing "reflection," Hegel taught, can man reach understanding and thereby discover his path to the future.[54] This final pageant of motifs – this "succession of Spirits, a gallery of images" – eloquently reifies in sound Hegel's concept of "comprehended History," events of the past thoughtfully recalled, and hence preserved, and organized in the self-conscious struggle to understand time.[55] And no one image is sufficient. The entire series of Spirit's shapes must be surveyed in order to comprehend the fullness of the historical process.[56] In the final measures of the *Ring*, the music drama reflects on itself, becomes self-conscious. Wagner's leitmotivic system reaches its apotheosis as the most perfect vehicle to communicate Hegel's philosophy of Spirit and the search for Absolute Knowing.

At the same time this process of capturing the shapes of the past necessarily becomes an aesthetic endeavor.[57] Like the poet, the historian "translate[s] what is externally present into the realm of mental representation."[58] Memory weighs, filters, and inevitably reconstructs lost time, creating patterns that are pleasing to our sense of order. The historical process so full of pain and suffering is transformed by Wagner's musical sequence into a beautiful Apollonian panorama. As Bancroft observed, "history calls [harmony] forth from the well-tuned chords of time."[59] At the same time, experiencing the whole course of history in one compelling sweep of sound, we can take Dionysian comfort in the "exuberant fertility of the universal will." "*[A]rt* approaches as a saving sorceress, expert at healing,"[60] allowing us to confront the terrors of existence with renewed faith in life.

Notes

1 Williams, *Wagner and the Romantic Hero*, 95: "Siegfried's heroism is fine when it is a question of dealing with a world where appearances do not deceive and evil declares itself in the form of a hideous dragon, but it is poor preparation for the social and political world."
2 Geck, *Richard Wagner*, 293.
3 Deathridge aptly captures the volte face in Siegfried's role as an abrupt transition from "the world of Sleeping Beauty" to "an almost Shakespearean world of human treachery and bloody intrigue." Deathridge, *Wagner*, 72.
4 Williams, *Wagner and the Romantic Hero*, 97: "this puzzling gap between Siegfried's character and Brünnhilde's praise of it, may be due to the immense time-lag between the composition of the poem and the music of *Götterdämmerung*." Kitcher and Schacht, *Finding an Ending*, 190: "The Siegfried we see on the stage is, in a sense, a fossil, remaining from an earlier version of Wagner's project in a final version to which he and his life and death are no longer central"; Shaw, *The Perfect Wagnerite*, 94: "When he scored Night Falls on the Gods, he had accepted the failure of Siegfried";

Spencer, "*Zieh hin!*," 105–6: noting "Wagner's altered attitude towards the old regime: there was no longer any room for men like Wodan in Wagner's ideal republic"; Darcy, "'The World Belongs to Alberich!,'" in *Wagner's Ring of the Nibelung: A Companion*, 52: "In 1872 Wagner could scoff at Siegfried's pretensions to free will. Siegfried's dramatic function had changed drastically"; Darcy suggests that the transformation in Siegfried's role was due to Wagner's new Schopenhauerian outlook after 1854: "yet where did all this [the referent is ambiguous but appears to be Wagner's 1856 Schopenhauerian ending for Brünnhilde] leave poor Siegfried?" *Id.*, 52.

5 Treadwell, *Interpreting Wagner*, 85: "One might explain the change as a response to the failure of Wagner's revolutionary ambitions in Dresden, were it not for the fact that the revision was made months *before* the abortive uprising. See also Darcy, "Everything that Is, Ends," 445, 445 n.6; Hollinrake "Epiphany and Apocalypse," 42–3; Hollinrake, *Nietzsche*, 33–5; Windell, "Hegel, Feuerbach and Wagner's *Ring*," 46–7. It also bears noting that the dramatic conception of Wotan's tragic failure had already been conceived well before *Der junge Siegfried* was drafted. As noted, Wagner explained in his autobiography that the opera on Barbarossa was to be about "the impossibility of realizing his highest ideals." In the *Wibelungen* essay, Wagner elaborated on this idea of Barbarossa's struggle. There he explained that Barbarossa "ever strove to realise his high ideal" and acted consistent with "the grand Idea informing him." Richard Wagner, "The Wibelungen: World History as told in Saga," in *Pilgrimage to Beethoven and Other Essays*, 290. But powerful forces were arrayed against him, not least the papacy. But even more significant were the Lombard communes who rebelled against his rule. Ironically, it was Barbarossa himself who had planted the seed of freedom in their hearts. "Friedrich, the representative of the last racial Ur-Folk-Kinghood, in mightiest fulfillment of his indeviable destiny, struck from the stone of manhood the spark before whose splendor he himself must pale." The terrible defeat of Barbarossa at Legnano by the Lombard Bond, which embodied "*the spirit of free Manhood loosed from the nature-soil of race*," "cried his world-plan final halt." *Id.*, 292. Initially Wagner viewed Siegfried as the mythic parallel to Barbarossa. But here also we see the fundamental outline of Wotan's tragedy. A great leader with a "world-plan" inspired by a "grand Idea" finds his defeat at the hands of free manhood, a freedom he himself has inspired.

6 Thomas Mann captured a measure of this paradox when he described Siegfried as a "harlequin, god of light, and anarchist social revolutionary, all in the same person" and then astutely asked, "what more could the theatre possibly ask for?" Thomas Mann, "The Sorrows and Grandeur of Richard Wagner," in *Pro and Contra Wagner*, 131.

7 Nietzsche, *The Birth of Tragedy*, 136.

8 See Walter E. Houghton, *The Victorian Frame of Mind: 1830–1870* (Yale University Press 1957), 310: "in the period of radical transition when men feel lost in a maze of ideas, they look to a savior."

9 Carlyle, *On Heroes*, 2.

10 Carlyle's lectures were not only about heroes, but about hero worship as well. In Carlyle's vision, great men were the groundwork for new myths to live by. Carlyle called "hero worship" "an eternal corner-stone, from which [men] can begin to build themselves up again." He explained further "That man, in some sense or other, worships Heroes; that we all of us reverence and must ever reverence Great Men: this is, to me, the living rock amid all rushings down whatsoever; – the one fixed point in modern revolutionary history, otherwise as if bottomless and shoreless." *On Heroes*, 24. In his first lecture he addressed the "Hero as Divinity," surmising that the pagan god Odin was simply the mythic abstraction of an actual man once revered for his strength and leadership. "Odin was a heroic Prince, in the Black-Sea region" who led his people out of Asia into Northern Europe and over time "came by and by to be worshipped as Chief God by these Scandinavians." *On Heroes*, 37.

11 Carlyle, *On Heroes*, 2.

12 Carlyle, *On Heroes*, 2; Williams, *Wagner and the Romantic Hero*, 86: *Nibelungenlied* acquired "the status of a national poem" and "made Siegfried into a German national hero"; Stewart Spencer, " *'Or Strike at Me Now as I Strangle thy Knee'*: A Note on the text and translation," *Wagner's Ring of the Nibelung*, 11: *Nibelungenlied* was hailed as a "German Iliad" and viewed as the "epitome of national aspirations." As the Young Germany movement contemplated the need for reform and revolution, they decried the ambivalence and apathy of the German people. Ludwig Börne, for one, characterized Germany as a Hamlet unable to rouse itself to action and revolution. The political rallying cry "*Deutschland ist Hamlet*" was popularized in 1844 by the poet Ferdinand Freiligrath. Germany could no longer afford dreamers and thinkers; it required men of action. Siegfried emphatically broke the Hamlet mold, setting a new example for engaged political activism. Unlike Hamlet, Siegfried's "native hue of resolution" had not been "sicklied o'er with the pale cast of thought."

13 Barry Millington, "*Der Ring des Nibelungen*: conception and interpretation," in *The Cambridge Companion to Wagner*, ed. Thomas Grey (Cambridge University Press 2008), 76.

14 Millington, "*Der Ring*," 76: "The legendary monarch was to wake from his slumber, return from the middle of the mountain to the real world and preside over a golden era of peace and justice."

15 Millington, "*Der Ring*," 78.

16 Wagner, "The Wibelungen," 289.

17 Eliade, *The Myth of the Eternal Return*, 35. See also Foster, *Wagner's 'Ring,'* 255: "myth aims at abolishing history by placing the story outside of time."

18 As Eliade recognizes, "[F]or the greater part of mankind, still clinging to the traditional viewpoint, history did not have, and could not have, value in itself. Every hero repeated the archetypal gesture, every war rehearsed the struggle between good and evil, every fresh social injustice was identified with the sufferings of the Saviour . . . each new massacre repeated the glorious end of the martyrs." Eliade, *The Myth of the Eternal Return*, 151–2.

19 Feuerbach, "Towards a Critique of Hegel's Philosophy," in Stepelevich, *The Young Hegelians*, 98.

20 See Mary A. Cicora, *Wagner's* Ring *and German Drama*, 9, 27: "The *Ring* . . . is a synthetic mythology, a nineteenth-century artistic myth that gives a quasi-mythological explanation of world-history"; "In writing his *Ring* tetralogy, Wagner used and refabricated myth as a metaphor for history." Or as Berry has put it, "Wagner wishes, in *his* mythical allegory of time, to write a true, eternal world history, albeit a history that aims at least to anticipate the revolution to come." Mark Berry, "Richard Wagner and the Politics of Music Drama," *The Historical Journal*, Vol. 47, No. 3 (2004), 683. Implicit in Berry's statement is the paradox that Wagner's drama aims to be an "mythical allegory" that at the same time contemplates the revolution. And in this regard he touches on Wagner's radical reinterpretation of the significance of myth. Wagner did not see myth's purpose as structuring a timeless framework for human existence. Rather, as Wagner wrote of Antigone's act of rebellion against the State, "[t]he necessity of this downfall was foreboded in the Mythos: it is the part of actual history to accomplish it" (OD 191). For Wagner, myth contained the inner truths of historical and indeed political necessity; it was the responsibility of man to recognize those truths and endeavor to bring them about in reality. Myth, then, in Wagner's view, paradoxically does not reinforce transcendent archetypes but lights the way to breaking the archetypes of the past.

21 See Mary Cicora's insightful analysis of Wagner's ironic treatment of Wotan's cosmology as a function of Wotan's self-reflective and self-questioning narrative stance. Cicora, *Mythology as Metaphor*, 142–3.

22 Spencer, "*Zieh hin!*," 107: "all Siegfried's actions are predetermined."

23 Geck, *Richard Wagner*, 293.

24 Emslie recognizes this problem, explaining that "the heroic deeds the hero performs ... are the result of others manipulating him." Emslie, *The Centrality of Love*, 76.

25 Darcy, "Everything that Is, Ends!," 447.

26 Porges, *Wagner Rehearsing the 'Ring,'* 104.

27 Heine, *On the History of Religion*, 79.

28 Wagner, *Beethoven* (Allen trans.), 195. Victor Hugo made a similar appraisal of the intellectual's role in world history just six years prior to *Beethoven*:

> It is time that the men of action should step back, and that men of thought should take the lead. The summit is the head. Where thought is, there power exists. It is time that the genius take precedence of the hero. It is time to render to Cæsar the things that are Cæsar's, and to the book the things that belong to the book. Such a poem, such a drama, such a novel, is doing more service than all the courts of Europe put together.
>
> (Victor Hugo, *William Shakespeare*, 408)

For Herzen, "The slowness of the historical process with its aberrations and deviations was hard to bear, but the events of 1848 and 1863 had shown the folly of attempts to speed it up by the use of force alone." As quoted in Kelly, *Discovery of Chance*, 519.

29 Carlyle, *On Heroes*, 20.

30 In this sense I agree with Kitcher and Schacht that *Götterdämmerung* enacts a *Heldendämmerung*, Kitcher and Schacht, *Finding an Ending*, 188, but not in the sense that there can be *no* heroic acts in the world, but rather that Siegfried's model of heroism is obsolete and that the world must recognize its debt instead to wise world-historical seers such as Brünnhilde. Köhler notes that by the end of the drama, the ring, the tarnhelm, the sword, and Hagen's "fatal potion" are reduced to "mere fairy tale symbols." Köhler, *Wagner*, 389.

31 Porges, *Rehearsing the 'Ring,'* 141.

32 As Williams rightly notes, "Siegfried never changes." Williams, *Wagner and the Romantic Hero*, 96.

33 Berry, Kitcher and Schacht, Corse, and Köhler all conclude that there is a measure of enlightenment in Siegfried's reawakening. Berry, *Treacherous Bonds*, 234: "the motif previously associated with Brünnhilde's awakening" indicates that "Siegfried and the revolution have at last been permitted similarly to awaken 'to light, to life, and the highest form of existence'"; Berry, "Nietzsche," 16: "In his death, Siegfried attains true consciousness, for the first time, of his revolutionary deeds"; Kitcher and Schacht, *Finding an Ending*, 188: "dying, he beings to grow up, and, for the first time, to understand what life and love are all about"; Köhler, *Wagner*, 404: As Siegfried dies "his self-consciousness returns with the sound of the six harps expressive of light"; Corse, *Wagner and the New Consciousness*, 184: "The music of this scene indicates that the hero reaches a new understanding of his relationship with Brünnhilde."

34 Williams, *Wagner and the Romantic Hero*, 96.

35 With characteristic acerbity, Shaw writes, "Siegfried . . . falls dead on his shield, but gets up again, after the old operatic custom, to sing about thirty bars to his love before allowing himself to be finally carried off to the strains of the famous *Trauermarsch*." Shaw, *The Perfect Wagnerite*, 82.

36 Treadwell, *Interpreting Wagner*, 100. As he states elsewhere, "in every case . . . rituals of prophecy founder on the loss of the future, the intractable sense of confronting an end." Treadwell, *Interpreting Wagner*, 93. Treadwell claims that he is not asserting a Schopenhauerian interpretation, *id.*, 100, but his image of endless repetition is not far from Schopenhauer's Buddhism-tinged teachings on the illusions of time and space.

37 Treadwell, *Interpreting Wagner*, 91, 93; Foster, *Wagner's 'Ring,'* 255–6: noting "linear circularity" of the theft of the gold theme in the *Ring*.

38 Treadwell, *Interpreting Wagner*, 93.

39 Ewans also recognizes that the breaking of the rope means that "eternal knowledge is at an end," but oddly attributes this to the continuing effect of Alberich's curse, itself a dramatic expression of the weight of fate. Ewans, *Wagner and Aeschylus*, 217.

40 Berry agrees that Wagner in *Götterdämmerung* rejects the concept of fate, but he claims that it is in favor of "a Schopenhauerian (neo-Kantian) conception of radical freedom" by virtue of Wotan's renunciation. Berry, *Treacherous Bonds*, 250–1.

41 See, e.g., Borchmeyer, *Drama and the World of Richard Wagner*, 235–7: "with . . . the return of the ring to the natural elements, the world is restored to its first paradisiacal state. By ending, it begins anew"; "In the history of myth, birth has always been what Mircea Eliade has termed a 'symbolic recapitulation of the cosmogony'"; see also Treadwell, *Interpreting Wagner*, 88: "In its first seconds, the *Ring* emerges out of an aboriginal silence; a return to nothingness consequently seems like its proper culmination"; Kitcher and Schacht, *Finding an Ending*, 181: "Fire and flood wipe the slate clean, reestablishing the primordial state of natural and human simplicity in which it all began"; Geck, *Richard Wagner*, 302: referencing theory of Sabine Henze-Döhring that the final theme is a "symbol of birth and – here – the rebirth of a state of paradisal innocence"; Deathridge, *Wagner*, 52: "a final scene that banishes history to celebrate the power of the natural elements"; Foster, *Wagner's 'Ring,'* 241–2: noting two alternative possibilities, namely that "the members of *das Volk* are now left alone in a state of nature" or that "nothing has changed and we are right back where we started."

42 Borchmeyer, *Drama and the World of Richard Wagner*, 235; Kitcher and Schacht, *Finding an Ending*, 181.

43 As Eliade explains, "Messianic beliefs in a final regeneration of the world themselves also indicate an antihistoric attitude." Eliade, *The Myth of the Eternal Return*, 111.

44 Nietzsche had also sounded the death knell of the thesis of the return of a natural golden age in *The Birth of Tragedy* where he debunked the "comfortable delight in an idyllic reality" that emerged out of the Rousseauvian project:

> This sentiment supposes that there was a primitive age of man when he lay close to the heart of nature, and, owing to his naturalness, had at once attained the ideal of mankind in a paradisiacal goodness and artistry. From this perfect primitive man all of us were supposed to be descended. We were even supposed to be faithful copies of him; only we had to cast off a few things in order to recognize ourselves once more as this primitive man, on the strength of a voluntary renunciation of superfluous learnedness, of superabundant culture.
>
> (*The Birth of Tragedy*, 117)

45 Kant, *Idea for a Universal History with a Cosmopolitan Purpose*.

46 Carlyle, *French Revolution*, 190.

47 Wagner, "Man and Established Society," 230.

48 *Id.*, 230.

49 Hegel, *History*, 79–80.

50 Carlyle completed his essay "Characteristics" with the lines: "My inheritance how wide and fair! Time is my fair seed-field, of Time I'm heir." "Characteristics," 356.

51 Hegel, *Phenomenology*, 492 (§808).

52 Hegel, *History*, 64–5.

53 See, e.g., Treadwell, *Interpreting Wagner*, 124–7: "[L]eitmotif turns out always to be a mode of narrative, not prophecy. . . . [I]ts direction is backward"; Abbate, 189: leitmotiv system represents "history not as progress but as a recurrent wrenching back, as error replayed"; Foster, *Wagner's 'Ring,'* 258–60.

54 Treadwell acknowledges how narrative "*does* something. . . . [I]t makes meanings, rather than just recording events," and yet refuses to recognize how such new meanings can point the way to the future. Treadwell, *Interpreting Wagner*, 129.

55 Hegel, *Phenomenology*, 493 (§808).

56 *Id.*, Hegel, *History*, 82.
57 See Joshua Foa Dienstag, "Building the Temple of Memory: Hegel's Aesthetic Narrative of History," *The Review of Politics*, Vol. 56, No. 4 (1994).
58 Hegel, *History*, 3.
59 Bancroft, *Progress*, 15.
60 Nietzsche, *The Birth of Tragedy*, 104, 60.

Bibliography

Abbate, Carolyn. *Unsung Voices: Opera and Musical Narrative in the Nineteenth Century.* Princeton: Princeton University Press, 1991.

Adorno, Theodor W. *In Search of Wagner.* Translated by Rodney Livingstone. London: Verso, 2005.

Allen, Roger. Introduction to *Richard Wagner's Beethoven (1870): A New Translation,* by Richard Wagner, translated by Roger Allen, 1–29. Woodbridge: The Boydell Press, 2014.

Ashton, Rosemary D. "Carlyle's Apprenticeship: His Early German Criticism and His Relationship with Goethe (1822–1832)." *The Modern Language Review* 71, no. 1 (Jan 1976): 1–18.

Badiou, Alain. *Five Lessons on Wagner.* Translated by Susan Spitzer. New York, NY: Verso, 2010.

Bakewell, Sarah. *How to Live, Or: A Life of Montaigne in One Question and Twenty Attempts at an Answer.* New York, NY: Other Press, 2010.

Bancroft, George. *The Necessity, the Reality, and the Promise of the Progress of the Human Race: Oration Delivered before the New York Historical Society, Nov. 20, 1854.* White-fish, MT: Kessinger Publishing's Legacy Reprints, 2010.

Beauchamp, Gorman. "Melville and the Tradition of Primitive Utopia." *The Journal of General Education* 33, no. 1 (Jan 1981): 6–14.

Beiser, Frederick C. "'Morality' in Hegel's *Phenomenology of Spirit.*" In *The Blackwell Guide to Hegel's 'Phenomenology of Spirit,'* edited by Kenneth R. Westphal, 209–25. Malden: Wiley-Blackwell, 2009.

Bell, Richard H. "Teleology, Providence and the 'Death of God': A New Perspective on the *Ring* Cycle's Debt to G.W.F. Hegel." *The Wagner Journal* 11, no. 1 (March 2017): 30–45.

Berlin, Isaiah. "Alexander Herzen." In *Russian Thinkers,* edited by Henry Hardy and Aileen Kelly, 2nd ed., 212–39. London: Penguin Classics, 2013.

———. *Political Ideas in the Romantic Age: Their Rise and Influence on Modern Thought.* Edited by Henry Hardy. Rev. 2nd ed. Princeton: Princeton University Press, 2014.

Berry, Mark. "The Positive Influence of Wagner Upon Nietzsche." *The Wagner Journal* 2, no. 2 (July 2008): 11–28.

———. "Richard Wagner and the Politics of Music-Drama." *The Historical Journal* 47, no. 3 (2004): 663–83.

———. *Treacherous Bonds and Laughing Fire: Politics and Religion in Wagner's* Ring. Burlington: Ashgate, 2006.

Bloom, Harold. *Shakespeare: The Invention of the Human.* New York, NY: Riverhead Books, 2015.

Borchmeyer, Dieter. *Drama and the World of Richard Wagner.* Translated by Daphne Ellis. Princeton: Princeton University Press, 2003.

Bortnichak, Edward A., and Paula M. Bortnichak. "The 'Missing Link' in the Evolution of Wagner's *Siegfried.*" *The Wagner Journal* 10, no. 2 (July 2016): 4–17.

Bradley, Andrew Cecil. "Lecture V: *Othello.*" In *Shakespearean Tragedy: Lectures on Hamlet, Othello, King Lear, Macbeth,* 16th imprint 2nd ed., 175–206. London: Macmillan and Co., 1922.

———. "Lecture VI: *Othello.*" In *Shakespearean Tragedy: Lectures on Hamlet, Othello, King Lear, Macbeth,* 16th imprint 2nd ed., 207–242. London: Macmillan and Co., 1922.

Brooks, Peter. *Flaubert in the Ruins of Paris: The Story of a Friendship, a Novel, and a Terrible Year.* New York, NY: Basic Books, 2017.

Budden, Julian. *From Don Carlos to Falstaff.* The Operas of Verdi, Vol. 3. Oxford: Oxford University Press, 1981.

Burwick, Frederick. "Shakespeare and Germany." In *Shakespeare in the Nineteenth Century,* edited by Gail Marshall, 314–31. Cambridge: Cambridge University Press, 2012.

Bykova, Marina F. "Spirit and Concrete Subjectivity in Hegel's *Phenomenology of Spirit.*" In *The Blackwell Guide to Hegel's 'Phenomenology of Spirit,'* edited by Kenneth R. Westphal, 265–95. Malden, MA: Wiley-Blackwell, 2009.

Canton, Kimberly Fairbrother. "Redeeming the Rhinemaidens: A Reconsideration of Their Dionysian and Apollonian Attributes." *The Wagner Journal* 2, no. 2 (July 2008): 40–54.

Carlyle, Thomas. "Characteristics." In *John Stuart Mill: Autobiography, Essay on Liberty. Thomas Carlyle: Characteristics, Inaugural Address, Essay on Scott,* edited by Charles William Eliot. The Harvard Classics, Vol. 25, 319–58. New York, NY: P.F. Collier & Son, 1909.

———. *The French Revolution: A History.* Reprint of 1837 1st ed. New York, NY: The Modern Library, 2002.

———. "Goethe." In *Critical and Miscellaneous Essays,* 204–64. Boston: Houghton, Mifflin and Company, 1881.

———. *On Heroes, Hero-Worship and the Heroic in History. Six Lectures.* London: James Fraser, 1841.

———. *Sartor Resartus.* Edited by Peter Sabor and Kerry McSweeney. Oxford: Oxford University Press, 2008.

Cicora, Mary A. *Mythology as Metaphor: Romantic Irony, Critical Theory, and Wagner's* Ring. Westport: Greenwood Press, 1998.

———. *Wagner's* Ring *and German Drama: Comparative Studies in Mythology and History in Drama.* Westport: Greenwood Press, 1999.

Cohen, Mitchell. "To the Dresden Barricades: The Genesis of Wagner's Political Ideas." In *The Cambridge Companion to Wagner,* edited by Thomas S. Grey, 47–64. Cambridge: Cambridge University Press, 2008.

Comay, Rebecca. *Mourning Sickness: Hegel and the French Revolution.* Stanford: Stanford University Press, 2011.

Comte-Sponville, André. *A Small Treatise on the Great Virtues: The Uses of Philosophy in Everyday Life.* Translated by Catherine Temerson. New York, NY: Metropolitan Books, 2001.

Cooke, Deryck. *I Saw the World End: A Study of Wagner's* Ring. London: Oxford University Press, 2002. Reprint of 1979 1st ed.

———. *An Introduction to 'Der Ring Des Nibelungen'.* London: Decca, 1967. 2 CDs, 443 581–2.

Corse, Sandra. *Wagner and the New Consciousness: Language and Love in the* Ring. Rutherford Fairleigh Dickinson University Press, 1990.

Dahlhaus, Carl. *Richard Wagner's Music Dramas*. Translated by Mary Whittall. Revised reprint of 1979 1st ed. Cambridge: Cambridge University Press, 1992.

Dale, Peter A. "*Sartor Resartus* and the Inverse Sublime: The Art of Humourous Deconstruction." In *Allegory, Myth, and Symbol*, edited by Morton W. Bloomfield, 293–312. Cambridge, MA: Harvard University Press, 1981.

Darcy, Warren. "'Everything That Is, Ends!': The Genesis and Meaning of the Erda Episode in 'Das Rheingold'." *The Musical Times* 129, no. 1747 (Sep 1988): 443–47.

———. "The Metaphysics of Annihilation: Wagner, Schopenhauer, and the Ending of the *Ring*." *Music Theory Spectrum* 16, no. 1 (1994): 1–40.

———. "The Pessimism of the Ring." *The Opera Quarterly* 4, no. 2 (1986): 24–48.

———. "'*The World Belongs to Alberich!*' Wagner's Changing Attitude Towards the 'Ring'." In *Wagner's Ring of the Nibelung: A Companion*, edited by Stewart Spencer and Barry Millington, 48–52. London: Thames and Hudson, 1993.

Deathridge, John. *Wagner Beyond Good and Evil*. Berkeley: University of California Press, 2008.

Diderot, Denis. "Extracts from the *Histoire Des Deux Indes*." In *Diderot: Political Writings*, edited and translated by John Hope Mason and Robert Wokler, 165–214. Cambridge: Cambridge University Press, 1992.

———. "The *Supplément Au Voyage De Bougainville*." In *Diderot: Political Writings*, edited and translated by John Hope Mason and Robert Wokler, 31–76. Cambridge: Cambridge University Press, 1992.

Dienstag, Joshua Foa. "Building the Temple of Memory: Hegel's Aesthetic Narrative of History." *The Review of Politics* 56, no. 4 (Autumn 1994): 697–726.

Donington, Robert. *Wagner's "Ring" and Its Symbols: The Music and the Myth*. 2nd ed. New York, NY: St. Martin's Press, 1969.

Eliade, Mircea. *The Myth of the Eternal Return: Cosmos and History*. Translated by William R. Trask. Princeton: Princeton University Press, 2005.

Emslie, Barry. "The Kiss of the Dragon-Slayer." *The Wagner Journal* 7, no. 1 (March 2013): 22–38.

———. *Richard Wagner and the Centrality of Love*. Woodbridge: The Boydell Press, 2010.

Ewans, Michael. *Wagner and Aeschylus: The* Ring *and the Oresteia*. London: Faber and Faber, 1982.

Feuerbach, Ludwig. *The Essence of Christianity*. Translated by George Eliot. New York, NY: Barnes & Noble Books, 2004.

———. "Principles of the Philosophy of the Future." In *The Fiery Brook: Selected Writings of Ludwig Feuerbach*, translated by Zawar Hanfi. Garden City: Anchor Books, 1972.

———. *Thoughts on Death and Immortality: From the Papers of a Thinker, along with an Appendix of Theological-Satirical Epigrams*. Translated by James A. Massey. Berkeley: University of California Press, 1980.

———. "Towards a Critique of Hegel's Philosophy." Excerpted in *The Young Hegelians: An Anthology*, edited by Lawrence S. Stepelevich, 95–124. Cambridge: Cambridge University Press, 1983.

Foster, Daniel H. *Wagner's Ring Cycle and the Greeks*. Cambridge: Cambridge University Press, 2010.

Gay, Peter. *Schnitzler's Century: The Making of Middle-Class Culture, 1815–1914*. New York, NY: Norton, 2002.

Geck, Martin. *Richard Wagner: A Life in Music*. Translated by Stewart Spencer. Chicago: The University of Chicago Press, 2013.

Gliboff, Sander. *H.G. Bronn, Ernst Haeckel, and the Origins of German Darwinism: A Study in Translation and Transformation*. Cambridge, MA: MIT Press, 2008.

Goethe, Johann Wolfgang von. *The Sorrows of Young Werther*. Translated by Michael Hulse. New York, NY: Penguin, 1989.

Greenblatt, Stephen. *The Swerve: How the World Became Modern*. New York: W.W. Norton & Co., 2011.

Grey, Thomas S. "Leitmotif, Temporality, and Musical Design in the *Ring*." In *The Cambridge Companion to Wagner*, edited by Thomas S. Grey, 85–114. Cambridge: Cambridge University Press, 2008.

Grillparzer, Franz. "Medea." In *German Classics of the Nineteenth and Twentieth Centuries*, translated by Theodore A. Miller (German Publication Society, 1914).

Guillin, Vincent. "Comte and Social Science." In *Love, Order, & Progress: The Science, Philosophy, & Politics of Auguste Comte*, edited by Michel Bourdeau, Mary Pickering and Warren Schmaus, 128–62. Pittsburgh: University of Pittsburgh Press, 2018.

HaCohen, Ruth. *The Music Libel against the Jews*. New Haven: Yale University Press, 2011.

Hauer, Stanley R. "Wagner and the 'Völospá.'" *19th Century Music* 15, no. 1 (Summer 1991): 52–63.

Hazlitt, William. *Characters of Shakespear's Plays*. London: C.H. Reynell, 1817.

Hegel, Georg Wilhelm Friedrich. *Introduction to "The Philosophy of History": with selections from "The Philosophy of Right"*. Edited and Translated by Leo Rauch. Indianapolis: Hackett Publishing Company, 1988.

———. *Lectures on the Philosophy of History*. Translated by Ruben Alvarado. Aalten: Wordbridge Publishing, 2011.

———. *Phenomenology of Spirit*. Translated by Arnold Vincent Miller. Oxford: Oxford University Press, 1977.

———. *Reason in History: A General Introduction to the Philosophy of History*. Translated by Robert S. Hartman. New York, NY: Collier Macmillan, 1985.

Heine, Heinrich. "Lucca, the City (in *Travel Pictures*, Part IV, 1831)." Excerpted in *On the History of Religion and Philosophy in Germany and Other Writings*, translated by Howard Pollack-Milgate, edited by Terry Pinkard, 127–29. Cambridge: Cambridge University Press, 2007.

———. *On the History of Religion and Philosophy in Germany*. Translated by Howard Pollack-Milgate. Edited by Terry Pinkard. Cambridge: Cambridge University Press, 2007.

———. "The Romantic School." Excerpted in *On the History of Religion and Philosophy in Germany and Other Writings*, translated by Howard Pollack-Milgate, edited by Terry Pinkard, 136–95. Cambridge: Cambridge University Press, 2007.

Heise, Paul. "The Wound that Will Never Heal." *Wagnerheim*. Accessed January 5, 2019. https://www.wagnerheim.com/page/988.

Hepokoski, James A. *Giuseppe Verdi: Otello*. Cambridge Opera Handbooks. Cambridge: Cambridge University Press, 1987.

Herwegh, Georg. *"Othello mit Ira Aldridge."* In *Der Freiheit Eine Gasse: Aus Dem Leben Und Werk Georg Herweghs*, edited by Bruno Kaiser, 298–99. Berlin: Verlag Volk und Welt, 1948.

Hollinrake, Roger. "Epiphany and Apocalypse in the 'Ring'." In *Wagner's Ring of the Nibelung: A Companion*, edited by Stewart Spencer and Barry Millington, 41–47. London: Thames and Hudson, 1993.

————. *Nietzsche, Wagner, and the Philosophy of Pessimism*. London: Allen and Unwin, 1982.

————. "Philosophical Outlook." In *The Wagner Compendium*, edited by Barry Millington, 143–46. London: Thames and Hudson, 1992.

Holloway, Robin. "Motif, Memory and Meaning in *Twilight of the Gods*." In *On Music: Essays and Diversions 1963–2003*. Brinkworth: Claridge Press, 2003.

Houghton, Walter E. *The Victorian Frame of Mind, 1830–1870*. New Haven: Yale University Press, 1957.

Hugo, Victor. "Introduction." In *Oeuvres Complètes de Shakespeare. Les Jaloux II: Cymbeline et Othello*, Tome V, translated by Francois-Victor Hugo. Paris: Pagnerre, 1860.

Hugo, Victor. *William Shakespeare*. Translated by Melville B. Anderson. 6th ed. Chicago: A.C. McClurg & Co., 1899.

Inwood, Margaret. *The Influence of Shakespeare on Richard Wagner*. Lewiston: Edwin Mellen Press, 1999.

Jacobs, Robert L. "The Shakespearean Element in the 'Ring'." *Wagner: New Series* 4, no. 1 (Jan 1983): 2–9.

Josserand, Frank B. "Wagner and German Nationalism." In *Penetrating Wagner's "Ring": An Anthology*, edited by John Louis DiGaetani, 205–18. Rutherford: Fairleigh Dickinson University Press, 1978.

Kant, Immanuel. "Idea for a Universal History with a Cosmopolitan Purpose." In *Kant: Political Writings*, edited by Hans Reiss, translated by H. B. Nisbet. Expanded 2nd ed., 41–53. Cambridge: Cambridge University Press, 1991.

Kaplan, Fred. *Thomas Carlyle: A Biography*. Berkeley: University of California Press, 1993.

Kelly, Aileen. *The Discovery of Chance: The Life and Thought of Alexander Herzen*. Cambridge, MA: Harvard University Press, 2016.

Kerlin, Robert. "Contemporary Criticism of Carlyle's "French Revolution"." *The Sewanee Review* 20, no. 3 (July 1912): 282–96.

Kitcher, Philip, and Richard Schacht. *Finding an Ending: Reflections on Wagner's* Ring. Oxford: Oxford University Press, 2004.

Köhler, Joachim. *Richard Wagner, the Last of the Titans*. Translated by Stewart Spencer. New Haven: Yale University Press, 2004.

Krasnoff, Larry. *Hegel's "Phenomenology of Spirit": An Introduction*. Cambridge: Cambridge University Press, 2008.

Krohn, Rüdiger. "The Revolution of 1848–49." In *Wagner Handbook*, edited by Ulrich Müller and Peter Wapnewski, translated by John Deathridge, 156–65. Cambridge, MA: Harvard University Press, 1992.

Lamartine, Alphonse de. *History of the Girondists: or, Personal Memoirs of the Patriots of the French Revolution*. Translated by H.T. Ryde. 3 vols. London: George Bell & Sons, 1905.

————. *Histoire des Girondins*. Bruxelles: Meline, Cans et Compagnie, 1847.

Laurentiis, Allegra de. "Absolute Knowing." In *The Blackwell Guide to Hegel's 'Phenomenology of Spirit'*, edited by Kenneth R. Westphal, 246–64. Malden: Wiley-Blackwell, 2009.

Lee, M. Owen. *Athena Sings: Wagner and the Greeks*. Toronto: University of Toronto Press, 2003.

Liébert, Georges. *Nietzsche and Music*. Translated by David Pellauer. Chicago: University of Chicago Press, 2004.

Magee, Bryan. *The Tristan Chord: Wagner and Philosophy*. New York, NY: Henry Holt and Co., 2000.

Magee, Elizabeth. *Richard Wagner and the Nibelungs*. Oxford: Clarendon Press, 1990.

Mah, Harold. "The French Revolution and the Problem of German Modernity: Hegel, Heine, and Marx." *New German Critique*, no. 50 (Spring-Summer 1990): 3–20.

Mann, Thomas. "Richard Wagner and *Der Ring Des Nibelungen,* November 1937." In *Pro and Contra Wagner*, translated by Allan Blunden, 171–93. Chicago: University of Chicago Press, 1985.

———. "The Sorrows and Grandeur of Richard Wagner, April 1933." In *Pro and Contra Wagner*, translated by Allan Blunden, 91–148. Chicago: University of Chicago Press, 1985.

Marcus, David. "The Break in the Ring." In *Penetrating Wagner's "Ring": An Anthology*, edited by John Louis DiGaetani, 197–204. Rutherford: Farleigh Dickinson University Press, 1978.

Melville, Herman. *Billy Budd, Sailor*. In *Billy Budd, Sailor and Other Stories*, edited by Frederick Busch. New York, NY: Penguin Books, 1986.

———. *Typee*. New York, NY: Penguin Books, 1996.

Mendelsohn, Moses. Review of *De Sacra Poesi Hebraeorum; Praelectiones Academicae Oxonii Habitae,* by Robert Lowth. In *Auseinandersetzung mit Shakespeare*, edited by Wolfgang Stellmacher. Berlin: Akademie-Verlag, 1976.

Mill, John Stuart. ""The Spirit of the Age" (1831)." In *The Spirit of the Age: Victorian Essays*, edited by Gertrude Himmelfarb, 50–79. New Haven: Yale University Press, 2007.

Millington, Barry. "*Der Ring des Nibelungen*: Conception and Interpretation." In *The Cambridge Companion to Wagner*, edited by Thomas S. Grey, 74–84. Cambridge: Cambridge University Press, 2008.

———, ed. *The New Grove Guide to Wagner and His Operas*. Oxford: Oxford University Press, 2006.

———. "Nuremberg Trial: Is There Anti-Semitism in 'Die Meistersinger'?". *Cambridge Opera Journal* 3, no. 3 (Nov 1991): 247–60.

———. *The Sorcerer of Bayreuth: Richard Wagner, His Work and His World*. New York, NY: Oxford University Press, 2012.

Montaigne, Michel de. *The Complete Works: Essays, Travel Journal, Letters*. Translated by Donald M. Frame. New York, NY: A.A. Knopf, 2003.

Morrow, John. *Thomas Carlyle*. London: Hambledon Continuum, 2006.

Newman, Ernest. *The Wagner Operas*. Princeton: Princeton University Press, 1991.

Nietzsche, Friedrich. "Attempt at a Self-Criticism." In *The Birth of Tragedy and The Case of Wagner*, translated by Walter Arnold Kaufmann. 17–27. New York, NY: Vintage Books, 1967.

———. *The Birth of Tragedy Or: Hellenism and Pessimism*. Translated by Walter Arnold Kaufmann. New York, NY: Vintage Books, 1967.

———. "The Case of Wagner." In *The Birth of Tragedy and The Case of Wagner*, translated by Walter Arnold Kaufmann. 153–92. New York, NY: Vintage Books, 1967.

Nietzsche, Friedrich, and Richard Wagner. *The Nietzsche-Wagner Correspondence*. Edited by Elisabeth Förster-Nietzsche, translated by Caroline V. Kerr. New York, NY: Boni and Liveright, 1921.

Nirenberg, David. *Anti-Judaism: The Western Tradition*. New York, NY: W. W. Norton & Company, 2013.

Nussbaum, Martha C. "The Transfigurations of Intoxication: Nietzsche, Schopenhauer, and Dionysus." *Arion: A Journal of Humanities and the Classics* 1, no. 2 (Spring 1991): 75–111.

Pinkard, Terry P. *Does History Make Sense?: Hegel on the Historical Shapes of Justice.* Cambridge, MA: Harvard University Press, 2017.

Pocock, John Greville Agard. *Barbarians, Savages and Empires.* Barbarism and Religion, Vol. 4. Cambridge: Cambridge University Press, 2005.

Porges, Heinrich. *Wagner Rehearsing the 'Ring': An Eye-Witness Account of the Stage Rehearsals of the First Bayreuth Festival.* Translated by Robert L. Jacobs. Cambridge: Cambridge University Press, 1983.

Praeger, Ferdinand. *Wagner as I Knew Him.* Middletown, DE, 2018. Reprint.

Proudhon, Pierre-Joseph. *What Is Property?* Edited and Translated by Donald R. Kelley and Bonnie G. Smith. Cambridge: Cambridge University Press, 2008.

Rapport, Michael. *1848, Year of Revolution.* New York, NY: Basic Books, 2008.

Rather, Leland J. *The Dream of Self-Destruction: Wagner's 'Ring' and the Modern World.* Baton Rouge: Louisiana State University Press, 1979.

Rosenberg, John D. *Carlyle and the Burden of History.* Cambridge, MA: Harvard University Press, 1985.

Ross, Alex. "Othello's Daughter: The Rich Legacy of Ira Aldridge, the Pioneering Black Shakespearean." *The New Yorker*, July 29, 2013, 30–35.

Rotenstreich, Nathan. "The Idea of Historical Progress and Its Assumptions." *History and Theory* 10, no. 2 (1971): 197–221.

Rousseau, Jean-Jacques. *A Discourse on Inequality.* Translated by Maurice Cranston. London: Penguin Books, 1984.

Ruge, Arnold. "Hegel's 'Philosophy of Right' and the Politics of Our Times." Excerpted in *The Young Hegelians: An Anthology*, edited by Lawrence S. Stepelevich, 211–36. Cambridge: Cambridge University Press, 1983.

Schiller, Friedrich. *On the Aesthetic Education of Man.* Translated by Reginald Snell. Kettering: Angelico Press, 2014. Reprint, Yale University Press, 1954 ed.

Schlegel, August Wilhelm von. *Lectures on Dramatic Art and Literature.* Translated by John Black. Revised by Rev. A. J. W. Morrison, 2nd ed. London: George Bell & Sons, 1904.

Schopenhauer, Arthur. *The World as Will and Representation.* Translated by E. F. J. Payne. 2nd ed., 2 vols. New York, NY: Dover, 1969.

Scruton, Roger. *The Ring of Truth: The Wisdom of Wagner's* Ring of the Nibelung. London: Penguin Books, 2016.

Shakespeare, William. *The Tragedy of Othello: The Moor of Venice.* Edited by Alvin B. Kernan. Revised 2nd ed. New York, NY: Signet Classic, 1998.

Shapiro, Alexander H. "McEwan and Forster: The Perfect Wagnerites." *The Wagner Journal* 5, no. 2 (July 2011): 20–45.

Shaw, George Bernard. *The Perfect Wagnerite: A Commentary on the Niblung's Ring.* New York, NY: Dover Publications, 1967.

Smith, Steven B. "Hegel and the French Revolution: An Epitaph for Republicanism." *Social Research* 56, no. 1 (Spring 1989): 233–61.

Solomon, Maynard. "Beethoven's Ninth Symphony: The Sense of an Ending." *Critical Inquiry* 17, no. 2 (Winter 1991): 289–305.

Spencer, Stewart. "The 'Romantic Operas' and the Turn to Myth." In *The Cambridge Companion to Wagner*, edited by Thomas S. Grey, 65–73. Cambridge: Cambridge University Press, 2008.

———. "'Or Strike at Me Now as I Strangle thy Knee': A Note on the Text and Translation." In *Wagner's Ring of the Nibelung: A Companion*, edited by Stewart Spencer and Barry Millington, 11–13. London: Thames and Hudson, 1993.

———. "'Zieh hin! Ich kann dich nicht halten!'" *Wagner: New Series* 2, no. 4 (Oct 1981): 98–120.

Steinberg, Michael P. "Music Drama and the End of History." *New German Critique*, no. 69 (Autumn 1996): 163–80.

Stepelevich, Lawrence S. Introduction to *The Young Hegelians: An Anthology*, edited by Lawrence S. Stepelevich, 1–15. Cambridge: Cambridge University Press, 1983.

Strauss, David Friedrich. "The Life of Jesus." Excerpted in *The Young Hegelians: An Anthology*, edited by Lawrence S. Stepelevich, 21–51. Cambridge: Cambridge University Press, 1983.

Tanner, Michael. *Wagner*. Princeton: Princeton University Press, 1995.

Tiffin, Sarah. *Southeast Asia in Ruins: Art and Empire in the Early 19th Century*. National University of Singapore Press, 2016.

Treadwell, James. *Interpreting Wagner*. New Haven: Yale University Press, 2003.

———. "The Urge to Communicate: The Prose Writings as Theory and Practice." In *The Cambridge Companion to Wagner*, edited by Thomas S. Grey, 177–91. Cambridge: Cambridge University Press, 2008.

Turner, Frank M. *European Intellectual History from Rousseau to Nietzsche*. Edited by Richard A. Lofthouse. New Haven: Yale University Press, 2014.

Volney, Constantin-François de. *The Ruins Or a Meditation on the Revolutions of Empires and the Law of Nature*. Translated by Peter Eckler. Middlesex: Echo Library, 2007. Reprint, 1890 American Edition.

Wagner, Cosima. *Cosima Wagner's Diaries*. Translated by Geoffrey Skelton. Edited by Martin Gregor-Dellin and Dietrich Mack. 2 vols. London: Harcourt Brace Jovanovich, 1978–80.

Wagner, Richard. "Annals." In *The Diary of Richard Wagner 1865–1882: The Brown Book*, edited by Joachim Bergfeld, translated by George Bird, 93–124. Cambridge: Cambridge University Press, 1980.

———. "Art and Climate." In *The Art-Work of the Future and Other Works*, translated by W. Ashton Ellis, 249–65. Lincoln: University of Nebraska Press, 1993. Reprint, from translation of Vol 1. of *Richard Wagner's Prose Works*, published by K. Paul, Trench, Trübner in 1895.

———. "Art and Revolution." In *The Art-Work of the Future and Other Works*, translated by W. Ashton Ellis, 21–67. Lincoln: University of Nebraska Press, 1993. Reprint, from translation of Vol 1. of *Richard Wagner's Prose Works*, published by K. Paul, Trench, Trübner in 1895.

———. *The Artwork of the Future*. Translated by Emma Warner. London: *The Wagner Journal*, 2013.

———. "The Art-Work of the Future." In *The Art-Work of the Future and Other Works*, translated by W. Ashton Ellis, 69–213. Lincoln: University of Nebraska Press, 1993. Reprint, from translation of Vol 1. of *Richard Wagner's Prose Works*, published by K. Paul, Trench, Trübner in 1895.

———. "Beethoven." In *Richard Wagner's "Beethoven" (1870): A New Translation*, translated by Roger Allen, 1–29. Woodbridge: The Boydell Press, 2014

———. "A Communication to My Friends." In *The Art-Work of the Future and Other Works*, translated by W. Ashton Ellis. 267–392. Lincoln: University of Nebraska Press, 1993. Reprint, from translation of Vol. 1 of *Richard Wagner's Prose Works*, published by K. Paul, Trench, Trübner in 1895.

———. *Gesammelte Schriften und Dichtungen*. 10 vols. Leipzig: E.W. Fritzsch, 1871–1883.

———. *Götterdämmerung,* Full Orchestral Score, A2355. Kalmus Orchestra Library, 1933.

————. *Götterdämmerung: Dritter Tag aus der Trilogie: Der Ring des Nibelungen*. Mainz: B. Schott's Söhne, 1876.

————. "Man and Established Society." In *Jesus of Nazareth and Other Writings*, translated by W. Ashton Ellis, 226–31. Lincoln: University of Nebraska Press, 1995. Reprint, from translation of Vol. 8 of *Richard Wagner's Prose Works*, published by K. Paul, Trench, Trübner in 1899.

————. *My Life*. Translated by Andrew Gray. Edited by Mary Whittall. Cambridge: Cambridge University Press, 1983.

————. *Opera and Drama*. Translated by W. Ashton Ellis. Lincoln: University of Nebraska Press, 1995. Reprint, from translation of Vol. 2 of 2nd ed. of *Richard Wagner's Prose Works*, published by K. Paul, Trench, Trübner in 1900.

————. "Religion and Art." In *Religion and Art*, translated by W. Ashton Ellis, 211–84. Lincoln: University of Nebraska Press, 1994. Reprint, from translation of Vol 6. of *Richard Wagner's Prose Works*, published by K. Paul, Trench, Trübner in 1897.

————. "The Revolution." In *Jesus of Nazareth and Other Writings*, translated by W. Ashton Ellis, 232–38. Lincoln: University of Nebraska Press, 1995. Reprint, from translation of Vol. 8 of *Richard Wagner's Prose Works*, published by K. Paul, Trench, Trübner in 1899.

————. *Der Ring des Nibelungen. Ein Bühnenfestspiel für drei Tage und einem Vorabend*. 2nd ed. Leipzig: J.J. Weber, 1873.

————. *Der Ring des Nibelungen. Ein Bühnenfestspiel für drei Tage und einem Vorabend*. Mainz: B. Schott's Söhne, 1876.

————. *Selected Letters of Richard Wagner*. Edited and Translated by Stewart Spencer and Barry Millington. London: J.M. Dent, 1987.

————. "Toast on the Tercentenary of the Royal Kapelle at Dresden." In *Pilgrimage to Beethoven and Other Essays*, translated by W. Ashton Ellis, 313–18. Lincoln: University of Nebraska Press, 1994. Reprint, from translation of Vol 7. of *Richard Wagner's Prose Works*, published by K. Paul, Trench, Trübner in 1898.

————. "The Wibelungen: World History as Told in Saga." In *Pilgrimage to Beethoven and Other Essays*, translated by W. Ashton Ellis, 257–98. Lincoln: University of Nebraska Press, 1994. Reprint, from translation of Vol 7. of *Richard Wagner's Prose Works*, published by K. Paul, Trench, Trübner in 1898.

Weiner, Marc A. *Richard Wagner and the Anti-Semitic Imagination*. Lincoln: University of Nebraska Press, 1995.

Weinstock, Herbert. *Rossini: A Biography*. New York, NY: A.A. Knopf, 1968.

Wernick, Andrew. "The Religion of Humanity and Positive Morality." In *Love, Order, & Progress: The Science, Philosophy, & Politics of Auguste Comte*, edited by Michel Bourdeau, Mary Pickering and Warren Schmaus, 217–49. Pittsburgh: University of Pittsburgh Press, 2018.

Westernhagen, Kurt von. *Richard Wagners Dresdener Bibliothek 1842–1849: Neue Dokumente zur Geschichte seines Schaffens*. Wiesbaden: Brockhaus, 1966.

Williams, Simon. *Wagner and the Romantic Hero*. Cambridge: Cambridge University Press, 2004.

Windell, George G. "Hegel, Feuerbach, and Wagner's *Ring*." *Central European History* 9, no. 1 (March 1976): 27–57.

Žižek, Slavoj. "Wagner, Anti-Semitism and 'German Ideology.'" Afterword to *Five Lessons on Wagner*, by Alain Badiou, translated by Susan Spitzer. New York, NY: Verso, 2010.

Index

Printed in Great Britain
by Amazon

39273766R00101